IoT, AI, and Blockchain for .NET

Building a Next-Generation Application from the Ground Up

Nishith Pathak
Anurag Bhandari

Apress®

IoT, AI, and Blockchain for .NET

Nishith Pathak
Kotdwara, Dist. Pauri Garhwal, India

Anurag Bhandari
Jalandhar, Punjab, India

ISBN-13 (pbk): 978-1-4842-3708-3
https://doi.org/10.1007/978-1-4842-3709-0

ISBN-13 (electronic): 978-1-4842-3709-0

Library of Congress Control Number: 2018952633

Managing Director, Apress Media LLC: Welmoed Spahr
Acquisitions Editor: Joan Murray
Development Editor: Laura Berendson
Coordinating Editor: Nancy Chen

Cover designed by eStudioCalamar

Cover image designed by Freepik (www.freepik.com)

Distributed to the book trade worldwide by Springer Science+Business Media New York, 233 Spring Street, 6th Floor, New York, NY 10013. Phone 1-800-SPRINGER, fax (201) 348-4505, e-mail orders-ny@springer-sbm.com, or visit www.springeronline.com. Apress Media, LLC is a California LLC and the sole member (owner) is Springer Science + Business Media Finance Inc (SSBM Finance Inc). SSBM Finance Inc is a **Delaware** corporation.

For information on translations, please e-mail rights@apress.com, or visit http://www.apress.com/rights-permissions.

Apress titles may be purchased in bulk for academic, corporate, or promotional use. eBook versions and licenses are also available for most titles. For more information, reference our Print and eBook Bulk Sales web page at http://www.apress.com/bulk-sales.

Any source code or other supplementary material referenced by the author in this book is available to readers on GitHub via the book's product page, located at www.apress.com/9781484237083. For more detailed information, please visit http://www.apress.com/source-code.

Printed on acid-free paper

Nishith dedicates this book to

Jai Gurudev

To the most important person in my life, my mother, the late Bina Pathak, for her guidance, sacrifices, prayers, and blessings, which made me what I am today. I miss her each day. To my father, Pankaj Pathak, for teaching me to do what I believe in. You are and will always be my role model and my hero for my entire life. To my Sadh-Gurudev, who has been an eternal guiding force and entirely changed my life. To my grandfather, the late Mahesh Chandra Pathak, for his blessings and moral values.

To my wife, Surabhi, for bearing with me, sacrificing her splendid career for our family, and always staying by my side through all the ups and downs. Getting married to you is the most beautiful thing in my life. You have given me the most precious diamond of my life, Shikhar, whom I love more than anyone else. I know this book has taken a lot of me and I haven't been able to spend enough time with you, Papa, and Shikhar for the past year since I've been working tirelessly to give this pleasant surprise. Surabhi and Shikhar, this book would not have been possible without all of your sacrifices.

To my lovely sister, Tanwi, and my niece, Aadhya—your smiling faces give me a lot of strength and inspiration to do better each day. To my Guruji, JP Kukreti, SS Tyagi, and Rajesh Tripathi, who have been there for me countless times and always provide me with comfort, understanding, spiritual beliefs, and lots of motivation.

Lastly, I thank God for blessing me with such wonderful people in my life.

*Anurag dedicates this book to his late grandfather—
Dr. Y.P. Bhandari—a tireless, unretired, and always learning doctor
who was an evergreen source of inspiration to Anurag and hundreds of
radiologists in India. To his late grandmother—Mrs. Kaushalya
Bhandari—an epitome of sacrifice, selflessness, and righteousness. Mrs.
and Dr. Bhandari passed away recently onto the heavenly realms a few
days after one another. To his maternal grandmother—Mrs.
Kailashwati Sood—for her unending love and motivation. To his
father—Pardeep Bhandari—for his sagely advice, composure, ideas,
and for always being there. To his mother (from whom he inherits his
creative genes)—Meenakshi Bhandari—for imparting him ethos and
values, and for being a constant motivation, apart from being ever-
caring and ever-forgiving. To his sister—Ashima Bhandari—for being
his best friend and biggest teacher and for being his "big data" memory
bank. To his wife—Divya Malhotra—for being understanding and
motivating, and for being the perennially cheerful person that she is.*

Table of Contents

About the Authors

Nishith Pathak is India's first artificial intelligence Microsoft Most Valuable Professional (MVP), a Microsoft Regional Director (RD), an architect, an international speaker and author, an innovator, and a strategist. He is a prolific author and has written more than half a dozen international books, articles, reviews, and columns for multiple electronic and print publications across the globe, including his latest book, *Artificial Intelligence for .NET* (Apress, 2017). Nishith is an international speaker, is featured in many big tech and research conferences as a panelist, and has given many keynotes across the globe.

Nishith has two decades of experience in IT, with expertise in innovation, research, architecting, designing, and developing applications for Fortune 100 companies using next-generation tools and technologies that incorporate AI, ML, cognitive services, Blockchain, and more.

Nishith is one of 19 Microsoft MVPs worldwide in AI and the only one in India. He was recently awarded elite Microsoft Regional Directors (RD), making him one of the 150 world's top technology visionaries chosen for their cross-platform expertise and community leadership. He is a gold member and sits on the advisory board of various national and international computer science societies and organizations. He has been awarded the Microsoft Most Valuable Professional (MVP) several times for his exemplary work and his expertise in Microsoft technologies. He is a member of various advisory groups for Microsoft. Nishith is currently the vice president of Accenture Technology Labs.

Anurag Bhandari is a researcher, educator, and programmer with a wealth of experience in architecting and developing end-to-end IT solutions for enterprises and startups. An early adopter of technologies, he has extensively worked on a breadth of artificial intelligence technologies, such as machine/deep learning, natural language processing, natural language understanding, and computer vision. A polyglot programmer, he specializes in creating rich applications for the web and for mobile.

As an educator, Anurag has developed multiple programming courseware. He has trained students in India and in the United States on various technologies, such as enterprise web development and data analytics. He has made significant contributions to several technical books, more recently as a contributing author of *Artificial Intelligence for .NET* (Apress, 2017).

Anurag is a graduate in computer science from National Institute of Technology, Jalandhar. He became a Microsoft Certified Professional at the age of 18. He is a member of Association of Computing Machinery (ACM), and has published research papers through reputed journals. He regularly speaks at national and international tech conferences. He is an ardent open-source evangelist, whose love for free software helped him found the Granular Linux project 11 years ago.

Anurag is currently a working as a senior researcher at Accenture Labs, where he designs next-generation AI, ML, and IoT solutions for clients.

About the Technical Reviewer

Fabio Ferracchiati is a senior consultant and a senior analyst/developer using Microsoft technologies. He works at BluArancio S.p.A (`www.bluarancio.com`) as a senior analyst/ developer and Microsoft dynamics CRM specialist. He is a Microsoft Certified Solution Developer for .NET, a Microsoft Certified Application Developer for .NET, a Microsoft Certified Professional, and a prolific author and technical reviewer. Over the past 10 years, he's written articles for Italian and international magazines and co-authored more than 10 books on a variety of computer topics.

About the Technical Reviewer

Acknowledgments

This book has been a team effort by some wonderful people. Nishith would like to thank his family, especially his wife, Surabhi, his father, Pankaj Pathak, and his son, Shikhar for being kind and supportive, believing in him, and making his dreams come true. He would like to thank his Guruji, Mr. J P Kukreti, for always inspiring and supporting him. You all are Most Valuable Person (MVPs) to me. Anything I do in my life would not be possible without you.

Anurag would like to thank his father (Pardeep Bhandari), mother (Meenakshi Bhandari), and sister (Ashima Bhandari) for their continuous push to question the status quo and learn new things; he thanks them for being his best critics. He would also like to thank his wife (Divya) for being patient and understanding all through the tough stretches of writing chapters, during which time he would disappear into his study room.

The authors thank all the people at Apress who put their sincere efforts into publishing this book. Gwenan deserves special thanks. Thanks to Nancy and Laura for doing a fabulous job of project management and constantly pushing us to do our best. We would also like to thank Fabio Ferracchiati for dedicating the many hours that went into an extensive tech review.

Introduction

We are in midst of a technological revolution. As with previous revolutions, an inability to adapt to the new ways will make your existing developer skills obsolete sooner than later. Starting with the Cloud revolution, Big Data, Internet of Things (IoT), and Artificial Intelligence (AI) have all changed the landscape of software development. As we enter a new era of AI and IoT, we have another technology currently creating disruptive waves across the globe. This new technology is Blockchain. The lethal combination of IoT and Blockchain, powered by AI, is ready to revolutionize software development yet again. We are talking about the AI 2.0 revolution.

This book introduces you to each component of AI 2.0 and Industry 4.0 in detail, viz. AI, IoT, Blockchain, and machine learning. Building on a strong conceptual base, it will provide methodical, hands-on and step-by-step approaches to solving practical real-world problems. In each "applied" chapter, you will build one module of our example solution for a fictional smart healthcare chain.

The book starts with quick and interesting introductions to AI, IoT, and Blockchain, and explains how these will be used in creating smart hospitals.

It then delves deeper into IoT concepts a developer must know and gives you a good understanding of Azure IoT Suite. From there, you build a centralized patient monitoring solution using real and fake IoT devices, leveraging the incredible power of IoT Suite.

The book then talks in detail about artificial intelligence, the various tasks that make up AI, and how developers—who do not need a background in applied mathematics—can use Azure Cognitive Services to make their applications smart and offer richer experiences to end users.

The book introduces the complex topic of Blockchain in ways that are easy to comprehend even by absolute beginners. It then teaches you to apply Blockchain in real life—using Azure Blockchain-as-a-Service—by letting you design your own trust-based security and inventory management solution for our fictional chain of smart hospitals.

Real-time analysis of data received by IoT devices is sometimes useful in extracting key insights and at other times imperative in making crucial business decisions. You will learn to perform real-time analysis of IoT data at scale—saving thousands of lives on the way—using Azure Stream Analytics and PowerBI.

The book concludes with a detailed understanding of crucial machine learning concepts and a hands-on exercise where you create an ML-based diabetes prediction solution in Azure Machine Learning Studio.

Who Is This Book For?

This book is targeted toward novice and intermediate developers who are curious about artificial intelligence, the Internet of Things (IoT), and Blockchain, and want to know how these work together to create next-gen software solutions. People who are curious about phenomena such as Industry 4.0 will also benefit. Developers and architects with no previous experience with .NET who want to apply the new technologies in their applications will benefit greatly from the discussion and code samples in this book.

Prerequisites

To get the most out of this book, you need the .NET Framework and an Internet connection, although not all the code samples are written in C#. We recommend using Microsoft Visual Studio 2017 as the development environment to experiment with the code samples, which you can find in the Source Code section of the Apress website (www.apress.com).

Obtaining Updates to This Book

As you read through this text, you may find the occasional grammatical or code error (although we sure hope not). If this is the case, our sincere apologies. Being humans, we are sure that a glitch or two may be present, regardless of our best efforts. You can obtain the current errata list from the Apress website (located once again on the home page for this book), as well as information on how to notify us of any errors you might find.

Contacting the Authors

If you have any questions regarding this book's source code, are in need of clarification for a given example, simply want to offer your thoughts regarding AI, or want to contact us for other needs, feel free to drop us a line at `nispathak@gmail.com` or `anurag.bhd@gmail.com`. We will do our best to get back to you in a timely fashion.

Thanks for buying this book. We hope you enjoy reading it and putting your new-found knowledge to good use.

CHAPTER 1

The Artificial Intelligence 2.0 Revolution

Once upon a time, computers were as big as rooms. They were capable of complex mathematical calculations. They were not, though, meant to be operated by people like me and you. Nor were they designed for creating documents and presentations, playing games, or surfing the web. Early computers were powered by vacuum tubes—just like most other sophisticated electronic devices of the time—and were used in scientific research. Then, the semiconductor revolution happened, and the *transistor* was born.

Note A vacuum tube is an electronic device that was a common component in old radio and television sets, amplifiers, and even computers. The tube is a glass enclosure that houses an anode and a cathode inside a vacuum (no air or gas). It's based on the principle that electric current can move through vacuum and does not need solid material for the purpose. The first vacuum tube was a diode that, unlike semi-conductor diodes of today, was large and fragile.

Transistors gave birth to microprocessors, and microprocessors eventually brought computers into our homes and allowed them to do much more than just record scientific data, crunch numbers, or break codes. The first IBM personal computer was powered by an Intel 8088 chip, which ran at a "blazing" speed of 4.77MHz. Processors soon went through a revolution of their own, one dictated by the famous Moore's Law. The processing power of computers roughly doubled every 18 months, allowing them to do tasks that could not be efficiently done on previous generation processors.

What is the common pattern here? All these revolutions have affected not just the performance or software development methods but also computing in general, in a way unimaginable before.

1

© Nishith Pathak and Anurag Bhandari 2018
N. Pathak and A. Bhandari, *IoT, AI, and Blockchain for .NET*, https://doi.org/10.1007/978-1-4842-3709-0_1

There have been other such historic revolutions—in parallel and subsequent—that have changed computing forever. Take a recent phenomenon for instance: the *Cloud* revolution. Back in 2010, when "cloud" was just a buzzword in newspapers and magazines, there was widespread confusion about the true meaning of cloud. Everyone talked about the disruptive potential and lasting benefits of Cloud, but only pockets of technology-savvy people actually understood it. A few years later everyone had adopted it. Cloud has affected not just businesses by offering entirely new business models to run their companies on but also affected our personal lives. Today, we cannot begin to imagine a world without Cloud: a world without online storage, unlimited music and video streaming, photo sharing, collaborative document editing, and social networking at the speed of light. Businesses have saved millions of dollars by basing the better part of their infrastructure on Cloud services rather than bearing steep costs of managing in-house networks of servers.

Cloud went on to become a key enabler of the *Big Data* revolution. Cloud computing gave us enough power to analyze billions of records, worth terabytes of data, exponentially quicker, and at considerably lower costs.

Let's try to understand the role of Cloud through an example. Consider an e-commerce website, say Amazon.com. At a high level, it stores two types of data about its users—transactional and non-transactional. Non-transactional data is information about customers (name, email, or address), items (name, price, discount, or seller), etc. Transactional data, on the other hand, is information about a particular transaction on the website, e.g., buying an item, submitting a product review, adding an item to wishlist or cart, etc. This type of data grows at a rapid pace on sites like Amazon. On Prime Day 2016, Amazon recorded sales of close to 600 items per second. That is 2.1 million items in one hour alone!

Storing such gigantic data was once prohibitively expensive, forcing companies to archive or remove transactional data after a set retention period (a few weeks to a couple of years). The potent combination of Cloud and Big Data technologies has not only enabled us to store (rather than throwing away) huge amounts of historic data at dirt cheap prices, but it has also allowed us to leverage the archived data to perform complex data analytics tasks over years' worth of data to derive meaningful statistics and graphs for customer behavior and buying trends—what were the top selling hundred items in each category during peak hours on sale day; which items were popular among users in terms of viewing but not in terms of buying?

Almost simultaneously came the *IoT* revolution. As with Big Data, Cloud is a key enabler of this revolution. Powered by a variety of sensors, IoT devices generate so much data that Big Data technologies usually go hand-in-hand with IoT. Cloud provides both storage and computing power to the otherwise lightweight devices on an IoT network. After helping spark two big revolutions, Cloud did it again with Artificial Intelligence (AI).

AI has surfaced and resurfaced in several waves, but it's only recently that it has become commonplace. The widespread affordability and use of AI in software development has been seen as a revolution. The first AI revolution, the one we are currently witnessing, is about AI-as-a-Service. The book *Artificial Intelligence for .NET: Speech, Language, and Search* (Apress, 2017) gives an in-depth of creating AI-enabled software applications. With advancements in IoT and the emergence of Blockchain, AI is on brink of a second revolution, one that involves creating complete product offerings with intelligent software and custom hardware.

Note   The "as a service" model is generally associated with Cloud infrastructure, and that is true here as well. World's top tech companies—Google, IBM, Microsoft, and Amazon—are offering AI services, in the form of SDKs and RESTful APIs, that help developers add intelligence to their software applications. Let's understand this in a little more detail.

Let's explore each component of the upcoming AI 2.0 revolution in detail.

Artificial Intelligence

The meaning of artificial intelligence (AI) has evolved over generations of research. The basic concepts of AI have not changed, but its applications have. How AI was perceived in the 1950s is very different from how it's actually being put to use today. And it's still evolving.

Artificial intelligence is a hot topic these days. It has come a long way from the pages of popular science fiction books to becoming a commodity. And, no, AI has nothing to do with superior robots taking over the world and enslaving us humans. At least, not yet. Anything intelligent enough, from your phone's virtual assistant (Siri and Cortana) to your trusty search engine (Google and Bing) to your favorite mobile app or video game, is powered by AI. Figure 1-1 shows an AI-powered intelligent chatbot.

Figure 1-1. *An intelligent chatbot that can place pizza orders by humanly understanding its users*

Interest in AI peaked during the 2000s, especially at the start of 2010s. Huge investments were made in AI research by both academia and corporations, investments that have not only affected these institutions but also its affiliates and users. For software developers, this has been nothing short of a boon. Advances made by companies such as Microsoft, Google, Facebook, and Amazon in various fields of AI, and the subsequent open-sourcing and commercialization of their products, has enabled software developers to create human-like experiences in their apps with unprecedented ease. This has resulted in an explosion of smart, intelligent apps that can understand their users just as a normal human would.

Have you, as a developer, ever thought about how you can use AI to create insanely smart software? You probably have, but did not know where to start.

Like all humans, developers have pre-conceived notions about products and technologies. In our experience with software developers at top IT companies, a common perception that we've found among both developers and project managers is that adding AI capabilities, such as natural language understanding, speech recognition, machine learning, etc., to their software would require a deep understanding of neural networks, fuzzy logic, and other mind-bending computer science theories. Well, let us tell you the good news. That is not the case anymore.

The intelligence that powers your favorite applications, like Google search, Bing, Cortana, and Facebook, is slowly being made available to developers outside of these companies: some parts for free and the others as SaaS-based paid commercial offerings.

AI in the Old Days

The term "artificial intelligence" was coined at a conference on the campus of Dartmouth College in the summer of 1956. The proposal for the conference included this assertion: "Every aspect of learning or any other feature of intelligence can be so precisely described that a machine can be made to simulate it." It was during this conference that the field of AI research was established, and the people who attended it became the pioneers of AI research.

During the decades that followed, there were major breakthroughs in the field of AI. Computer programs were developed to solve algebra problems, prove theorems, and speak English. Government agencies and private organizations poured in funds to fuel the research. But the road to modern AI was not easy.

The first setback to AI research came in 1974. The time between that year and 1980 is known as the first "AI Winter." During this time, a lot of promised results of the research failed to materialize. This was due to a combination of factors, the foremost one being the failure of scientists to anticipate the difficulty of the problems that AI posed. The limited computing power of the time was another major reason. As a result, a lack of progress led the major British and American agencies that were earlier supporting the research to cut off their funding.

The next seven years, 1980-87, saw a renewed interest in AI research. The development of expert systems fueled the boom. Expert systems are rule engines designed for specific domains; they are fed with a set of logical rules derived from the knowledge of experts; decisions are calculated for each input using the fed rules. They were getting developed across organizations, and soon all big giants started investing huge amount of money in artificial intelligence. Work on neural networks laid the foundation for the development of optical character recognition and speech recognition techniques. The following years formed the second AI Winter, which lasted from 1987 to 1993. Like the previous winter, AI again suffered financial setbacks.

1993-2001 marked the return of AI, propelled in part by faster and cheaper computers. Finally, older promises of AI research were realized because of access to faster computing power, the lack of which had started the first winter. Specialized computers were created using advanced AI techniques to beat humans. Who can forget the iconic match between IBM's Deep Blue computer and the then reigning chess champion Garry Kasparov in 1997?

AI was extensively used in the field of robotics. The Japanese built robots that looked like humans and even understood and spoke human languages. The western world wasn't far behind, and soon there was a race to build the most human-like mechanical assistant to man. Honda's ASIMO is a brilliant example of what could be achieved by combining robotics with AI: a 4'3" tall humanoid that can walk, dance, make coffee, and even conduct orchestras.

Status Quo

AI started off as a pursuit to build human-like robots that could understand us, do our chores, and remove our loneliness. But today, the field of AI has broadened to encompass various techniques that help in creating smart, functional, and dependable software applications.

With the emergence of a new breed of technology companies, the 21st Century has seen tremendous advances in artificial intelligence, sometimes behind the scenes in the research labs of Microsoft, IBM, Google, Facebook, Apple, Amazon, and more. Perhaps one of the best examples of contemporary AI is IBM's Watson, which started as a computer system designed to compete with humans on the popular American TV show "Jeopardy!". In an exhibition match in 2011, Watson beat two former winners to clinch the $1 million prize money. Propelled by Watson's success, IBM soon released the AI technologies that powered its computer system as individual commercial offerings. AI became a buzzword in the industry, and other large tech companies entered the market with commercial offerings of their own. Today, there are startups offering highly specialized but accurate AI-as-a-Service offerings.

AI has not been limited to popular and enterprise software applications. Your favorite video games, both on TV and mobile, have had AI baked for a long time. For example, when playing single player games, where you compete against the computer, your opponents make their own decisions based on your moves. It is even possible to change the difficulty level of the opponents: the harder the difficulty level, the more sophisticated the "AI" of the game, and the more human-like your opponents will be.

The Buildup to AI 1.0 Revolution

Commoditization of AI, as highlighted in the previous section, was made possible because of the development of key enabling technologies such as machine learning. This term is best explained by the help of an example.

Microsoft Bing, the popular search engine from Microsoft, can not only perform keyword-based searches but also search the Web based on the intended meaning of your search phrase. So doing a simple keyword search like "Taylor Swift" will give you the official website, Wikipedia page, social media accounts, recent news stories, and some photos of the popular American singer-songwriter. Doing a more complex search like "Who is the president of Uganda?" will give you the exact name in a large font and top web results for that person. It's like asking a question of another human, who knows you do not mean to get all web pages that contain the phrase "Who is the president of Uganda," just the name of the person in question.

In both examples (Taylor Swift and President of Uganda), Bing will also show, on the left, some quick facts about the person: date of birth, spouse, children, etc. And depending on the type of person searched, Bing will also show other relevant details, such as education, timeline, and quotes for a politician, and net worth, compositions, and romances for a singer. How is Bing able to show you so much about a person? Have Bing's developers created a mega-database of quick facts for all the famous people in the world (current and past)? Not quite.

Although it is not humanly impossible to create such a database, the cost of maintaining it would be huge. Our big, big world, with so many countries and territories, will keep on producing famous people. So there's a definite scalability problem with this database.

The technique Microsoft used to solve this problem is called *machine learning*. We look at machine learning in a bit. Similarly, the thing that enables Bing to understand the meaning of a search phrase is *natural language understanding* (NLU). You can ask the same question of Bing in a dozen different ways and Bing will still arrive at the same meaning every time. NLU makes it smart enough to interpret human languages in ways humans do subconsciously.

Machine Learning

The term *machine learning* was coined by Arthur Samuel in his 1959 paper "Some Studies in Machine Learning." As per Samuel, machine learning is what "gives computers the ability to learn without being explicitly programmed". We all know a computer as a machine that performs certain operations by following instructions supplied by humans in the form of programs. So how is it possible for a machine to learn something by itself?

Machine learning is the very fundamental concept of artificial intelligence. ML explores the study and construction of algorithms that can learn from data and make predictions based on their learning. ML is what powers an intelligent machine; it is what *generates* artificial intelligence.

A regular, non-ML language translation algorithm would have static program instructions to detect which language a sentence is written in: words used, grammatical structure, etc. Similarly, a non-ML face detection algorithm would have a hard-coded definition of a face: something round, skin colored, having two small dark regions near the top (eyes), etc. An ML algorithm, on the other hand, doesn't have such hard-coding; it learns by examples. If you train it with lots of sentences that are written in French and some more that are not written in French, it will learn to identify French sentences when it sees them. Figure 1-2 shows how an ML algorithm iteratively uses sample data to create a trained model that can make predictions based on new inputs.

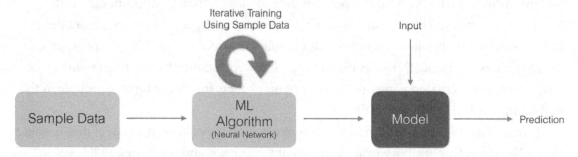

Figure 1-2. *Large amounts of training data are supplied to an ML algorithm, such as a neural network, to create what is called a "trained model". A trained model can then be used to quickly make predictions against the specified input data.*

A lot of real-world problems are nonlinear, such as language translation, weather prediction, email spam filtering, predicting the next president of the United States, classification problems (such as telling apart species of birds through images), and so on. ML is an ideal solution for such nonlinear problems where designing and programming explicit algorithms using static program instructions is simply not feasible.

Creating AI-Enabled Applications

We know now how precious ML is for solving nonlinear problems. Technically, AI is seen as a wide research area whose goal is to explore fields of computer science and to create technologies to lend machines human-like intelligence. One major field of AI—and the one used the most—is natural language processing or NLP. It is an umbrella term that is used to represent various related and independent tasks related to processing natural languages, languages that humans speak. Understanding the basic communication medium of humans is the foundation of intelligence in our world, is it not? Among the various NLP tasks are language understanding (NLU), machine translation (language translation), speech recognition (speech to text), etc.

Another major field of AI is computer vision (CV), the field that deals with making machines intelligent enough to interpret visuals (images and videos) the way humans do. Some common CV tasks include face detection and recognition, object detection and recognition, optical character recognition (OCR), image classification, etc.

Each of the NLP and CV tasks is a nonlinear problem that can be solved through machine learning. In technical terms, we can create machine learning models for each of them using sufficiently large amounts of training data (usually in gigabytes). Creating one ML model, let alone all, is intellectually challenging and expensive. Even if you have a team of computer science and math people armed with ML skills, there's the cost of extremely expensive hardware to take care of to develop those models. It may take up to 2-3 months to accurately train an ML model on high-end machines running 24x7, using the currently available deep learning toolkits such as Microsoft CNTK, Google Tensorflow, and Torch. Although specialized ML-friendly microprocessors are being developed (iPhone's A11 Bionic and Google's TPU) and hardware costs are coming down further, it's still exponentially easier and cheaper to use commercially available AI services.

AI services—such as Microsoft's Cognitive Services APIs—can be used in virtually any code to incrementally add intelligence. This task has been reduced to a matter of a few REST API calls. All of the following use cases are not cumbersome to implement anymore:

- Adding face detection in a security system's software to detect intruders

- Adding face recognition in social apps to identify friends

- Adding language understanding in chatbots for automated support, ticket bookings, etc.

- Extracting text from images using OCR

The AI 1.0 revolution is literally changing the way software is written. AI is no longer a dominion of enthusiasts. The practicality and accuracy of contemporary AI solutions have compelled even the most traditional IT and software companies to adopt it. IT companies are using AI to create innovative new solutions and to redesign existing software for their clients. And an increasing number of clients are themselves demanding AI-enabled software.

What Is AI 2.0?

The next generation of AI technologies will take software solutions several steps ahead. AI 2.0 is something bigger than AI alone. It's no longer about just creating intelligent software.

This has been made possible by recent advancements in cognitive technologies (AI), the Internet of Things (IoT), and Blockchain. Figure 1-3 highlights this equation. IoT and Blockchain are relatively recent developments but have co-existed with AI for some time now.

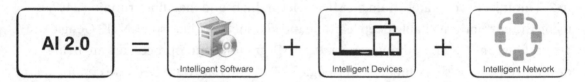

Figure 1-3. AI 2.0 is a combination of AI (intelligent software), IoT (intelligent devices), and Blockchain (intelligent network)

Improvements in AI technologies have made it increasingly easier to develop "complete" product offerings using AI, IoT, and Blockchain. To reiterate, it's not about just software anymore but it's about software and hardware on top of a highly secure and flexible network.

The following sections list three possibilities opened by AI 2.0. Try to imagine more.

Early Warning Systems for Wildlife

Some rural areas across the globe are hotbeds of human-animal conflict, one of the most common being humans versus elephants. Humans are known to illegally poach elephants for their tusks. In retaliation, elephants often trample humans' crop fields. As per WWF, current intrusion prevention systems, such as electric fencing, are expensive, difficult to maintain, and sometimes life-threatening for elephants. Intelligent early warning systems that work based on real-time data collected from IoT monitoring devices can be a cost-effective and highly scalable solution for this sensitive problem.

Smart Lean Manufacturing

Manufacturing practices have become highly optimized. But there is still room for improvement. IoT devices can be used to monitor machines and environment. Intelligent analytics can then be performed over the collected monitoring data to generate insights to help further optimize manufacturing processes. Blockchain can help in securely and reliably distribute optimized parameters across a string of connected manufacturing plants. Supply chain can also be effectively managed using Blockchain.

Connected Homes

Mark Zuckerberg, founder and CEO of Facebook, conducted and published a famous AI experiment in 2016. Jarvis was a custom home automation solution built using several open source and in-house AI libraries. AI 2.0 will allow us to easily create not just one such smart home but an ultra-secure network of connected smart homes. You can read more about his experiment at `https://www.facebook.com/notes/mark-zuckerberg/building-jarvis/10154361492931634/`.

Azure Cognitive Services

Cognitive Services is a set of software-as-a-service (SaaS) commercial offerings from Microsoft related to artificial intelligence. Cognitive Services is the product of Microsoft's years of research into cognitive computing and artificial intelligence, and many of these services are being used by some of Microsoft's own popular products, such as Bing (search, maps), Translator, Bot Framework, etc.

Microsoft has made these services available as easy-to-use REST APIs, directly consumable in a web or a mobile application. As of writing this book, there are 30 available cognitive services, broadly divided into five categories Vision, Speech, Language, Search, and Knowledge.

The Internet of Things

The Internet of Things is a routinely misunderstood term. In fact, Internet itself is highly misunderstood, let alone "things?" So, what is the Internet and what are the things? And more importantly, how are things connected to the Internet (and each other)?

The Internet was invented to connect two computers, sitting in two different parts of the world, with each other. It was not invented, as is a common misconception, to help you browse websites. Sometimes, the terms Internet and WWW (world wide web or just Web) are used interchangeably. This is a dangerous error. They are not the same. It's like saying that Facebook and status updates are the same thing, which they are not because updating status is just one part of Facebook among dozens of other features, such as photos, apps, games, check-ins, etc.

Using the same analogy, Web is just one aspect of the Internet. It is Internet, and not Web, that allows you to check emails, watch videos, send IM messages, make video calls, and a hundred other things. Each of the Internet's "functionalities" is supported by a different protocol. Web uses HTTP, email uses IMAP/SMTP, video streaming uses RTSP, instant messaging uses Jabber, video calling uses VoIP, and so on. So, the next time you hear somebody say, "check the latest prices for this product on the Internet," interrupt them politely by pointing out that they actually meant Web and not Internet.

During its initial days, the Internet was composed only of computers, which were large and bulky (although not big-as-room bulky). Back then, the Internet connected computers with servers or with each other. There were few or no other devices that could be connected to the Internet. This changed with the introduction of smartphones. They were tiny, pocket-sized computers that could be connected to the Internet. While on Internet, they could do most things a regular computer could—browse websites, check email, send IM, etc. Then came tablets. And then, smart TVs. After that, smartwatches. You have probably witnessed the trend yourself. We even have smart thermostats, fridges, printers, cameras, music systems, cars, toasters (!), and so on. In other words, our Internet now has millions of these non-computer items connected to it (see Figure 1-4). These non-computer items are the "things" in IoT. Each thing is individually called an IoT device.

Figure 1-4. *This illustration shows many different things connected to the Internet*

A More Technical Definition

IoT is the global network of "smart" versions of regular physical objects. What makes an object smart? Its ability to do its tasks automatically and more efficiently through the help of embedded computing hardware, sensors, actuators, and software. But the defining feature that makes an object smart is its ability to connect to the Internet, which opens a bunch of possibilities. For instance, a regular thermostat installed at home must be manually set with a desired temperature to control air conditioning. A smart thermostat can be remotely controlled via a mobile app (because it's connected to the Internet) to make the house warmer when it starts snowing so that you get a cozy feeling once you reach home from the office.

We'll explore IoT devices in more detail in Chapter 2, including the technologies that help in converting regular electrical and electronic items into IoT devices.

What's the Use of IoT?

The smart thermostat example illustrates an IoT device's remotely controlling use case. The same use case can be extended to smart bulbs, smart fans, smart CCTVs, smart washing machines, etc., to collectively build a *smart home*. The devices that make a smart home are also called home automation systems/solutions.

However, the most common use case of IoT devices is that of data collection. Most IoT devices have one or more sensors for measuring certain parameters. Smartwatches come with a heart-rate sensor, a pedometer (to measure steps), barometer (to measure pressure), etc. Sensors continuously record and store data in devices. This data is then analyzed on a device or saved in the Cloud for later analysis. The result of analysis is a lot of meaningful information—average vitals during the day, the hour of maximum activity, total number of steps walked, total calories burned (as a result of walking/running), etc. Specialized wearables are sometimes used to keep track of patients' health. So, another useful application of IoT is that of *health monitors* and *remote patient monitoring systems.*

A smartwatch is usually a complex, expensive IoT device. We may have simpler IoT devices that have only one purpose and, thus, one sensor. In a typical manufacturing plant, these could be a device to monitor room temperature, another device to monitor humidity, another one to record video, and yet another one to record the rotations of a running machine. The result is a *connected factory,* where the collected data can be analyzed to extract results to optimize the efficiency of machines and processes.

You will learn more about capturing real-time data in Chapter 9. Analyzing the captured data to generate insights is covered in Chapter 10.

Try to imagine more applications of IoT in the fields of agriculture, transportation, environment, and public infrastructure.

Azure IoT Suite

IoT suite is a collection of services, from Microsoft, to manage small to large networks of IoT devices. The services are especially useful in large setups, where managing hundreds or thousands or even millions of IoT devices manually just isn't possible. A typical setup, aka IoT solution, is composed of two major components: IoT devices and a solution backend. The Cloud-based solution backend is where data collected by devices is stored and analyzed. Azure IoT Suite provides end-to-end implementations for pre-configured or custom IoT solutions, such as remote monitoring (monitoring status of devices), predictive maintenance (anticipating maintenance needs of devices to avoid downtime), and connected factory (manage industrial devices).

The suite usually goes with the following five Azure services:

- **IoT Hub**—Enables secure, bi-directional communication between IoT devices and solution backend. Azure IoT device SDKs for various languages and platforms are provided to enable devices to reliably connect with their solution backend. IoT Hub provides solutions for problems such as device identity management, device twins, per-device authentication, routing device-to-Cloud messages to Azure services, etc.

- **Machine learning**—A fully-managed Cloud service that enables you to easily build, deploy, and share predictive analytics solutions. Machine Learning Studio is a browser-based, drag-and-drop authoring environment that allows you to create ML models for your analytics needs. It comes with support for R and Python, languages commonly used for creating statistical, predictive solutions. ML Studio also provides a fully managed service you can use to deploy your predictive models as ready-to-consume web services.

- **Stream analytics**—Develop and run real-time analytics on data streams captured by IoT devices. Analytics programs are written in an SQL-like declarative language, with support for JavaScript user-defined functions for temporal logic. Parallel real-time analytics on multiple IoT streams is supported. It is also possible to call Azure Machine Learning models for predictive scoring on streaming data.

- **Notification hubs**—A mobile push notification engine to send out notifications at scale about various IoT events. It's a common requirement to receive notifications on mobile about job completion, regular monitoring updates, impending device failure, etc. Notification hubs can send out notifications to millions of mobiles at once. All popular mobile platforms are supported, including Android, iOS, and Windows.

- **Power BI**—A suite of business analytics and intelligence tools to create dashboards and charts using the results of analytics performed on data collected by IoT devices. Integrates well with stream analytics to create dashboards with real-time insights.

You will learn more the IoT suite and its services in Chapter 2. In Chapter 3, you will use Azure IoT Hub and other services with your own devices to create real-world connected networks.

Blockchain

Suppose you bought a new car. If, like me, you live in India, it is compulsory to buy car insurance before taking your new car out on the road. This is not just to protect your car against damages but also to provide for medical costs for a person who may get injured in an accident because of your driving. Anyway, let's say you are a careful driver and even after a year of driving your new car you haven't injured anyone. Then one fateful day, you were driving carefully as usual when another car comes speeding from nowhere and hits your car from the side. You are devastated. You had kept your car like new for all that time. And now, because of no fault of your own, your precious car has a dent as deep as a black hole.

To make things worse, when you submit your claim, get bogged down by a complicated claims process and are eventually paid unfairly. The insurer says that they weren't able to access whether the damage was the other guy's fault or your own.

Cases like this happen by the thousands on a daily basis around the world. Blockchain is the revolution that can change this forever. Not only do customers benefit but so do the insurers. Before you see how, let's first understand what Blockchain is.

What Is Blockchain?

In the simplest of words, Blockchain is a document full of entries that are shared with a group of people and organizations. The entries can be anything related to people/organizations within the sharing group: items owned, money sent/received, items sold/bought, etc. For security purposes, the shared document is encrypted and verified to ensure the data it stores is always correct (true to everyone). As everyone in the group has access to the exact same entries, there is no need for a central authority—a bank, the police, a judge, or any other arbitrator—to validate a transaction between two people in the group. Everyone knows about the said transaction that occurred between those two people. Also, the entries are immutable: once created, they cannot be updated or deleted. They cannot be tampered with!

In slightly more technical terms, Blockchain is a *decentralized* network—as seen in Figure 1-5—where each transaction involving two or more members on the network is recorded on a block in a giant write-once *ledger*. Think of a block as a page in the ledger. In this sense, a ledger can be thought of as a chain of blocks. Everyone in the network has the same copy of the ledger. Each time a transaction takes place, it is added to the ledgers of the members involved. Then, quickly and securely, all other copies of the ledger on the network are updated to ensure that all copies are kept in sync. There is no "master" ledger. There are as many ledgers as there are members on the network.

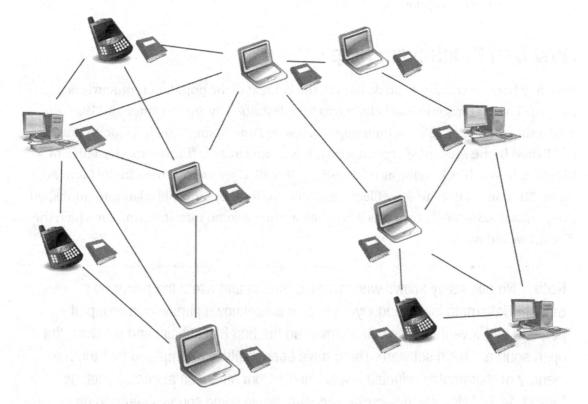

Figure 1-5. *A decentralized network of computers and mobile devices (collectively called "nodes"). Each node has a copy of the ledger.*

For the sake of emphasis, let us recap what we have learned so far about Blockchain:

- Blockchain is decentralized. There is no central authority to provide guarantees or validations for transactions that happen on the network. It's the direct opposite of a bank that acts as a middleman for all financial transactions between two or more entities.

- Nobody on a Blockchain network owns the ledger. Because of its decentralized nature, everyone on the network has a copy of the ledger.

- Records in the ledger are immutable. This is to disallow fraudulent tampering.

- All ledger copies are always kept in sync. If everyone has the same information about each other, the risk of a fraud is nullified.

- Blockchain provides a mechanism to verify each transaction through strong encryption.

How Can Blockchain Help?

You may have heard about Blockchain in the context of the popular cryptocurrency Bitcoin. The precursor to Blockchain was first described by Stuart Haber and W. Scott Stornetta, as early as 1991, in their paper "How to Time-Stamp a Digital Document," published in the *Journal of Cryptography*. It was only in 2008 that the modern idea of Blockchain—or block chain, as it was originally called—was presented in the famous paper "Bitcoin: A Peer-to-Peer Electronic Cash System" by Satoshi Nakamoto published at `metzdowd.com`. Blockchain was described as the backend infrastructure on which the Bitcoin would work.

Note   No one really knows who invented Bitcoin and wrote the paper on it. Satoshi Nakamoto is a pseudonym used by an unknown person or a group of persons that invented Bitcoin, implemented the first Blockchain, and released the open source Bitcoin software. There have been multiple attempts to find the real identity of Nakamoto, including involvements from American agencies such as Department of Homeland Security and NSA. While some sources claim to have found the real person(s) behind the mysterious pseudonym, there is no consensus. To this day, Nakamoto remains a hidden figure potentially worth billions of U.S. dollars because of his or her initial stock of Bitcoins.

Bitcoin is a virtual, electronic currency. It is not issued by a bank, and no government or authority in the world endorses it. There are no official Bitcoin currency notes and physical coins. So, how does it work? Why does it have credibility? Let's see. We learned in Blockchain's simpler definition that it can be thought of as a big shared database of transactions. In the case of Bitcoin, its Blockchain network started off with a small amount of coins (money). These coins were then distributed among the network's members. New coins can be introduced into the chain through a time- and resource-intensive process, aka *Bitcoin mining*. Each time coins are redistributed or added, a transaction is securely recorded in the Blockchain's ledgers. So, if Person A gives Person B a certain amount of money, the transaction is replicated at each and every ledger. In effect, everyone on the network knows that Person A has given x money worth coins to Person B. As everyone knows about this transaction, there is no dispute. Person B cannot lie about getting money less than x, and Person A cannot lie about giving money more than x. The economics of demand and supply decide the real-world worth of a Bitcoin. As of writing this book, 1 Bitcoin (BTC) was valued over U.S. $4000!

Now let's apply the same logic to the car insurance situation we saw earlier. If there were a Blockchain network consisting of customers, insurers, repair shops, and hospitals, everyone on the network would know of your insurance contract with an insurer. In the case of a medical claim for the person you injured, the hospital can instantly check your insurance contract to quickly facilitate the claim. In the case of a car damage claim, chances of getting unfairly duped by the insurer because of a complicated process would reduce. With the help of an IoT device installed in your car, the insurer can find out various parameters during the accident such as speed, location, photo, etc. This would help the customer get fair claims. For the insurer, this would mean no exaggerated claims. As per a Deloitte report (`https://www2.deloitte.com/content/dam/Deloitte/ch/Documents/innovation/ch-en-innovation-deloitte-blockchain-app-in-insurance.pdf`), some customers are known to indulge in a practice called "crash for cash," in which deliberately cause an accident to make claims. IoT devices with accurate sensors would prevent such scenarios. Another thing an insurer is protected from is multiple claims fraud. Scammers buy insurance policies from multiple insurers under made-up identities. Through a staged crash, they make multiple claims against the same accident. Such frauds are currently difficult to detect, as data is not shared by different insurers. A Blockchain network where multiple insurers are present and where fraudulent identity management is enforced will make it easy to detect a multiple claims fraud.

Blockchain is explained in further detail in Chapter 7.

Azure Blockchain Solutions

Deploying a Blockchain network is not easy. Microsoft Azure makes it easy to develop, test, and deploy Blockchain applications through something called Blockchain as a Service (BaaS). Blockchain is an open concept, with several open source and commercial implementations. Some implementations are existing deployments that run a digital currency while others are offered as platforms that can be installed on one's own infrastructure. Azure offers the latter implementations—Blockchain platforms—as part of BaaS. Each Blockchain platform or solution must be installed on one or more Linux or Windows virtual machine (VM) for your Blockchain network to come into effect. BaaS provides pre-configured VM templates to automate the task for installation and deployment. The tools and libraries required to develop applications for these Blockchain solutions are also installed along with the network.

Some Blockchain solutions offered as part of BaaS are:

- Ethereum Consortium

- STRATO Blockchain LTS

- Chain Core Developer Edition

- Ethereum Studio

- Emercoin Blockchain

You will learn about implementing one of these BaaS solutions in Chapter 8.

It Is All About Data

In the revolutions we have talked about, the real hero is not Cloud, nor it is AI or IoT or Blockchain. These are only the enablers. What do they enable? That's easy—data, which will always be the real hero in all important revolutions. Think about it. Data is what's collected (IoT). Data is what's analyzed (AI). Data (results) is what's stored and propagated (Blockchain).

Why Is Data So Important?

The first computer programs were written specifically to collect and analyze data—from recording weather data to making predictions to intercepting encrypted messages and using them to recognize patterns for code breaking, you may also be able to think of numerous other such examples.

Most of the software that we create today also depends on data in one form or another. While some apps come preloaded with their data, a sizable number of them depend on data collected from users. And, usually, there is an end goal to be met or insights to be obtained using the collected data, which may vary from a few kilobytes to gigabytes to terabytes in size. Through each revolution, it's always been our intention to put the data to use as intelligently as possible.

Take for instance a simple TODO application. The whole point of its existence is to provide a means to store user's notes (data) to help them remember things. A simple, static TODO app will do just that. A more sophisticated TODO app will continuously analyze your notes (and probably your emails, SMS, calendar, etc.) to offer you suggestions on what you may need reminding.

A social network is built totally on user data. Your status updates, comments, likes, photos, and so on, make Facebook the lively place that it is. Why is Facebook—the nicest thing on planet for some—offered absolutely free of cost? It's because of data: the data it collects from me, you, and millions of other people. Based on your activity (likes, location, friends, and apps) on the social network, it cleverly shows your promotions and advertisements, things that Facebook actually gets paid for by publishers and companies. The same goes for Twitter, Instagram, YouTube, Gmail, and more.

A search engine may use search trends to offer customized ads. A travel app may share (at a cost) users' booking and search data with airlines and hotels to allow them to offer better prices based on demand and supply. A maps app may collect users' location data to offer real-time traffic predictions.

Can you think of the importance of data in other domains, such as academia, research, health, stock markets, banking, education, and entertainment?

How Data Collection Has Evolved

There are two aspects of data collections—how it is collected, and where is it stored. Both these aspects have evolved immensely between the revolutions.

How Data Is Collected

Early computer programs were not user-facing. They were used by academicians and researchers to solve scientific problems. When software became accessible to commercial and non-commercial organizations, data collection was largely a paper-and-pen based process. Thousands of paper-based applications and forms filled up by customers had to be manually fed into the system by following a manual, labor-intensive process.

The Internet revolution brought about an explosion of user-facing applications. Through websites and desktop software, users and customers could themselves submit data. The smartphone revolution took this to an unimaginably new level. These smart pocket devices not only allowed users to explicitly submit data whenever and wherever they wanted, they also allowed collection of implicit user data—data collected without the intervention of the user: location, audio, images, etc.

We are currently in the midst of IoT revolution that has taken implicit user data collection further. Smartwatches automatically collect data about various health parameters, smart thermostats automatically collect temperature data, and custom IoT devices can be built with sensors to collect the desired data from a user's surroundings.

Where Data Is Stored

We started with files, the sort of text files that you create in Notepad. Logs, configuration data, and even user data was stored in text files. Writing to text files was fast and simple. Large amounts of data could be split among several files for convenience. Reading data from files was a challenge, though. As we know, data stored in unstructured or partially structured formats is difficult to search and use for analysis. This gave rise to spreadsheets and relational databases, where data could be stored in orderly formats made up of rows and columns. Storing and looking up large amounts of data became easy. They also made it easy to generate reports and insights. Major RDBMSs, such as SQL Server, offer reporting and intelligence functionalities such as SSRS and SSIS. The problem with RDBMSs is that they weren't made to handle billions of records. That's where NoSQL came into picture.

NoSQL databases are non-relational and do not enforce a set schema. Popular options, such as MongoDB and Cassandra, can store massive amounts of data (billions of records) in a way that is exponentially faster to save and retrieve. They are especially useful for storing semi-structured or unstructured data, and are used in environments where performance and speed are of utmost priority. Unstructured data is the one that grows at a rapid pace, as opposed to structured (relational) data, and analyzed to derive useful insights. And then there is Hadoop, a key driver of the Big Data revolution.

Hadoop is capable of storing massive amounts of unstructured and structured data. Additionally, it provides the means to perform data analytics on the stored massive amounts of data to generate reports and dashboards.

Now we have Blockchain, a mechanism to openly and securely store large amounts of data that is available to each member on the network. Blockchain should not be thought of as a replacement to other data storage mechanisms discussed here. Its use is only with transactional data, and it is often used in conjunction with NoSQL and relational databases.

Smart Hospitals

Throughout this book, you will learn and use the technologies that make up AI 2.0. You will see how AI 2.0 can be used to build real-world solutions. For the purpose of this book, we'll be focusing on the smart hospitals use case. *Asclepius* (pronounced ess-clip-ee-us) *Consortium* is our fictitious global network of 3+ star-rated hospitals that want to work together to save more lives and make easier the lives of their patients through data sharing.

We will build an AI 2.0 offering for the Asclepius Consortium that works in the following ways. All member hospitals and a bunch of insurance companies will be part of a dedicated Blockchain network. Medical records of patients across hospitals will be published on the Blockchain, including real-time patient monitoring data recorded through IoT devices. This will facilitate transparent sharing of patient data across hospitals and insurers.

AI will facilitate real-time analytics on patient monitoring data, leading to better diagnoses. Patient data collected from across hospitals can also be centrally analyzed to generate results that can be later used to make life-saving predictions in the case of other patients.

A network of such hospitals can keep track of all of medical inventory (equipment, machines, medicines, etc.) across hospitals. This will be helpful in the event of shortages of medical supplies.

Along the same lines, it will be possible to create highly-accessible organ banks, including a blood bank and an eye bank.

Transactions in which customers buy medical or life insurance from one of the insurers on this network will also be recorded. Availability of insurance records to hospitals will automate the claim process, making it simpler and time-saving. Availability of health records of patients to insurers will prevent potential frauds.

Recap

This chapter introduced you to the concepts and technologies that you will use to create the next generation of software solutions. You learned about:

- The upcoming revolution in software development called AI 2.0

- Various use cases involving AI 2.0

- Basics and evolution of Artificial Intelligence (AI)

- An overview of the Internet of Things (IoT)

- A simplistic understanding of Blockchain

- The importance of data in ongoing and upcoming revolutions

In the next chapter, you learn in detail about IoT in general and Azure's enterprise IoT offerings.

CHAPTER 2

Understanding the Internet of Things and Azure IoT Suite

A few years ago, Internet of Things (IoT) was an emerging trend. Today, it is part of modern arsenal of IT solutions. In the consumer space, IoT is generally perceived as smartwatches, fridges, TVs, etc.—age-old things that are now connected to the Internet. It is seen more as a convenience feature than a solution to an existing problem (smart thermostats and remote pet food dispensers, anyone?).

At the enterprise level, IoT has been a boon, especially in automation. Take for instance an automobile factory set up with hundreds of machines working hard-to-manufacture cars. Each machine may have lots of moving parts, which are susceptible to wear and tear. There are several parameters that must be regularly checked to ensure a 100% safe and operational working environment at all times. Such monitoring is largely a manual process at typical factories, done by humans. Data is recorded digitally or on paper and analyzed later to identify machines (or specific parts) that need repair or replacement. This is a slow and expensive process. Monitoring of manufacturing equipment can be automated by retrofitting cheap IoT devices into these machines. IoT devices can be customized to have specialized sensors to monitory specific parameters for different machines. In a world where Cloud storage and Big Data analysis is cheap, the IoT devices can run 24x7 to record and store monitoring data. This large feed of data can then be automatically analyzed later or in real time to detect potential problems. Factory supervisors can then be automatically intimated through text and notification messages.

© Nishith Pathak and Anurag Bhandari 2018
N. Pathak and A. Bhandari, *IoT, AI, and Blockchain for .NET*, https://doi.org/10.1007/978-1-4842-3709-0_2

What was the dominion of electrical and electronics engineers until a few years ago is now part of solution offerings at every major IT firm, making IoT a vital skill to have for computer and software engineers. To put it a little differently, what was a hardware and embedded software affair earlier is now writing normal software programs for tiny computers (IoT devices).

In this chapter, you learn about:

- The history of IoT

- IoT devices, including enablers such as Raspberry Pi

- Network connectivity, including messaging and protocols

- Practical use cases

- Configuring and deploying a single IoT device

- Azure IoT Suite and its components

- Azure IoT Hub architecture

- Configuring and deploying multiple IoT devices at scale using the Azure IoT Hub

The History of IoT

Like artificial intelligence, the central idea behind IoT is not new. The phrase "Internet of Things" was coined by Kevin Ashton in 1999, but the origin of the concept goes way back to early 80s. In 1982, a re-engineered Coke bottle dispensing machine—at Carnegie Mellon University's computer science department—became the first appliance to be connected to the Internet (ARPANET, as it was called during its formative years). With the help of micro-switches and sensors, the Coke machine could continuously report its inventory status (number of bottles remaining, number of warm versus cold bottles, etc.). So instead of students visiting the machine and then being disappointed on finding no chilled bottles, students could log in to a website and check its status. The famed Coke machine is still connected to the Internet, and even has a page on CMU's website to tell its own story.

John Romkey, creator of TCP/IP stack for IBM PCs, created a toaster in 1990 that could be turned on or off over the Internet. In 1993, Quentin Stafford-Fraser connected a coffee pot to the Internet to monitor its pot levels.

Mark Weiser's popular article on ubiquitous computing, called "The Computer for the 21st Century," explored this idea in detail. So, you see, the idea was there but it did not get widespread attention as the Internet itself was in its infancy. It is said that when Kevin Ashton showed his presentation on a revolutionary new idea on RFIDs to his management at P&G, he called it the "Internet of Things" to in order to attract immediate interest, as the Internet was a red hot topic in those days.

The RFID revolution indeed provided a thrust to the then future IoT revolution as we know it today. Digitally identifying real-world physical things using fingertip-small circuits was a powerful concept that enabled digital representations of these on the Internet.

In the early 2000s, IoT as a term started getting traction. It was being mentioned in scientific journals, at conferences, and in magazines. It was not until 2009 that it was officially born, when (according to Cisco) the number of devices that were connected to the Internet exceeded the number of people in the world. The release of Raspberry Pi in 2012 and the subsequent wave of tiny system on a chip (SoC) computers were major contributors to the IoT phenomenon. IoT started receiving widespread industry adoption starting in 2014; the trends have not looked back since.

Figure 2-1 summarizes the timeline of IoT.

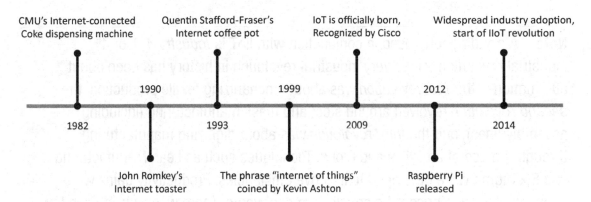

Figure 2-1. *IoT timeline chart that summarizes the milestones*

IoT Devices

There should be no confusion in the fact that "things," devices, and IoT devices are all the same in an IoT network. As we saw at the start of this chapter, IoT devices can be thought of as being of two types—consumer and enterprise. In fact, there is a formal way of categorizing IoT itself:

- **Consumer IoT**: Consists of readymade devices for direct consumption by end users. Examples include smartwatches, smart TVs, and smart speakers. Devices are usually connected to each other or to the local network via Bluetooth or WiFi.

- **Industrial IoT**: Consists of devices custom-made for specific enterprise and industrial scenarios. The car factory example we talked about earlier falls in this category. It is important to note that *custom-made* does not mean that all electronic components of a device are manufactured or even assembled. As you'll see a little later, there are "boilerplate" enabler devices that can be customized or extended for creating large solutions. Devices are usually connected directly to the Internet via Ethernet or WiFi.

Note   A trending term used in conjunction with IIoT is *Industry 4.0* (or 4th industrial revolution, 4IR). Every industrial revolution in history has been about automation—the *first revolution* was about mechanizing textile production, the *second revolution* revolved around steel and mass manufacturing (including assembly lines), and the *third revolution* was about digitizing manufacturing through the use of analytics and Cloud. Techniques such as Lean Manufacturing and Six Sigma were developed to improve efficiencies. Productivity gains were huge initially, but dipped substantially in recent years. There was a strong need to look to other ways to improve efficiencies.

Industry 4.0 is about improving efficiencies through complete digital transformation using leading contemporary digital technologies—IIoT, Big Data, Cloud Computing, Augmented Reality, Robotics, etc. What started off with manufacturing now covers other industries such as healthcare, agriculture, logistics, and more. Benefits include decreased unplanned downtime, lower maintenance costs, reduced power consumption, and improved performance.

It is easy to confuse the third industrial revolution with the fourth. The key differentiating factor is undoubtedly advancements in machine and deep learning, which gave rise to artificial intelligence, robotic process automation, and cognitive services as we know them today.

Sensors and Actuators

No discussion about IoT devices is complete without talking about their core building blocks—sensors and actuators.

A *sensor* is a small electronic component that is designed to sense (detect) a specific parameter—sound, light, temperature, humidity, pressure, GPS coordinates, acceleration, etc. Our mobile phones come loaded with half a dozen sensors.

An *actuator* is an electrical or mechanical device that performs an action or a movement (push, pull, or rotate). LEDs, motors, speakers, and vibrators are a couple of examples.

An actuator is the logical opposite of sensor. How? Both sensors and actuators are *transducers* that convert one form of energy into another. A sensor converts a physical phenomenon into an electrical signal—a microphone converts sound vibrations into signals, a temperature sensor converts heat into its representative analogue or digital value. On the contrary, an actuator converts electrical signals into physical actions (rotation, light, sound, etc.).

An IoT device is defined by the sensors and actuators it comes with. These may come either built into the device or as separate pluggable components. They can be controlled by the operating system of their IoT device. Because of this, sensors and actuators may work independently or in tandem.

Figure 2-2 shows how an actuator complements a sensor on the same IoT device.

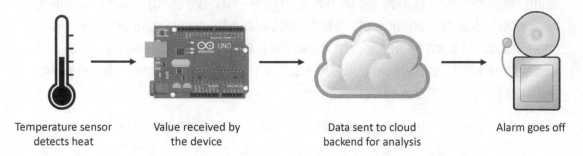

| Temperature sensor detects heat | Value received by the device | Data sent to cloud backend for analysis | Alarm goes off |

Figure 2-2. *Workflow of an alarm going off on receiving a high temperature signal from sensor*

Enablers

As noted earlier, for several years IoT was the dominion of electrical, electronics, and embedded engineers. In the early days of IoT revolution, network connectivity hardware was built into industrial machines and electronic products by manufacturers. Alternatively, custom or existing programmable microcontrollers were used as embedded devices on machines. Software for such systems were written either in assembly language or using specialized programming languages, often proprietary for the specific microcontroller. The release of Raspberry Pi in 2012 completely changed the status quo and virtually sparked off the modern IoT revolution.

Raspberry Pi

Raspberry Pi or RPi or just Pi is a system on a chip (SoC) device that has an ARM-based microprocessor, RAM, graphics processor, and various I/O and network connectivity options built on top of a single credit card-sized printed circuit board. In other words, it is a tiny general-purpose computer.

Pi was launched as a cheap, affordable self-learning toolkit for school students and electronics enthusiasts by a not-for-profit organization based in the UK. It was complemented with a well-documented website containing tutorials for building all sorts of projects—from simple LED blinkers to full-blown theft prevention systems.

Figure 2-3 shows a Raspberry Pi.

Figure 2-3. *Raspberry Pi 2 Model B*

Being a cheap (just $35) and sufficiently sophisticated SoC, Raspberry Pi offered limitless possibilities. At that price point, one can finally afford a general purpose computer rather than a single board microcontroller. Microcontrollers are similar to SoCs in that they have a CPU, small amount of memory, and some I/O. But they are less sophisticated than SoCs. While a microcontrollers are designed for embedded applications using specialized programming techniques/languages, a SoC has a microprocessor and a decent amount of RAM that allows it to run a full-blown operating system such as Linux and Windows, on which can be run general purpose computing applications written in all major high-level programming languages (Java, Python, C#, Perl, Ruby... you name it).

As the Pi came with an Ethernet adapter and four USB ports to add more network adapters, such as Bluetooth and WiFi, it did not take much time for developers to leverage it as an IoT device. A question may pop in your mind at this point—IoT devices have sensors and/or actuators, so what about Raspberry Pi? To answer that question, look at Figure 2-4, which shows the schematics of a Pi.

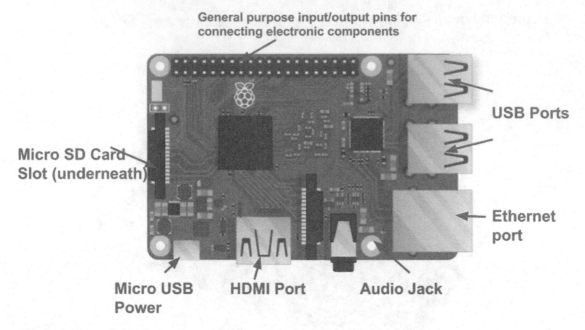

Figure 2-4. *The schematics of a Raspberry Pi*

Raspberry Pi does not come with sensors and actuators of its own. But it does come with something called general purpose input-output (GPIO) pins. These pins are a bridge between the outside world and the internals of Pi. You can connect electronic components (sensors, actuators, and more)—such as LEDs, motors, buttons, or other boards and microcontrollers—with a Pi through its GPIO pins. Connected electronic components can then be controlled via software programs that run on top of the operating system installed on that Pi. Many popular programming languages provide easy APIs to interact with GPIO pins. Python is the most popular choice, and something used in code samples provided on RPi's official documentation.

A Pi can easily be fitted with sensors and store and run programs written to send data collected from sensors to a Cloud backend. With the hardware configuration that is has, a Pi can also be used in edge computing use cases. You will learn more about edge computing in the Network Connectivity section a bit later. Since a Pi is a tiny general-purpose computer, it can also be used without sensors or actuators, in use cases such as a web server or a media streaming platform.

RPi comes in two major variants—the Raspberry Pi and the Raspberry Pi Zero, the former having four further variants and the latter having two (with and without WiFi). Price starts at $5 and goes up to $35.

Arduino

Arduino is one of the most popular single board microcontrollers. Unlike the Raspberry Pi, Arduino is not an SoC and does not have a microprocessor. It has a lower performance CPU and a few KBs of RAM. Due to this, it manages to be even cheaper than Raspberry Pi Zero. But even a low hardware configuration is mostly sufficient to allow it to be used as an IoT device that just has to capture sensor data and send it to a Cloud backend for storage and processing.

Like the RPi, Arduino has digital input-output pins that can be connected with electronic components to extend it as an IoT device. It also comes with a USB port that can be used to power or program the board. It does not run an OS, so programs have to be uploaded from a regular computer (PC, laptop, etc.) through a USB cable. What makes Arduino stand out from other microcontrollers is its ability to be programmed without a separate hardware (programmer). Arduino provides an IDE software to write code and upload it onto the board.

Figure 2-5 shows a diagrammatic representation of an Arduino UNO board.

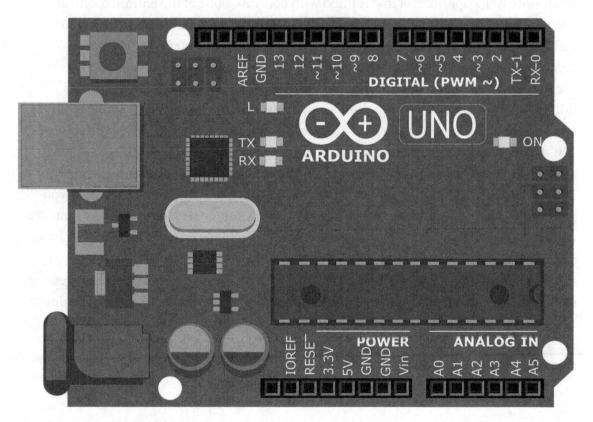

Figure 2-5. *Arduino UNO*

Arduino is open source, meaning its blueprint and architecture have been openly made available online for any one to refer or even use to build their own Arduino boards. This is another reason behind Arduino's popularity since now there are hundreds of small to medium-sized board makers that produce Arduinos globally.

Arduino has dozens of official variants, the most popular one being Arduino UNO, which is well-suited to beginners who want to learn about the board.

BLE Beacons

Bluetooth low energy beacons or simply Beacons are a very different class of IoT enablers. A beacon is a dead-simple, battery-powered, thumb-sized device whose sole purpose is to transmit Bluetooth signals containing its universally unique identifier (UUID). Several beacons can be deployed in a hall or a building. A mobile app can then be designed to detect Bluetooth signals coming from all the beacons in range and perform a specific action based on the closest beacon.

Perhaps beacons are best understood through its retail store use case. Imagine a retail store or a supermarket that is fitted with beacons—one at the entrance, one at checkout, and one each in every aisle. Each beacon regularly transmits its UUID. You walk into the store with the store's official app installed on your phone. The app is designed to interact with the store's beacons. The moment you enter, your app detects the beacon at the entrance. The app's developers have programmed it to trigger a notification message on coming close to each beacon. On coming in proximity to the entrance beacon, you instantly get a notification that says something like, "Welcome to ABC Store. This is an excellent time to check in, as we have plenty of discounts. Check aisle 7 through 13 for maximum discounts." The beacon didn't send this message, your app did (there's possibly an if-else logic for each beacon's UUID). Similarly, when you pass through an aisle, you get an aisle-specific notification, "Hey, did you know that your favorite oats are 15% off?" In this way, retail store owners can make shopping more engaging, increasing their revenues in the process.

Apart from being able to retrieve a beacon's UUID, an app may also use its Bluetooth signal strength value to roughly calculate its distance (in meters) from the mobile device.

Both iOS and Android offer native APIs to interact with beacons. Apple calls its API set iBeacon, while Google calls it EddyStone. AltBeacon is a popular open alternative, created by Radius Networks.

Other Honorable Mentions

Intel's family of IoT devices—Edison, Joule, Arduino 101, Curie, and Galileo—all based on Intel processors. Edison and Joule are powerful but expensive alternatives to Raspberry Pi.

BeagleBone—another worthy RPi alternative—comes with a large number of analog and digital I/O pins.

Products

By now you have learned about the building blocks of an IoT device—sensors, actuators, and IoT enabler devices. You have seen various options for building an IoT device of your own at home. Now let's spend a quick minute or two to check another type of IoT devices: ones that are factory fitted by manufacturers into electronic items and home and electrical appliances. These are IoT devices whose hardware cannot be customized or extended, but which may allow software customizations through a companion mobile app.

A popular category of IoT products is *wearables*. These are devices that can be worn, things such as:

- Smartwatches—Monitor heart rate, distance run, altitude variations, sleep patterns, and more. Examples: Apple Watch, Moto 360, Samsung Galaxy Gear, Fossil SmartWatch.

- Fitness bands—Similar to smartwatches, sans the clock aspect. Examples: Fitbit, Pebble, and Mi Band.

- Smartglasses—Come with a camera and motion sensors, are often used with computer vision and augmented reality applications. Examples: Google Glass, PivotHead, Vuzix, and Microsoft HoloLens.

- Shoes—Come with various health tracking sensors. Examples: Nike+ and Under Armor Speedform.

Apart from wearables, other electronic and even simple home devices that may be IoT-enabled are TVs, speakers, washing machines, thermostats, door locks, switches, plugs, cameras, and light bulbs. Amazon's Dash buttons also quality as IoT devices.

Network Connectivity

Their ability to connect to a network for sharing data is what sets IoT devices apart from regular electronic devices. However, contrary to the name "Internet" of Things, devices do not have to be connected to the Internet all the time to qualify as IoT devices. They may operate in offline mode most of the time and connect to the Internet only occasionally to sync data with their Cloud backend. Monitoring devices in a factory setup where real-time updates is not crucial may operate in this mode.

Alternatively, IoT devices may be connected to each other locally without an active Internet connection. For example, consider a media streaming device connected to a TV and various stream sources (mobile, laptop, PC, etc.) on a local WiFi network.

Depending on connectivity options available on the device, it may be connected to other devices or the Internet through Bluetooth or Ethernet. ZigBee is another popular option for low-powered devices.

Since IoT is all about transportation of data (from sensors or otherwise) from one device to others or to a Cloud backend, let's take a quick glimpse at some popular messaging protocols used with IoT devices.

Messaging

Suppose yours is an IoT device with just one transducer—a temperature sensor. The only job of your device is to continuously detect the temperature inside your room and send the reading to a Cloud backend after every minute. For sending data from device to Cloud, you probably wrote a RESTful API that could be called from the device. This API accepts just one parameter—temperature—and stores it in some sort of a database. This, perhaps, is the simplest use case imaginable for an IoT device. In the real world, however, things are more complicated.

In a typical IoT setup, hundreds or thousands of IoT devices must simultaneously send their recorded data every second or few seconds to the Cloud. Many of these devices may have multiple sensors and, thus, as many data streams to send. In the room temperature device example, sending data reliably wasn't difficult. A very small amount of data had to be sent over the Internet after a considerable amount of time (one minute is comfortably long between API calls). There was negligible chance of data congestion and delivery failure.

But when large amounts of data need to be sent, things get different. We must be ready for the following questions:

- How do we ensure all data is sent in the timely manner set for each device?

- How do we ensure all data is sent by devices and received at the Cloud backend reliably (that is, no data message is dropped on the way)?

- How do we ensure large amount of data doesn't congest the network connection?

If you have worked with large-scale software, you know an efficient queuing technique can address these questions. A suitable messaging, data queuing, and routing technique is all the more important in IoT to deal with large volumes of data to be transferred rapidly over the Internet. This is where messaging protocols come to the rescue. More often than not, the protocols work with an existing or custom messaging middleware (broker) for desired results.

Figure 2-6 shows how data flows from a device to the Cloud using proper messaging.

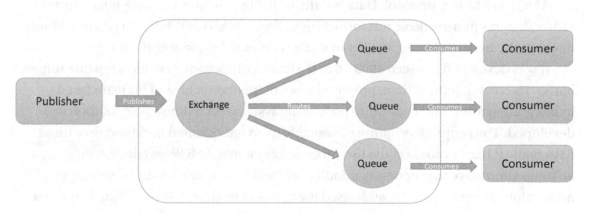

Figure 2-6. *Example messaging flow using a protocol and a broker*

All protocols discussed next are neither new nor were they created specifically for IoT. They are application layer protocols for message-oriented communication. Their low power consumption and reliable messaging make them a suitable choice for data transfer in the case of IoT devices.

AMQP

Advanced Message Queuing Protocol is perhaps the most popular choice for writing enterprise IoT applications. AMQP makes extensive use of queuing for reliably routing messages from source to destination. Routing is based on publish-and-subscribe model, and queuing is done using the store-and-forward technique. A *publisher* (source) generates a message and sends it to the *exchange*. The exchange redirects the message to one of several *message queues*. The message is stored in its queue until the *subscriber* (destination) is ready to receive it. At an appropriate time, the queue forwards the message to subscriber, thus completing its reliable delivery of the message.

AMQP is known for its rich set of features, including restricting access to queues and other fine-grained controls over its components. A message can have properties and a header. It provides three message-delivery guarantees—*at-most-once* (fire and forget mode: message is delivered once or never), *at-least-once* (message is guaranteed to be delivered, but could be sent multiple times), and *exactly-once* (message is delivered certainly and only once). Because of these features, AMQP is an ideal choice for developing highly scalable enterprise applications where reliability and security are crucial.

AMQP is a binary protocol. Data is transported in machine-readable binary format rather than human-readable text format (as in the case of HTTP, FTP, SMTP, etc.). Binary data has the benefit of being smaller in size as compared to plain-text data.

It was developed between 2003-06 at JPMorgan Chase, one of world's top investment banks. Its creator, John O'Hara, proposed it out of frustration he and his team faced in integrating front- and back-office processing systems each time a new solution was developed. The proprietary nature of available message-oriented middleware of those days made it hard to connect the two processing systems. AMQP was developed as an open alternative to proprietary middleware, and so interoperability was a major motivation. The protocol also addressed the issues of reliable delivery owing to the fact that in banking each message delayed or failed could have economic implications.

JP Morgan still uses AMQP to process a billion messages a day, and so do companies such as a NASA and Google. The world's largest biometric and identity database—India's UIDAI or Aadhaar project—also uses the protocol to serve 1.2 billion people.

In sum, the defining features of AMQP are *queuing, reliability,* and *security*.

MQTT

Message Queue Telemetry Transport protocol is simpler and more focused than AMQP. Like AMQP, it uses the publish-and-subscribe model for messaging, but unlike AMQP it does not use message queues (you read it right—no message queues, despite the name). MQTT is intentionally designed to have a low footprint. It is especially suited to low-powered, resource constrained devices operating over low-bandwidth, high-latency networks.

MQTT is also a binary protocol, where messages are smaller due to compressed headers and the lack of message properties. It is ideally suited to IoT devices that send out simple data messages, such as temperature and humidity values, stock prices, mobile notifications, etc.

Defining features are *simplicity* and a *lower footprint*.

STOMP

Simple Text Oriented Message Protocol is a text-based protocol with simplicity and interoperability as key design goals. Unlike AMQL and MQTT, messages are transmitted in human-readable plaintext format. This makes communication between the server possible with a wide-range of clients (including telnet).

STOMP does not use message queues, but the messages support AMQP-like properties and headers. The protocol is simple and easy to implement, as its design follows closely that of how HTTP works. The creators of STOMP claim that developers have been able to write a STOMP client program in a couple of hours.

Defining features are *simplicity* and *interoperability*.

XMPP

Extensible Messaging and Presence Protocol is another text-based protocol suited to applications that require real-time exchange of structured information. Messages are transmitted in XML format, allowing for extensive interoperability since XML is understood by a wide variety of systems and programming languages. XMPP is a secure protocol that allows for authentication mechanisms and end-to-end encryption of communication. Also known as Jabber (after the open source community that originally developed it), XMPP is widely used in instant messaging applications including Google Talk. It also facilitates the exchange of presence information (online, offline, busy, away, etc.) across contact-based IM applications.

Defining features are *structured messaging* (via XML) and *real-time communication*.

Edge Computing

In an IoT network, things that form the network are often pretty low configuration devices whose sole purpose is to capture data and send it over to a powerful Cloud backend for storage, processing, and analysis. Such devices do not have computational power or memory to do analytics on their own. With the explosion of IoT enabler devices, things are changing rapidly.

The new breed of IoT devices come with decent compute power at a low cost. The $5 Raspberry Pi Zero comes with 1GHz single core processor (same as Model B+) and 512MB RAM. Compare this with the original Raspberry Pi (Model B gen 1)—launched in 2012 at $35—that came with 700MHz single-core processor and the same amount of RAM!

By utilizing this increased compute power and memory clubbed with modern machine learning techniques, basic analysis of captured data can be performed on the device itself. In an IoT network, devices are connected to the Cloud backend via gateways, routers, and servers. While Cloud backend sits at the center, devices form the "edge" of the network. So, pushing data storage and analysis to the logical extremes of a network is called *edge computing*. Edge devices may be connected to a source of data (motor, turbine, pump, or another machine part) or may itself be the source of data. Results obtained from edge computing may later be synced with a Cloud backend for permanent storage and further analysis. As you might instantly imagine, performing computation at or near source of data has several benefits:

- **Instant action**: Since a device can perform basic analysis by itself and doesn't have to wait for data to upload and Cloud backend to respond, it can take immediate actions based on calculated decisions. For example, calling off an alarm proactively when detecting a particular temperature predictive trend. The ability to perform instant actions is a godsend in cases where network connectivity is slow.

- **Reduced network usage**: The Cloud backend does not have to be updated as frequently as in normal scenarios. Results obtained through edge computing may be stored on the devices and synced with Cloud every few hours or minutes rather than seconds. In this way, a lot of network bandwidth (and, thus, costs) may be saved, especially in setups involving hundreds or thousands of devices.

- **Ability to work offline**: In certain scenarios, edge computing may allow devices to work completely offline without the need to connect with a Cloud backend. This might not require sufficiently powerful IoT devices, depending on the use case. Autonomous vehicles, such as self-driving cars, are a good use case.

- **Security and compliance**: Sometimes security constraints of organizations, such as banks and government agencies, mandate data to be stored only on the intranet and not cross over to Internet Cloud servers. This is to make it harder for hackers to penetrate their data. Edge computing can fill in for the lack of a Cloud backend.

Note   *Fog computing* is a conceptually similar term, sometimes (incorrectly) used interchangeably with edge computing. In both cases, data processing happens near the source of data. The difference is exactly where on the edge. In the case of edge computing, processing happens on the device itself. On the other hand, in fog computing processing happens on IoT gateways. A gateway is a powerful, server-like routing and compute device that connects several IoT devices to the Internet or rest of the network. So, data processing happens nearer the source of data in the case of edge computing.

Practical Use Cases

By now, you probably already have a very good idea about where and how IoT can be useful. We still want to introduce you to four very different use cases in the hopes that they prove thought-provoking and instigate in you a motivation to build something of your own.

Use Case 1: Home Automation

There are various aspects of a home that can be automated. Whether it is a physical disability that prevents one from manually accessing parts of a home or just sheer convenience, automation can be really useful in those crucial moments.

A visitor sounds the doorbell. A camera mounted strategically at the door is triggered to record a photo/video of the visitor. The camera, which is connected to the Internet, sends the recorded media over to a Cloud backend for face recognition. If the face matches one in the "friends and family" database, the door unlocks automatically. In the meantime, a notification is sent to the home owner's phone about the visitor. The visitor identification system can be programmed to not unlock the door if no one is at home. This idea can be extended to allow only those people to automatically enter who have an appointment with the home owner during that time as per their online calendar.

A home intrusion system can be built on similar lines. A high-priority notification can be sent to the owner and local police authorities if someone unknown tries to trespass.

The weather is melting hot. The home owner is on this way from office to home. Fifteen minutes before her estimated time of arrival (perhaps as per the navigation system on car or mobile), a message is sent to the bedroom's air conditioner to turn on to make the room temperature comfortable once the owner is home.

We are sure that you can think of a dozen more such convenient use cases. The idea of home automation can also be extended to create a *connected home,* a place where appliances talk to each other and all connected appliances are accessible to the owner via a mobile app: smartwatch asking the room lights to turn off when the wearer falls asleep, home owner activating the pet feeder remotely using mobile app, and so on.

For a person suffering from a severe physical disability, such as in the case of ALS or quadriplegia, the ability to control the home is a necessity rather than a convenience. Imagine such a person, wearing a smartglass, and being able to switch the lights on and off just by blinking and double-blinking their eyes.

Since such a person would be home-bound most of the time, it would make great sense to notify their caretaker who is out at work. If the patient's vitals, being monitored by a fitness band, come to a critical level, the caretaker automatically receives a pre-recorded urgent call to pull them out of their work.

Use Case 2: Indoor Navigation

GPS is a cool technology to navigate us from one place to another. While it works great outside, GPS fails indoors owing to the fact that its signals find it difficult to penetrate the concrete and other construction materials used in building our homes and offices. For going from one place to another inside a building, we need another technology.

We learned earlier that signals received from beacons not only tell their UUID but also their rough distance from the phone receiving those signals. This information, when clubbed with pedestrian dead reckoning (PDS) algorithms, can be used to precisely estimate a person's location as they walk through a building. Beacons serve as checkpoints, whereas PDS provides the route information to navigate from one checkpoint to another.

Indoor navigation is especially useful to people suffering from vision impairment.

Use Case 3: Pet Monitoring

An IoT device (microcontroller, RFID tag, or beacon) attached to a pet can check on its various health parameters. It can also constantly monitor the pet's position and immediately sound an alarm when they cross the house's boundary. This use case can be extended to farm animals, where it is easy for them to go astray and difficult for the farm owner to manually keep track of all the livestock. A simple location monitoring device may keep an animal safe from being run over by a vehicle or eaten by a larger wild animal.

Use Case 4: Process Optimization

Have you ever been to a large kitchen, the kind where meals are produced in very large quantities to be served to the general public? If you have then you know that a good amount of food is wasted every time. Such kitchens use huge containers to cook food in bulk quantities. It's not unusual for a container's food to overcook due to a miscalculation on the cook's part. Food waste is a big problem, especially for NGOs working to provide free mid-day meals to thousands of needy people. The cost of wasted food can easily accumulate to thousands of dollars per month.

IoT devices can be installed inside these food containers to sense temperature and other parameters. Sensing overcooking, alerts may be sounded. Through this approach, waste can be diminished and food quality made consistent.

Configuring and Deploying a Single IoT Device

In the "IoT Devices" section earlier, you learned about some popular enabler devices. The three important ones we discussed were Raspberry Pi, Arduino, and beacons. The process of deploying code varies from device to device.

Raspberry Pi

Rpi, being an SoC, offers a PC-like hardware configuration. It can ably run a regular operating system, such as Windows or Linux. As a result, running code and programs on a Pi is similar to doing so on a regular computer. People can connect their Pis to their TVs or monitors, plug a keyboard into one of the USB ports, and start coding. Sensors and actuators can be installed via the RPi's GPIO interface, whose pins can be controlled directly through code.

A Pi's operating system may be run in headless mode, meaning without the OS's graphical interface. Headless mode is useful because of two reasons—the GUI consumes precious memory and computing resources, which may otherwise be used to speed up data analysis on the device and the environments where IoT devices are deployed usually do not have a need for a TV/monitor screen. Even without a GUI, a developer may log into their Pi through SSH or a similar technology. This is also the standard industry practice. While logged in via SSH, it is easy to write and update code, calibrate sensors, and configure and optimize the device.

Arduino

An Arduino connects via a USB cable to a regular computer, where the developer uses Arduino IDE to write code and upload it to and run it on the device. Electronic components can be attached through its digital I/O pins. Since Arduinos cannot run operating systems, it is not possible to write code by "logging in".

Beacons

Beacons are the simplest of IoT devices. They neither have a processor nor memory. The code to interact with them is installed on a mobile device. How the app uses the Bluetooth signals emanated by one or more beacons is totally up to the app.

What About Deploying Code to Multiple IoT Devices at Once?

Dealing with IoT devices can be simple and fun as long as you are doing that with one or two devices, maximum. Things start getting frustratingly complicated and laborious when you have to deal with hundreds of similar or even different devices (think Pis and Arduinos). In an enterprise scenario, the following must be addressed:

- Managing network connectivity for all devices

- Continuous monitoring of all devices

- Deploying code updates on all devices

- Adding new devices to the network

- Security and identity management

Azure IoT Suite

We have said it half a dozen times before and we'll say it again, "IoT is centered on data. Data is the fuel of an IoT network, its most valuable asset." Through its Azure Cloud services, Microsoft has been targeting data for some time now. Its data storage, processing, and analytics services are stable and evolved. It was natural, then, that with the onset of the IIoT revolution Microsoft would be one of the first to offer a well-tested set of services to manage large-scale enterprise IoT solutions.

The Azure IoT Suite is a set of new and existing Cloud services to comprehensively cover all IIoT needs. While *machine learning, PowerBI,* and *Notification Hubs* are veteran services that were reused in the suite, *IoT Hub* and *Stream Analytics* are new additions specially created for enterprise IoT.

It is important to note that the Azure IoT Suite is about managing IoT devices at scale: not one or two or a dozen devices, but hundreds or thousands or millions of them. You can, of course, use the services with fewer devices but the real cost benefit is seen with a large set of devices.

IoT Solution Architecture

Before going into the details of each service, let's look at the architecture of a typical IoT solution. Figure 2-7 shows the key components of an IoT solution architecture.

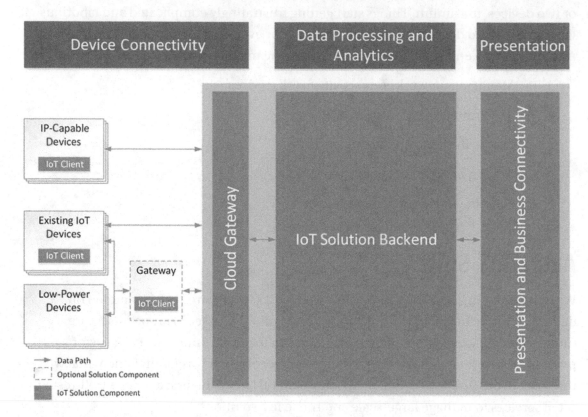

Figure 2-7. *IoT solution architecture*

Figure 2-7 shows how data flows within a solution. Data originates at the IoT devices, gets routed through a Cloud gateway over to a Cloud backend (IoT solution backend), and after the data has been processed in the backend, it is presented in human-readable format as graphs and charts. At all stages of this workflow, there is something that is facilitating data flow, as can be seen at the top of the diagram.

Device connectivity is fully managed by IoT Hub. It is responsible for connecting, authenticating, configuring, updating, and deploying millions of IoT devices.

Data processing and analytics is done using the machine learning and Stream Analytics services. It helps in extracting meaningful insights and making predictions that are relevant to optimizing or growing business.

Presentation is facilitated by PowerBI, which can generate elegant and easy-to-understand dashboards using raw data insights produced by ML and Stream Analytics services. Decision-makers in an organization can refer to the dashboards, rather than being bogged down by Excel sheets, to quickly make decisions.

At each stage in the workflow, it may be required to notify stakeholders and users of that stage of important events, such as device malfunction, security breach, completion of analytics, etc. Notification Hubs is a multi-platform push-notification engine that can send notification messages at scale to mobile devices, including iOS, Android, and Windows devices.

Preconfigured Solutions

The Azure IoT Suite provides a set of three preconfigured end-to-end solutions that cover the most common real-world use cases. So, instead of starting from scratch, one can use a preconfigured solution either directly (if it fulfills are business requirements) or as base template that will undergo customizations. Deploying a preconfigured solution takes only a few minutes and is supported by Azure's Resource Manager deployment model.

Remote Monitoring

This preconfigured solution targets a scenario where various assets of a workshop, factory, office, or other similar establishments produce telemetry data that must be constantly monitored to keep track of critical events.

For simplicity's sake, take for instance a workshop that has a furnace, an engine, and a lathe machine. All three produce data for various telemetry parameters: furnace (temperature, humidity, pressure), engine (fuel level, vibration), and lathe machine (rotations per minute, temperature). Using the remote monitoring solution, it's easy to set up alarms for events such as when:

- Pressure inside the furnace is greater than 220 psi

- Fuel level of the engine is less than five liters

- Temperature of the lathe machine is more than 50 degrees Celsius

Predictive Maintenance

This solution is helpful in predicting maintenance needs of machines well ahead of their imminent failure.

Consider a factory with hundreds of machines with moving parts. Each machine is susceptible to fail at some point due to wear and tear. Each time a machine fails, part of the production halts until it is fixed or replaced. Such delays due to unplanned downtimes result in monetary losses to the factory. The predictive maintenance solution can regularly highlight machines that will fail in the near future, and, thus, help them save costs by doing fewer planned maintenances rather than several unplanned ones.

Connected Factory

This solution is similar to remote monitoring one, except automated actions can be taken in addition to raising alarms. The solution can help in:

- Monitoring assets and generating key performance indicator (KPI) values

- Using the Azure Time Series Insights service to analyze telemetry data

- Taking actions to fix issues based on alarms by sending commands to devices

For each solution, a predefined set of Azure services gets activated. In the case of remote monitoring:

- IoT Hub (device connectivity and maintenance)

- Container services (hosts and manages microservices)

- Web apps (host custom application code)

- Cosmos DB (data storage)

For this connected factory, the following two services get activated in addition to the ones in the case of remote monitoring:

- Time Series Insights (analyze and display telemetry data)

- Azure Tables (store NoSQL data)

Azure IoT Hub

IoT Hub is a fully managed service that enables reliable and secure two-way communications between a large number of IoT devices and a solution backend. It is the answer to our earlier question about connecting and deploying code to multiple IoT devices at once.

Figure 2-8 shows the architecture diagram of IoT Hub. It is a focused and more detailed version of the IoT solution architecture we saw earlier.

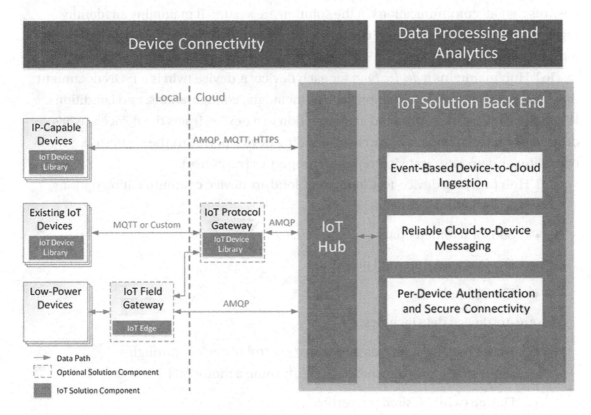

Figure 2-8. *Azure IoT Hub architecture*

In Figure 2-8, IoT Hub is the interface between devices and backend. We saw earlier how connectivity options vary across devices. In order to standardize connectivity to the solution backend, IoT Hub provides *device SDKs* for C, Python, Node.js, Java, and .NET.

IoT Hub natively understands only three protocols—MQTT, AMQP, and HTTPS. For devices that use different messaging protocols, IoT Hub provides a *protocol gateway* to translate messages from their protocol to one it understands.

Configuring and Deploying Multiple IoT Devices at Scale

IoT Hub is designed to manage millions of devices simultaneously. It provides secure bidirectional communication between devices and the solution backend. Devices can send their telemetry data to the backend. Conversely, the backend can send commands to stop/restart a device, turn actuators on or off, and so on.

Security is the utmost, the number one consideration in IoT Hub's design. Hub ensures that all communications in the solution are secure. It maintains an identity registry that has a record of each trusted device's identity. Unauthorized devices cannot join the network.

IoT Hub maintains a *device twin* for each device. A device twin is a JSON document that stores device state information such as metadata, configurations, and conditions. When the backend needs to send an instruction to a device, it sets the device's twin's desired properties (request). The corresponding device performs the requested operation and updates its twin's reported properties (response).

IoT Hub provides device-to-Cloud and Cloud-to-device communication options. Device-to-Cloud data includes:

- Sensor telemetry data

- Device twin's reported properties

- File uploads

Cloud-to-device data includes:

- Direct methods, such as interactive control of devices through a request-response mechanism (e.g., turning a motor off)

- Device twin's desired properties

- One-way notifications to the device app

Recap

In this chapter, you learned about IoT and devices (or things) in detail. You also had a glimpse of the Azure IoT Suite and its components and saw how it can help manage massive IoT solutions. The chapter included:

- An introduction to IoT: its meaning, history, and practical use cases

- A quick discourse on IoT devices: building blocks, types, and deployment methods

- A discussion of network connectivity options with IoT devices

- A discussion of Azure IoT Suite components and architecture

In the next chapter, you use the Azure IoT Suite to create and manage your own IoT solution.

CHAPTER 3

Creating Smart IoT Applications

In Chapter 2 we learned about the Internet of Things, IoT devices, practical use cases, and messaging protocols. We also gained the conceptual understanding of Azure IoT Suite and its various components, especially Azure IoT Hub. Armed with this knowledge, it is time to create an IoT solution ourselves. We will create our own IoT network and write applications for devices in that network to solve a real-world problem.

By the end of this chapter, you will learn to:

- Write applications for IoT devices using Azure's device SDK
- Create simulated IoT devices
- Create an IoT Hub
- Perform device-to-Cloud and Cloud-to-device communication
- Use the Notification Hubs service to send out push notifications

Use Case: Centralized Patient Monitoring

Our use case will revolve around solving a problem for Asclepius Consortium. Refer the section called "Smart Hospitals" in Chapter 1 for more details about this fictional association.

The Problem

The member hospitals of Asclepius Consortium are all faced with the same problem. A doctor or nurse cannot be with each patient at all times, even with patients in the ICU, in order to attend to other existing and new incoming patients. Normally, a nurse visits

© Nishith Pathak and Anurag Bhandari 2018
N. Pathak and A. Bhandari, *IoT, AI, and Blockchain for .NET*, https://doi.org/10.1007/978-1-4842-3709-0_3

a patient after set regular intervals to administer medications and check vital statistics, but sometimes this is not enough. There have been instances when complications occurred—severe and otherwise—due to delay in providing necessary care when the patient's vitals started to deteriorate just because nurses and doctors could not be timely notified.

Clearly, a solution that could automate monitoring and notifications would be a godsend in such a typical healthcare scenario.

The Solution

The simplest solution involves creating a network of two IoT devices—connected via an Azure IoT Hub—one for collecting patient data (device with sensors) and the other for taking action based on collected data (device with actuator). Data is processed and the action to be taken is calculated over at the hub. Depending on the size of hospital and other factors, an actual deployment of such a solution would be larger and more sophisticated than our two-device setup, but the basics would remain the same. Our simplified solution will give you a good starting point to build upon. Azure IoT makes it super easy to scale solutions by providing a fully managed interface to add, remove, and maintain virtually unlimited IoT devices later.

Figure 3-1 is a visual depiction of the proposed solution.

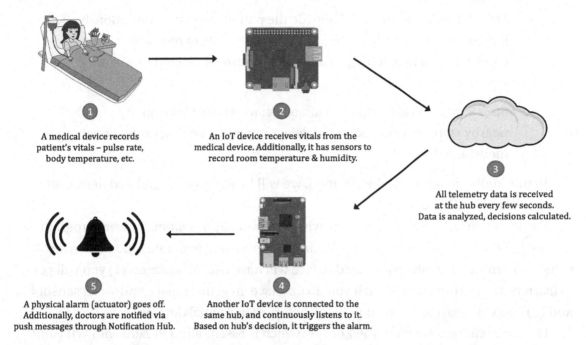

Figure 3-1. *Dataflow of the proposed centralized patient monitoring solution*

Here's a step-by-step breakdown of how this solution will work:

- **Step 1**. A standard medical device connected to the patient
  constantly records their vitals—body temperature, pulse rate,
  respiration rate, and blood pressure.

- **Step 2**. An IoT device (Device 1) is connected to patient's medical
  device through GPIO or a wireless interface. Device 1 receives all
  data being recorded by the medical device. Apart from that, it has its
  own sensors to measure room's temperature and humidity values. A
  combination of all these statistics is necessary to reliably monitor the
  patient's health.

- **Step 3**. Device 1 sends out the combined telemetry data to our IoT
  Hub. An application (solution backend) written to receive hub's
  incoming messages constantly analyzes the input stream of data. If
  the values lie within normal ranges, no action is taken. Conversely,
  if our logic detects an anomaly it sends out a message to Device 2
  to trigger an alarm. As an added precaution, a push notification is
  relayed to doctors' phones through an Azure Notification Hub.

- **Step 4**. Device 2—installed outside the patient's room—continuously listens to our IoT Hub. Depending on the severity of message received from hub, it triggers a physical alarm connected to it as an actuator.

- **Step 5**. A physical alarm immediately catches the attention of nearby staff, reducing potential delays in patient getting professional medical help.

In our implementation of this solution, we will be using one simulated device and one actual device (Raspberry Pi).

Device 1 will be a simulated device, which is basically a custom software program that uses Azure's device SDK to simulate an IoT device and generate random sensor values. Learning to create a simulated device will have two advantages: (1) you will get to learn how IoT Hub works even if you do not have an actual device and/or its sensors, and (2) you will learn to test your network before using actual devices.

Device 2 will be a Raspberry Pi Zero W, which is essentially a Pi Zero with WiFi and Bluetooth pre-installed. Pi Zero W is cheap ($10) and easy-to-use.

Getting an Azure Subscription

If you already have an Azure account, feel free to skip this section. Utilizing the services in Azure IoT Suite, including IoT Hub, will require you to have a valid Azure subscription. An Azure subscription is different from simply having a free Microsoft Live ID (@outlook.com or @hotmail.com email account). A subscription can be obtained several ways, including creating an account on Azure's website using your credit card and getting it bundled with Visual Studio Professional. For the purposes of this book, we'll explore the former option.

Signing up for an Azure account is easy, but requires you to have a Microsoft account—get it free at signup.live.com if you already don't have one. You have two options to sign up for an Azure account—get a Pay-As-You-Go subscription or start with a 30-day free trial.

With a Pay-As-You-Go subscription, you pay monthly charges for services that you use, as per you use them. The subscription is a no-commitment one, meaning it does not require you to pay any additional initial or fixed monthly charges. For example, if the only service you are availing is a VM that costs $20/month, then that's all what you pay monthly, for as long as you use it. Likewise, if you have activated the free tier of an IoT Hub, you pay $0 or nothing if you stay within the bounds imposed by the free tier.

The 30-day free trial is your safest bet and is highly recommended if you are a first-time user. With the trial, you get a complimentary $200 (subject to change at any time) credit in your Azure account. You can use this credit however you like. Once you have exhausted your free credits—which is usually an unlikely scenario—you will be asked to pay for the additional paid services. After the 30 days of the trial period are over, you will be given an option to switch to Pay-As-You-Go subscription. If you don't, you will lose access to the services you'd set up during the trial period. Your Azure Portal access, however, will remain intact. But unlike how trials go usually, Azure does not automatically upgrade you to a paid plan after your trial expires. So there is zero risk of your credit/debit card getting involuntarily charged.

It is worth mentioning that Visual Studio Professional and Enterprise subscribers get complimentary Azure credits every month—$50 for Professional and $150 for Enterprise subscribers. This amount is automatically credited every month to the Microsoft account linked to a Visual Studio subscription.

Assuming that you do not have an existing Azure account, let's sign up for the free trial. With a Microsoft account, head over to `https://azure.microsoft.com/en-in/free` and click the Start Free button. You may be asked to log in using your Microsoft account at this point. Once you do, you will receive a message about your account having no existing subscriptions.

Click on the Sign Up For a Free Trial link. This will bring up a signup form where you will need to supply basic information about yourself, as can be seen in Figure 3-2.

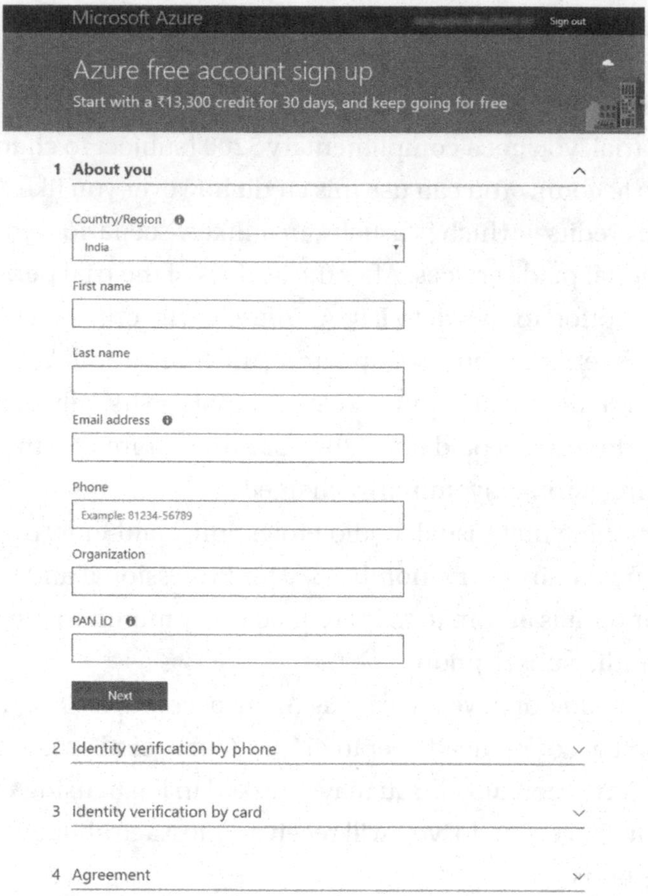

Figure 3-2. *Azure trial signup form*

Next, you will be asked to enter some additional information for identity verification purposes. This includes your mobile number and credit card details. Please note that credit card details are required only for verification. You may be charged a minor phony amount during signup, but that transaction would be instantly reversed. As stated by Microsoft on their website—*We keep prices low by verifying that account holders are real people, not bots or anonymous trouble makers. Don't worry, your card will not be charged unless you explicitly convert to a paid offer, although you might see a temporary authorization hold.*

Once your identity is verified, you will need to accept the subscription agreement to complete your application. At this point, it's a good idea to spend a few minutes quickly scanning through the agreement terms and offer details, links to both of which are given in the Agreement section of the application form. Once you've accepted the agreement and clicked the Sign Up button, you will be redirected to the subscriber's page. Here, click the button to go to Azure Portal.

Creating an IoT Hub

IoT Hub sits at the core of our network. It is the entity that allows devices to securely communicate with the solution backend and vice versa. We'll create this first and deal with the devices later. With an Azure subscription at our disposal, go ahead and create a hub.

Head to `https://portal.azure.com` and access your Azure Portal. From the left side menu, click on **New**. From the resulting blade, select Internet of Things ➤ IoT Hub, as seen in Figure 3-3. Alternatively, search for "iot hub" in the Search the Marketplace textbox.

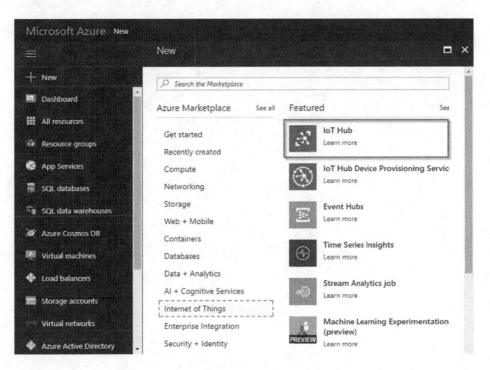

Figure 3-3. *The new resource blade in Azure*

In the resulting form (see Figure 3-4), enter a unique name for your hub. As a matter of practice, we follow the notation *<nickname>-<resource type>-<application name>* but you can use your own as long as the name is globally unique. Change the pricing tier from S1 (paid) to F1 (free). The free tier has a daily message limit of 8000, which is sufficient for our testing. Alternatively, you can utilize the free credits you received with Azure's trial subscription to opt for a paid account in case you plan to take our experiment to the next level, since you will not be able upgrade to a higher plan if you create a free-tier hub. IoT Hub Units and Device-to-cloud Partitions fields will be disabled in free tier: the former pertains to management of daily message quota, and the latter affects availability and consistency of the hub as it decides the number of concurrent readers that can connect to your hub (a concept taken directly from Azure's Event Hubs). You can ignore these values for now and proceed to create the hub.

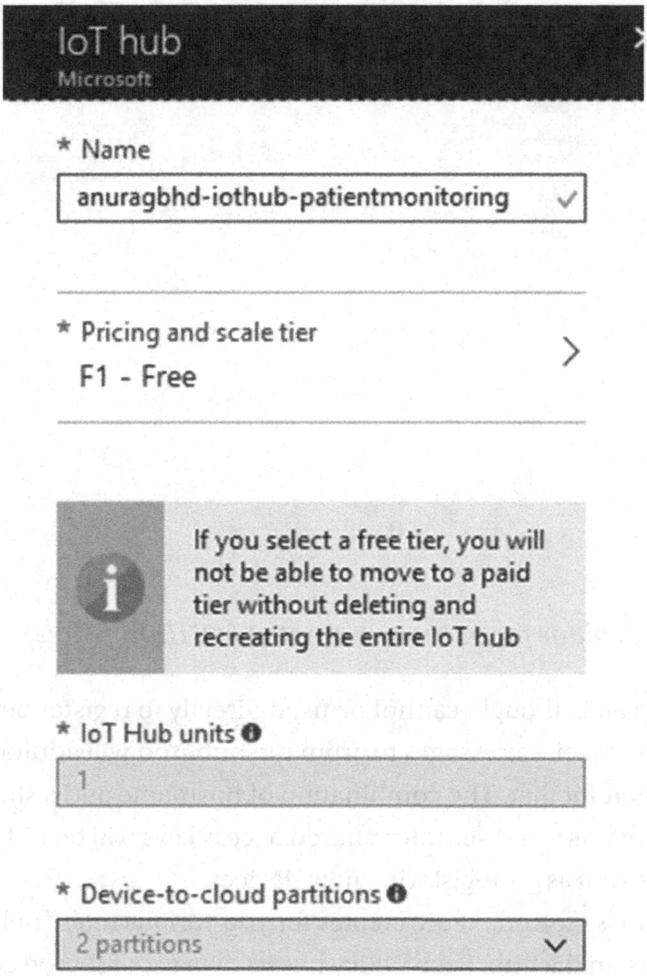

IoT hub
Microsoft

* Name

anuragbhd-iothub-patientmonitoring   ✓

* Pricing and scale tier
F1 - Free   >

> ℹ If you select a free tier, you will
>   not be able to move to a paid
>   tier without deleting and
>   recreating the entire IoT hub

* IoT Hub units ❶

1

* Device-to-cloud partitions ❶

2 partitions   ⌄

Figure 3-4. *New IoT Hub form*

It normally takes 1-2 minutes for Azure to finish creating a new hub. Once your hub is ready, you will see a notification in the Notifications center at the top. Click the notification to open the hub's details page, as seen in Figure 3-5. Take a note of the Hostname field. This is the URL where your hub is hosted, and what devices and solution the backend will interact with.

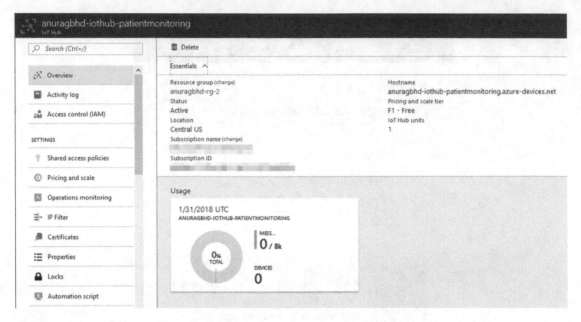

Figure 3-5. *Details blade for our newly created IoT Hub*

The Hostname value, though, cannot be used directly to register devices or by applications to send/receive messages to/from the hub. You will additionally need a shared access key pair for that. The combination of hostname and a shared access key is a connection string. As you'll see later, shared access keys will be different for each registered device as well as for registering new devices.

When a new hub is created, Azure creates for you various roles (policies) with varying permissions on the hub. Each policy has its own set of shared access keys. For the purposes of our solution, let's retrieve the connection string corresponding to the policy with full permissions. In a production setup, you might want to use a more restrictive policy.

In your IoT Hub's details blade, navigate to Settings ➤ Shared Access Policies ➤ iothubowner. In the resulting right sidebar (see Figure 3-6), scroll down to locate Connection String—Primary Key. Note it down.

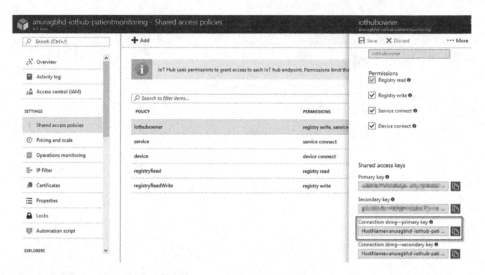

Figure 3-6. *Getting the connection string of the IoT Hub*

Creating Device Identities

The next step in sequence is to register our the devices in the hub's registry. You saw in Chapter 2 how security is the number one concern of an IoT Hub. A device cannot connect to a hub if it is not registered with it. So, even before we create our simulated device (Device 1) and configure our Pi Zero (Device 2), we will create their device identities. Each device identity is associated with a device ID and a key. Our client applications, running on the devices, will need these values to identify themselves to the hub.

There are two ways to create a device identity—using code and through Azure Portal. We will explore both.

Using Code

This method requires using Azure's Devices SDK to write a few lines of code. It may be a little bit cumbersome to register just one or two devices using this method, but it is extremely helpful while registering hundreds or thousands of devices, or when automating device registration.

We'll create a simple C#-based Windows Console App. Fire up your Visual Studio. Go to File ➤ New ➤ Project, and choose Console App under Visual C# ➤ Windows Classic Desktop. Refer to Figure 3-7.

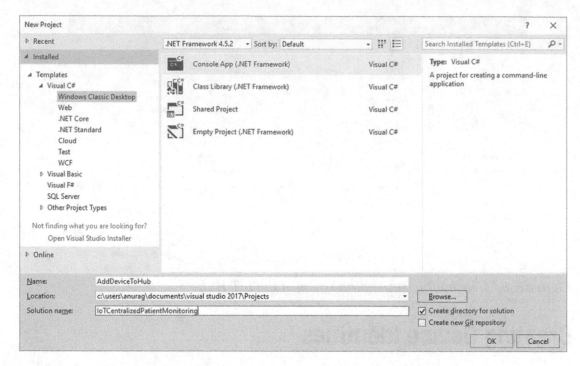

Figure 3-7. *Creating a new console app in Visual Studio 2017*

Once Visual Studio has finished creating the new application, right-click the AddDeviceToHub project in Solution Explorer and select Manage NuGet Packages. In the package manager window, switch to Browse tab, search for Microsoft.Azure.Devices and install the first package in the list (that exactly matches the searched name). You may be prompted to install several dependencies along with the Azure IoT Devices SDK; choose to install all.

Note   The version we used for all subsequent code examples is Visual Studio Professional 2017. If you do not have Professional 2017 or are running an older version, we highly recommend that you upgrade. VS Community 2017—available completely free of cost—will work equally well.

Next, add a new app setting for IoT Hub's connection string in `App.config`. Add the following code. Replace the value attribute's value with the connection string you noted at the end of "Creating an IoT Hub" section earlier.

```
<appSettings>
  <add key="connectionString" value="" />
</appSettings>
```

In **Program.cs**, copy-paste the following code:

```
using System;
using System.Threading.Tasks;
using Microsoft.Azure.Devices;
using Microsoft.Azure.Devices.Common.Exceptions;

namespace AddDeviceToHub
{
    class Program
    {
        static RegistryManager registryManager;
        static string connectionString = System.Configuration.
        ConfigurationManager.AppSettings["connectionString"];

        static void Main(string[] args)
        {
            registryManager = RegistryManager.CreateFromConnectionString
            (connectionString);
            RegisterDeviceAsync().Wait();
            Console.ReadLine();
        }

        private static async Task RegisterDeviceAsync()
        {
            string deviceId = "medicaldevice-patient1";
            Device device;
            try
            {
```

```
            device = await registryManager.AddDeviceAsync(new
            Device(deviceId));
        }
        catch (DeviceAlreadyExistsException)
        {
            device = await registryManager.GetDeviceAsync(deviceId);
        }
        Console.WriteLine("Device shared access key:" + device.
        Authentication.SymmetricKey.PrimaryKey);
    }
  }
}
```

Let's break down this program to understand what's happening in each section.

Adding a NuGet package automatically adds its DLLs in the project's references, but its corresponding using statements need to be manually placed in the code. That is why we have the following two lines at the top:

```
using Microsoft.Azure.Devices;
using Microsoft.Azure.Devices.Common.Exceptions;
```

We need a reference to hub's registry manager. So, we created a new static field:

```
static RegistryManager registryManager;
```

We also created a static field for the connection string:

```
static string connectionString = System.Configuration.ConfigurationManager.
AppSettings["connectionString"];
```

The ConfigurationManager class is, by default, not present in the System.Configuration namespace. We have to add a reference to the System. Configuration DLL in our project. Right-click References in Solution Explorer and scroll down to add the needed reference, as shown in Figure 3-8.

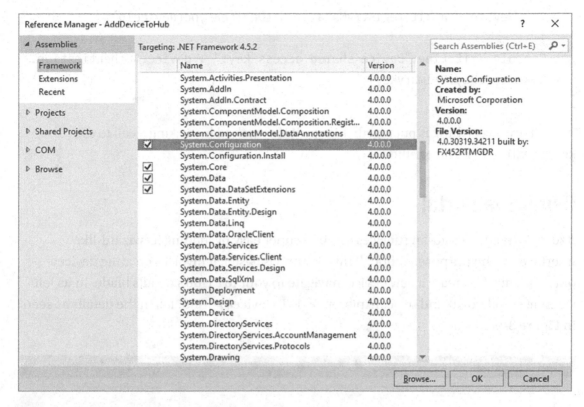

Figure 3-8. Adding a reference to System.Configuration

RegisterDeviceAsync is the actual method that registers our device. We use it to register only Device 1. It tries to add the device in our hub's registry. If the device with the specified device ID already exists, an instance of the existing device is fetched. The shared access key of the added device is then printed to the console.

```
private static async Task RegisterDeviceAsync()
{
    string deviceId = "medicaldevice-patient1";
    Device device;
    try
    {
        device = await registryManager.AddDeviceAsync(new Device(deviceId));
    }
    catch (DeviceAlreadyExistsException)
    {
```

```
        device = await registryManager.GetDeviceAsync(deviceId);
    }
    Console.WriteLine("Device shared access key:" + device.Authentication.
    SymmetricKey.PrimaryKey);
}
```

Finally, everything is put together in the `Main` method by making a call to the `RegisterDeviceAsync` method.

Using the Portal

Azure Portal makes adding devices to a hub super easy by lending its wizard-like interface for the purpose. Although this method is easier, it involves creating devices one at a time. To create a new device, navigate to your IoT Hub's details blade. In its left sidebar, scroll down and select Explorers ➤ IoT Devices ➤ Add. Fill in the details as seen in Figure 3-9.

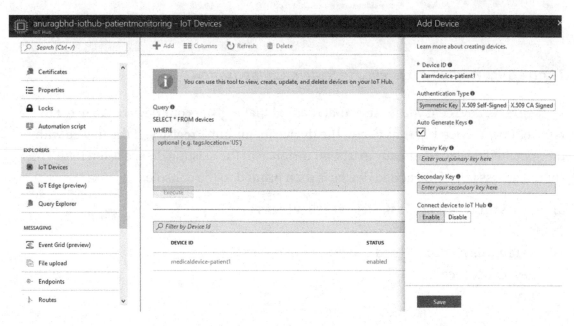

Figure 3-9. *Adding a device through Azure Portal*

Once the device is added successfully, it will be listed in the device explorer alongside Device 1 that we added using code earlier. If added device's status shows as "disabled," enable the device by opening its Device Details blade.

Creating a Simulated Device

With our hub created and devices registered with it, let's create our simulated device that will periodically send patient telemetry data to the hub.

Creating the Application

The steps are similar to what we saw in Creating Device Identities section. In Visual Studio, create another console application called `SimulatedDevice` in the same solution `IoTCentralizedPatientMonitoring`. Install the NuGet package `Microsoft.Azure.Devices.Client` to the new project. Like before, add a reference to `System.Configuration` in order to read app settings from `App.config`.

In `App.config`, add the following key-value pairs:

```
<appSettings>
  <add key="iotHubHostname" value="" />
  <add key="deviceId" value="medicaldevice-patient1" />
  <add key="deviceSharedAccessKey" value="" />
</appSettings>
```

The value of `iotHubHostname` is the hostname we noted down in the "Creating an IoT Hub" section rather than the connection string. `deviceSharedAccessKey` is the output that was printed at the end in the "Using Code" subsection of "Creating Device Identities". If you did not get a chance to note it down, you can easily get it from IoT Devices explorer of your hub in Azure Portal; take the primary key value from there.

Add the following code in `SimulatedDevice` project's `Program.cs` file:

```
static void Main(string[] args)
{
  deviceClient = DeviceClient.Create(iotHubHostname, new DeviceAuthentication
  WithRegistrySymmetricKey(deviceId, deviceSharedAccessKey), TransportType.Mqtt);
  deviceClient.ProductInfo = "Asclepius Consortium Vitals Recorder";
  SendPatientTelemetryToHubAsync();
  Console.ReadLine();
}
```

```csharp
private static async void SendPatientTelemetryToHubAsync()
{
  // Minimum values for telemetry parameters
  double minBodyTemperature = 36.5; // degrees Celsius
  double minPulseRate = 60; // beats per minute
  double minRespirationRate = 12; // breaths per minute
  double minRoomTemperature = 18; // degrees Celsius
  double minRoomHumidity = 30; // percentage

  Random random = new Random();

  while (true)
  {
    // Pretentiously received from the medical device
    double currentBodyTemperature = minBodyTemperature + random.
    NextDouble() * 4; // 36.5-40.5 deg
    double currentPulseRate = minPulseRate + random.NextDouble() * 40;
    // 60-100 per min
    double currentRespirationRate = minRespirationRate + random.
    NextDouble() * 4; // 12-16 per min
    // Pretentiously received from on-board sensors
    double currentTemperature = minRoomTemperature + random.NextDouble() * 12;
    // 18-30 deg
    double currentHumidity = minRoomHumidity + random.NextDouble() * 30;
    // 30-60%

    // Combined telemetry data
    var deviceTelemetryData = new
    {
      messageId = Guid.NewGuid().ToString(),
      deviceId = deviceId,
      patientBodyTemperature = currentBodyTemperature,
      patientPulseRate = currentPulseRate,
      patientRespirationRate = currentRespirationRate,
      rooomTemperature = currentTemperature,
      roomHumidity = currentHumidity
    };
```

```
    // Serialize and send data to hub
    var messageString = JsonConvert.SerializeObject(deviceTelemetryData);
    var message = new Message(Encoding.ASCII.GetBytes(messageString));
    await deviceClient.SendEventAsync(message);

    // Output the sent message to console
    Console.WriteLine("Message at {0}: {1}", DateTime.Now, messageString);

    // Wait for 3 seconds before repeating
    await Task.Delay(3000);          }
}
```

Let's break down the code as before.

We start by adding the required using statements:

```
using System.Threading.Tasks;
using Microsoft.Azure.Devices.Client;
using Newtonsoft.Json;
using System.Configuration;
```

We create an instance of DeviceClient, the class that exposes methods to communicate with the hub. We also read app setting values into class fields.

```
static DeviceClient deviceClient;
static string iotHubHostname = ConfigurationManager.
AppSettings["iotHubHostname"];
static string deviceId = ConfigurationManager.AppSettings["deviceId"];
static string deviceSharedAccessKey = ConfigurationManager.AppSettings
["deviceSharedAccessKey"];
```

In the SendPatientTelemetryToHubAsync method, we start by setting minimum values for telemetry parameters that will be recorded (simulated) by the device.

```
double minBodyTemperature = 36.5; // degrees Celsius
double minPulseRate = 60; // beats per minute
double minRespirationRate = 12; // breaths per minute
double minRoomTemperature = 18; // degrees Celsius
double minRoomHumidity = 30; // percentage
```

Next, we start an infinite loop that:

1. Generates fake sensor values.

```
// Pretentiously received from the medical device
double currentBodyTemperature = minBodyTemperature + random.
NextDouble() * 4;
// 36.5-40.5 deg
double currentPulseRate = minPulseRate + random.NextDouble() * 40;
// 60-100 per min
double currentRespirationRate = minRespirationRate + random.
NextDouble() * 4;
// 12-16 per min
// Pretentiously received from on-board sensors
double currentTemperature = minRoomTemperature + random.
NextDouble() * 12; // 18-30 deg
double currentHumidity = minRoomHumidity + random.NextDouble() * 30;
// 30-60%
```

2. Builds the telemetry data object.

```
var deviceTelemetryData = new
{
  messageId = Guid.NewGuid().ToString(),
  deviceId = deviceId,
  patientBodyTemperature = currentBodyTemperature,
  patientPulseRate = currentPulseRate,
  patientRespirationRate = currentRespirationRate,
  rooomTemperature = currentTemperature,
  roomHumidity = currentHumidity
};
```

3. Serializes and sends the data to hub.

```
var messageString = JsonConvert.SerializeObject(deviceTelemetryData);
var message = new Message(Encoding.ASCII.GetBytes(messageString));
await deviceClient.SendEventAsync(message);
```

4. Waits for 3000 milliseconds (three seconds) until repeating.

```
await Task.Delay(3000);
```

Running the Application

Set SimulatedDevice project as the startup project in Visual Studio and press the F5 button on the keyboard (or the Start button in VS) to run the application. A Command Prompt window will pop up and display a message every three seconds that we are outputting on console. Figure 3-10 shows sample output.

```
                                                                        \SimulatedDevice.exe    —    □    ×
Message at 01-Feb-18 3:52:07 PM: {"messageId":"3a99abcf-859f-4aa3-bba1-d936ce90e4f4","deviceId":"medicaldevice-patient1"
,"patientBodyTemperature":39.17493883675806,"patientPulseRate":96.8494126558534,"patientRespirationRate":12.82646078282
3368,"rooomTemperature":19.28888913490292,"roomHumidity":46.063031412690428}
Message at 01-Feb-18 3:52:10 PM: {"messageId":"d652375c-2476-44ee-b7bd-9ea0d522a753","deviceId":"medicaldevice-patient1"
,"patientBodyTemperature":37.219585674218642,"patientPulseRate":74.27182324895243,"patientRespirationRate":13.560730575
379324,"rooomTemperature":22.893884228958694,"roomHumidity":56.748704727156415}
Message at 01-Feb-18 3:52:14 PM: {"messageId":"2b8d60ef-bab9-4bdb-83b3-ead59c966d1e","deviceId":"medicaldevice-patient1"
,"patientBodyTemperature":39.66031812873625,"patientPulseRate":90.0426336890285,"patientRespirationRate":14.74215743818
4208,"rooomTemperature":18.220760543002172,"roomHumidity":38.694870294395308}
Message at 01-Feb-18 3:52:17 PM: {"messageId":"ceb605eb-3f87-48b1-a7cc-690a826058bf","deviceId":"medicaldevice-patient1"
,"patientBodyTemperature":40.156435636643522,"patientPulseRate":76.2842459493709,"patientRespirationRate":15.33524322106
2815,"rooomTemperature":26.308651566649161,"roomHumidity":49.388649775361941}
Message at 01-Feb-18 3:52:21 PM: {"messageId":"ac5e072d-55c9-4eca-8dab-ccfce321c839","deviceId":"medicaldevice-patient1"
,"patientBodyTemperature":39.147522664930449,"patientPulseRate":85.114640716982365,"patientRespirationRate":12.041439395
417198,"rooomTemperature":26.513598593191055,"roomHumidity":44.251560691861229}
Message at 01-Feb-18 3:52:25 PM: {"messageId":"0ae8d01b-0137-42b1-9d07-e6a5cdf05679","deviceId":"medicaldevice-patient1"
,"patientBodyTemperature":36.684504635717957,"patientPulseRate":91.760690357424636,"patientRespirationRate":14.964790228
272225,"rooomTemperature":18.649434339557512,"roomHumidity":54.757716606723946}
```

Figure 3-10. *Output from the simulated device console application*

To verify whether messages are being successfully sent to the hub, open the hub's details blade in Azure Portal. You should see the usage count increase, as shown in Figure 3-11.

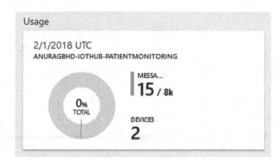

Figure 3-11. *Daily usage—messages exchanges—for a hub can be checked in Azure Portal*

Creating the Solution Backend

We have created a simulated client, sent messages from it, and verified their count in Azure Portal. The next step is to create a very basic solution backend that can:

- Show messages in the console received from the device (device-to-cloud)

- Analyze received messages and make decisions

- Send messages to another device (Cloud-to-device)

- Send push notifications to Android phones through Notification Hubs

Creating the Application

As previously, we'll create the solution backend as a console application. In Visual Studio, add a new console app project called SolutionBackend to the IoTCentralizedPatientMonitoring solution.

Creating a Notification Hub

Doing this is similar to creating an IoT Hub. On Azure Portal, go to New ➤ Web+ Mobile ➤ Notification Hubs. Create a new hub as shown in Figure 3-12.

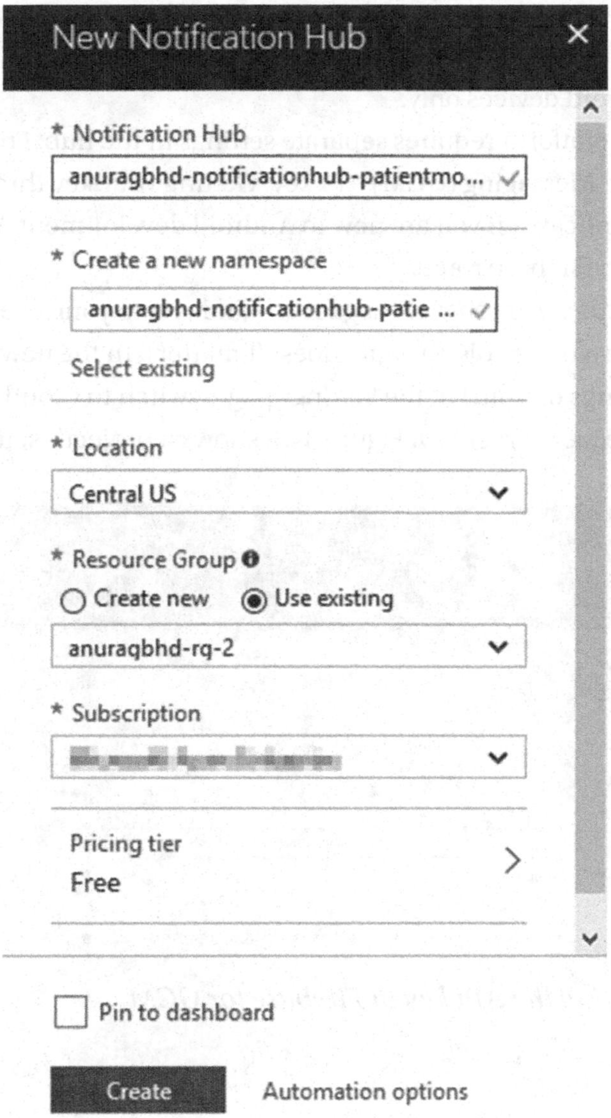

Figure 3-12. *Creating a Notification Hub in Azure*

Keep the hub name that you use here handy, as you'll use it later. The Namespace field can have the same value as hub name field. Stick to the free tier for this exercise. It comes with a generous limit of 1 million push notifications and 150 registered devices (to which notifications can be sent via the hub).

Azure Notification Hubs supports all major device platforms to send out notifications to—iOS, Android, Windows, Windows Phone, etc. In this exercise, we'll limit our push notifications to Android devices only.

Sending to each platform requires separate settings in the hub. For Android, we need a Google Cloud Messaging (GCM) API key. Getting your key through the standard process may be complicated if you are new to Android development. We'll take a shortcut by going the Firebase route.

Head over to `https://firebase.google.com` and create your free account. On the Console page, create a new project (name doesn't matter). In the newly created project, find the project settings option. On the Settings page, switch to Cloud Messaging tab and copy the value for Legacy server key. Figure 3-13 shows a project's settings page.

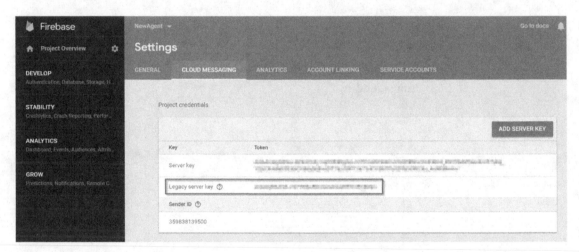

Figure 3-13. Locating the API key in Firebase for GCM

Once Azure has finished creating our notification hub, go to Notification Settings ➤ Google (GCM). Paste the key we copied above in API Key textbox, as shown in Figure 3-14.

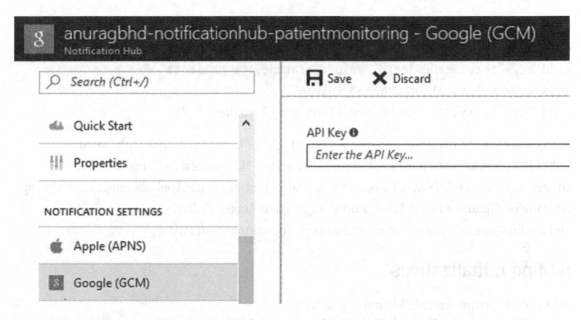

Figure 3-14. Setting the GCM API key in notification hub to allow it to send messages to Android devices

Adding Dependencies

We need three NuGet packages—Microsoft.ServiceBus.Messaging (for reading device-to-Cloud messages), Microsoft.Azure.Devices (for sending Cloud-to-device messages), and Microsoft.Azure.NotificationHubs (for sending push notifications). Install them for this project via the NuGet Package Manager. As usual, we also need to reference app settings in App.config. So, add a reference to System.Configuration.

When all dependencies are installed, add the following using statements at the top in Program.cs:

```
using Microsoft.ServiceBus.Messaging;
using Microsoft.Azure.Devices;
using Microsoft.Azure.NotificationHubs;
using Newtonsoft.Json;
using System.Configuration;
```

Adding App Settings

Add the following settings in `App.config`:

```
<add key="connectionString" value="" />
<add key="deviceToCloudEndPoint" value="messages/events" />
<add key="receiverDeviceId" value="alarmdevice-patient1" />
<add key="notificationHubName" value="" />
<add key="notificationHubConnectionString" value="" />
```

connectionString will be what we noted in the "Creating an IoT Hub" section. notificationHubName will be what we noted in the "Creating a Notification Hub" subsection just a while ago. To retrieve the value for notificationHubConnectionString, on your notification hub's Azure Portal page, go to Access Policies ➤ DefaultFullSharedAccessSignature and copy the connection string.

Adding Initializations

Add the following static fields in `Program.cs`:

```
static EventHubClient eventHubClient;
static ServiceClient serviceClient;
static NotificationHubClient notificationHubClient;
static string connectionString = ConfigurationManager.AppSettings
["connectionString"];
static string deviceToCloudEndPoint = ConfigurationManager.AppSettings
["deviceToCloudEndPoint"];
static string receiverDeviceId = ConfigurationManager.AppSettings
["receiverDeviceId"];
static string notificationHubName = ConfigurationManager.AppSettings
["notificationHubName"];
static string notificationHubConnectionString = ConfigurationManager.AppSet
tings["notificationHubConnectionString"];
```

Initialize them in the `Main` method as shown here.

```
// Initialize event hub client to receive device to cloud messages
eventHubClient = EventHubClient.CreateFromConnectionString(connectionString,
deviceToCloudEndPoint);
```

```
// Initialize service client to send cloud to device messages
serviceClient = ServiceClient.CreateFromConnectionString(connectionString);
// Initialize notification hub client to send cloud to mobile push notifications
notificationHubClient = NotificationHubClient.CreateClientFromConnectionStr
ing(notificationHubConnectionString, notificationHubName);
```

Receiving Messages from Devices

Let's create a new method for receiving messages sent to our IoT Hub by connected devices (only the medical device in our case).

```
private static async Task ReceiveMessagesAsync(string partition)
{
  // Create a receiver to read messages written to the given partition
  starting at given date-time
  var eventHubReceiver = eventHubClient.GetDefaultConsumerGroup().
  CreateReceiver(partition, DateTime.UtcNow);

  // Start receiving messages
  while (true)
  {
    EventData eventData = await eventHubReceiver.ReceiveAsync();
    if (eventData == null) continue;
    // Extract the message
    string serializedMessage = Encoding.UTF8.GetString(eventData.
    GetBytes()); // serialized JSON string
    // Display the message on console
    ShowMessageOnConsole(serializedMessage);
    // Analyze the message
    AnalyzeMessage(serializedMessage);
  }
}
```

In the infinite while loop, we are constantly checking to see incoming messages on the hub. We can do all sorts of things with received messages. In our code, we are writing them to the console and then performing basic analysis to make decisions. It's important to note that messages are received as serialized JSON strings as we sent them in SimulatedDevice project.

ShowMessageOnConsole() method is simple beyond your imagination:

```
private static void ShowMessageOnConsole(string message)
{
  Console.WriteLine();
  Console.WriteLine("Message received: " + message);
}
```

We'll look at the AnalyzeMessage() method in a bit. First, let's hook up the receive messages method in the Main() method. Add the following lines at the end of Main:

```
// Get the first partition
var firstPartition = eventHubClient.GetRuntimeInformation().PartitionIds[0];
// Start receiving messages from medical device
ReceiveMessagesAsync(firstPartition).Wait();
```

Although IoT Hub's free tier (F1) allows for two partitions, we are reading the first partition for keeping our code simple. For this simplicity, we are sacrificing receiving messages written to the second partition. A production application will typically have even more partitions (4 and above).

Analyzing Received Messages

Add the following method in Program.cs:

```
private static void AnalyzeMessage(string messageJSONString)
{
  // Deserialize the message
  var messageType = new
  {
    messageId = "",
    deviceId = "",
    patientBodyTemperature = 0.0d,
    patientPulseRate = 0.0d,
    patientRespirationRate = 0.0d,
    rooomTemperature = 0.0d,
    roomHumidity = 0.0d
  };
```

```
var message = JsonConvert.DeserializeAnonymousType(messageJSONString,
messageType);

// If patient's body temperature is more than 102 deg Fahrenheit:
// 1. send an alert to the alarm device to inform hospital staff
// 2. send a push notification to registered phones to inform doctors
if (message.patientBodyTemperature > 38.89)
{
  Console.WriteLine("SENDING HIGH BODY TEMPERATURE ALERT TO PATIENT'S
  ALARM DEVICE.");
  SendMessageToDeviceAsync(receiverDeviceId, "high-body-temp-alert").Wait();
  Console.WriteLine("SENDING HIGH BODY TEMPERATURE ALERT TO NOTIFICATION
  HUB.");
  SendPushNotificationAsync("ALERT: Patient in Room 1 has high fever.").
  Wait();
}
}
```

The code is pretty much self-explanatory. As the received message is a serialized JSON string, we convert it into a C# object before we can start analyzing it. Once that is done, we perform a simplistic analysis of checking the patient's body temperature.

Sending Messages to Device

As with other things in Azure IoT devices SDK, sending messages to a device is dead simple.

```
private async static Task SendMessageToDeviceAsync(string deviceId, string
message)
{
  var commandMessage = new Message(Encoding.ASCII.GetBytes(message));
  await serviceClient.SendAsync(deviceId, commandMessage);
}
```

Check the call to this method in the AnalyzeMessage() method in the last section.

Sending Push Notifications

Sending messages to the notification hub to be further relayed as push notifications is equally simple.

```
private async static Task SendPushNotificationAsync(string message)
{
  await notificationHubClient.SendGcmNativeNotificationAsync("{ \"data\" :
  {\"message\":\"" + message + "\"}}");
}
```

Running the Application

Our simple solution backend is now ready to be tested. Before running, verify the app settings in App.config. Incorrect app settings values is a common cause of issues.

To be able to test the solution backend, you will need the SimulatedDevice project to be running simultaneously. Otherwise, the backend will have no messages to receive and analyze. Visual Studio provides an easy way to run multiple projects at once. In Solution Explorer, right-click the solution IoTCentralizedPatientMonitoring and select Properties. In Common Properties ➤ Startup Project, select the Multiple Startup Projects option. Set Start as the action for both the SimulatedDevice and SolutionBackend projects. Click OK to save.

Click the Run button or press F5 to start the application. Both projects should now run at the same time. Sample output from the solution backend is shown in Figure 3-15.

SolutionBackend.exe

Message received: {"messageId":"8e5c1a5a-6bd5-466f-907f-7fb914d6f15d","deviceId":"medicaldevice-patient1","patientBodyTe
mperature":38.823668749222378,"patientPulseRate":64.375618903141287,"patientRespirationRate":13.481506227274196,"rooomTe
mperature":26.794193776694218,"roomHumidity":33.966556919723075}

Message received: {"messageId":"4a341008-0c10-4e04-8c8f-0910c5065a55","deviceId":"medicaldevice-patient1","patientBodyTe
mperature":38.8623929593537,"patientPulseRate":89.401421895903269,"patientRespirationRate":13.673512565751333,"rooomTemp
erature":23.352033753577636,"roomHumidity":33.71023059529729}

Message received: {"messageId":"1fcdb984-590f-449b-b15a-69f6f3dd95e3","deviceId":"medicaldevice-patient1","patientBodyTe
mperature":36.633689126062059,"patientPulseRate":89.9371032556226,"patientRespirationRate":15.423932876169651,"rooomTemp
erature":26.282195961234251,"roomHumidity":39.610214591776121}

Message received: {"messageId":"9fbf338c-a5bc-489f-a127-9978a0590729","deviceId":"medicaldevice-patient1","patientBodyTe
mperature":39.738786762225807,"patientPulseRate":75.168425056696137,"patientRespirationRate":12.693389777417011,"rooomTe
mperature":29.770688753468306,"roomHumidity":49.076249412762117}
SENDING HIGH BODY TEMPERATURE ALERT TO PATIENT'S ALARM DEVICE.
SENDING HIGH BODY TEMPERATURE ALERT TO NOTIFICATION HUB.

Message received: {"messageId":"b635680f-cbd2-4bda-9486-470a323c7ac2","deviceId":"medicaldevice-patient1","patientBodyTe
mperature":37.443723574720195,"patientPulseRate":79.243644093742432,"patientRespirationRate":15.259510116306837,"rooomTe
mperature":19.656673702251481,"roomHumidity":51.382313748533981}

Message received: {"messageId":"d471b0bd-7b49-4c6f-b7e3-dadaa7f1fd62","deviceId":"medicaldevice-patient1","patientBodyTe
mperature":39.909501034491463,"patientPulseRate":67.732484325641991,"patientRespirationRate":15.634497107767732,"rooomTe
mperature":21.048645711992236,"roomHumidity":42.667345200976051}
SENDING HIGH BODY TEMPERATURE ALERT TO PATIENT'S ALARM DEVICE.
SENDING HIGH BODY TEMPERATURE ALERT TO NOTIFICATION HUB.

Figure 3-15. *Messages that were sent by the simulated device are received by the solution backend*

As you can see in Figure 3-15, there were a couple of instances when a patient's body temperature was high and alerts were sent to the alarm device and notification hub. In the next section, we write and run an application on an actual Raspberry Pi Zero. That is when you'll be able to see the alerts received from the solution backend, routed through IoT Hub.

If you want to test receiving notification hub messages, you will need to create an Android application and run it on a mobile. To save you time and effort, the Azure team has created a ready-to-use Android application for the purpose. Visit https://github.com/Azure/azure-notificationhubs-samples/tree/master/ Android/GetStartedFirebase to learn more. Figure 3-16 is a screenshot of a push notification our Android mobile received from our solution backend.

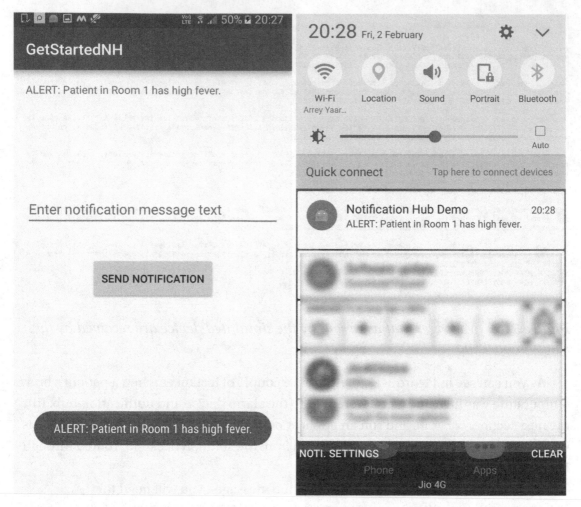

Figure 3-16. *Alert notifications received from the hub by Azure's IoT Hub demo Android app: (left) in-app notification in the form of a toast and (right) message in the phone's notifications shade*

Tip   You can write additional code in the Android app to make the phone vibrate strongly and play a sharp, persistent ringtone whenever an alert notification is received to immediately catch doctors' attention.

Writing an IoT Application for Raspberry Pi

The thing that you were waiting for is here. Time has come to finally put your Pi to use. The joy of watching a physical device do wonderful things is beyond compare.

Tip   It's okay if you do not have a physical Pi Zero. Azure's Raspberry Pi web simulator is a great way to test your code in the absence of a real device. It runs completely in a browser and has two components—a Pi with its circuit configuration on the left and a code editor on the right. As of writing this book, the simulator is in early preview stage and doesn't allow for modifying the pre-configured circuit. But that may change in future. The Pi web simulator is available at `https://azure-samples.github.io/raspberry-pi-web-simulator`.

The build-up to this section has already taught you a lot of things you need to know about writing applications for IoT devices. You have already created a simulated device using Azure IoT devices SDK. Developing for an actual device will be similar, as you will be using the same SDK. But this time you will be writing the application not in C# but in JavaScript (using node.js). This is because Linux is the most common operating system available for the Pi. Running .NET applications on Linux is possible through Mono, but it's notoriously tricky to set up and maintain properly. Python and node.js are popular choices for developing applications for Pi and several other IoT devices.

Note   Instructions in this section apply not only to Pi Zero but all other models of Raspberry Pi as well, including Model 1 B+, 2, and 3.

Setting Up Your Pi

If you are new to Pi and have not set it up before, Raspberry Pi's official documentation is a great place to start. Visit `https://www.raspberrypi.org/learning/software-guide` to get started. Alternatively, find the software installation guide on Raspberry Pi website's Help page. You will be instructed to:

- Choose the right operating system (Raspbian is an officially supported flavor of Linux)

- Download and install the operating system on a microSD card

- Connect Pi to LAN or WiFi networks, etc.

We recommend that you install Raspbian. Once you have your Pi all set up, ensure you have SSH access and I2C interface enabled. Doing so is as easy as running the `raspi-config` command; you will find detailed instructions on Pi's website.

Connecting to Pi via SSH

There are several ways to connect to a Pi from a computer to write and deploy software on it. Remote access via SSH is the most common and secure method. You could also simply connect a monitor/TV and a keyboard to your Pi and start coding as you normally would on your laptop. Or, access Pi's desktop using VNC or xrdp. Both methods will allow you to connect Pi's graphical interface, much like when you use RDP to connect to a remote Windows VM. Connecting via SSH is faster and requires less hardware. The only downside is SSH allows only for command-line access. You do not get to access the graphical interface. But, why worry? We are developers! We love to write code and execute commands.

For connecting to SSH in Windows, you need a third-party software such as PuTTY. Download and install PuTTY from `https://www.putty.org`. While setting up your Pi, you might have already connected to it via SSH at least once. If not, find instructions to do that on Pi's documentation. Figure 3-17 shows how one typically connects to a Pi through PuTTY and Figure 3-18 shows Pi's command-line interface after connecting.

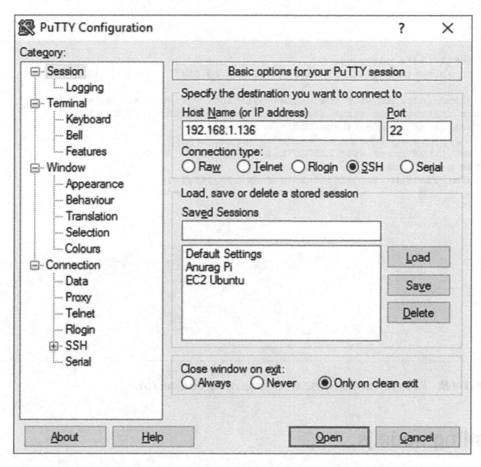

Figure 3-17. *Connecting to Pi via SSH using PuTTY*

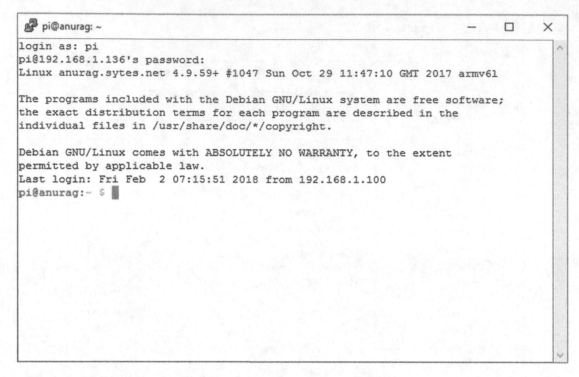

Figure 3-18. Pi's command-line interface after connecting

Installing node.js

Node.js is a server-side implementation of JavaScript. It provides ultra-fast APIs for accessing I/O (files, databases, etc.) and other system-level resources. In other words, Node is an application server to run JavaScript-based applications. Learn more about Node at https://nodejs.org.

There is more than one way to install the latest version of node.js in Raspbian. It's best to follow the official installation instructions as mentioned at https://nodejs.org. Since Raspbian is a Debian-based Linux OS, follow the instructions to install node via package manager (apt-get). The following two commands should ideally do the trick:

```
curl -sL https://deb.nodesource.com/setup_9.x | sudo -E bash -
sudo apt-get install -y nodejs
```

To verify if node was installed correctly, run this command:

```
node -v
```

Note   Skip the following instructions if the package manager installation of nodejs worked for you.

You should get an output such as v9.5.0. If this method does not work, go to the Downloads page on nodejs.org and download the Linux Binary (ARM) package corresponding to your Pi's model. For example, for Pi Zero you download the ARMv6 package:

```
wget https://nodejs.org/dist/v9.5.0/node-v9.5.0-linux-armv6l.tar.xz
```

Next, extract the downloaded tarball archive to a globally-accessible location. Run the following three commands:

```
sudo mkdir /usr/lib/nodejs
sudo tar -xJvf node-v9.5.0-linux-armv6l.tar.xz -C /usr/lib/nodejs
sudo mv /usr/lib/nodejs/node-v9.5.0-linux-armv6l /usr/lib/nodejs/node-v9.5.0
```

Add the above directory permanently to your PATH environment variable. Open the .profile file in a text editor:

```
nano ~/.profile
```

And add these lines to the end of the document:

```
export NODEJS_HOME=/usr/lib/nodejs/node-v9.5.0
export PATH=$NODEJS_HOME/bin:$PATH
```

Finally, refresh your PATH:

```
. ~/.profile
```

Creating the Application

Create a new directory to store the application and enter into it:

```
mkdir AlarmDevice
cd AlarmDevice
```

Initialize this directory as a node application:

```
npm init
```

You will be asked a series of questions, at the end of which a new file called package.json will be generated.

Installing Dependencies

Now, install Azure IoT devices SDK dependencies. This step is similar to installing NuGet packages in Visual Studio. Run the following command:

```
npm install --save az-iot-bi, azure-iot-device, azure-iot-device-mqtt, wiring-pi
```

This will install the required dependencies in a new folder called node_modules and update the package.json file. Our final package.json file looked like this:

```
{
  "name": "alarmdevice",
  "version": "1.0.0",
  "description": "Azure IoT app to receive messages from Remote Patient
  Monitoring IoT Hub.",
  "main": "index.js",
  "dependencies": {
    "az-iot-bi": "^0.1.20",
    "azure-iot-device": "^1.3.0",
    "azure-iot-device-mqtt": "^1.3.0",
    "wiring-pi": "^2.2.1"
  },
  "devDependencies": {},
  "scripts": {
    "test": "echo \"Error: no test specified\" && exit 1"
  },
  "author": "Anurag Bhandari",
  "license": "MIT"
}
```

Note If the installation of the `wiring-pi` package fails, ensure that you have Git installed in Raspbian. To install Git, run the `sudo apt-get install git-core` command.

Connecting an Actuator

The simplest actuator that we can use in an alarm device is an LED that provides a visual indication about an event. LEDs are cheap and very easily available. We will connect a red LED to our Pi Zero's GPIO. You can do the same or connect a sound device such as a buzzer. The wiring connection will pretty much remain the same.

GPIO pins work in two modes—input (for sensors) and output (for actuators). In output mode, a pin's voltage may be set to high (1) or low (0) through code to turn an actuator on or off. Although there are 40 GPIO pins on recent Pi models, not all of them can be usable by sensors and actuators. Also, there are more than one pin numbering systems. Visit https://pinout.xyz/pinout/wiringpi to see Pi Zero's pin layout. As we are using the wiring-pi node module for interacting with pins, we'll follow its numbering system.

Connect an LED to ground and pin 15. These are the third and fourth pins from the left in the first row. The LED's short leg (cathode, -ve) will go in ground and the long leg (anode, +ve) will go in pin 15, as shown in Figure 3-19.

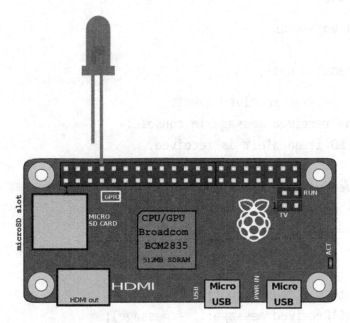

Figure 3-19. *Circuit layout for our Pi Zero. The LED is connected to pin 15 (WiringPi notation)*

Writing the Code to Receive Messages and Take Action

Create a new file called index.js in the current directory:

nano index.js

And paste the following code:

```
// Required dependencies
const wpi = require('wiring-pi');
const deviceClient = require('azure-iot-device').Client;
const message = require('azure-iot-device').Message;
const protocol = require('azure-iot-device-mqtt').Mqtt;

// App settings
const connectionString = '<connection string of alarmdevice-patient1 in IoT
Devices explorer in Azure Portal>';
const LEDPin = 15;

// Other global variables
var client;
var blinkLEDTimeout = null;

/** Handler for message received event.
 *  Displays the received message in console.
 *  Blinks an LED if an alert is received.
 */
function receiveMessageCallback(msg) {
  var message = msg.getData().toString('utf-8');
  if (message === "high-body-temp-alert") {
    blinkLED();
  }
  client.complete(msg, function () {
    console.log('Received message: ' + message);
  });
}
```

```
/** Lights up the LED for 5 secs.
 */
function blinkLED() {
  if(blinkLEDTimeout) {
      clearTimeout(blinkLEDTimeout);
   }
  wpi.digitalWrite(LEDPin, 1);
  blinkLEDTimeout = setTimeout(function () {
    wpi.digitalWrite(LEDPin, 0);
  }, 5000);
}

// Set up wiring
wpi.setup('wpi');
wpi.pinMode(LEDPin, wpi.OUTPUT);

// Create a device client using IoT Hub connection string
client = deviceClient.fromConnectionString(connectionString, protocol);

// Handler for hub connection opened event
client.open(function (err) {
  if (err) {
    console.error('[ERROR] IoT Hub connection error:' + err.message);
    return;
  }
  else {
    console.log('Connected to IoT Hub.');
  }

  // Attach the cloud-to-device method callback
  client.on('message', receiveMessageCallback);
});
```

You will notice that, although the code is in a different language, the structure is pretty much the same. Go through it a couple of times and refer to the comments in the code for hints.

Running the Application

Run the application using the following command:

```
node index.js
```

If the connection to the IoT Hub is successful, you will see the message "Connected to IoT Hub" printed in console. At this point, the alarm device is listening to the hub for incoming messages.

Fire up Visual Studio again, open the IoTCentralizedPatientMonitoring solution, and run it. Make sure both the SimulatedDevice and SolutionBackend projects are set as startup projects. When the solution backend encounters the high body temperature condition, it will send an alert message to the alarm device. Wait for this condition to occur. When it does, go back to PuTTY and check for the alert message (see Figure 3-20). Do not forget to check out your LED light blinking on each alert.

```
Connected to IoT Hub.
>
Received message: high-body-temp-alert
>
Received message: high-body-temp-alert
>
Received message: high-body-temp-alert
>
Received message: high-body-temp-alert
```

Figure 3-20. *Console output from the node.js application running on Pi*

Congratulations. You have successfully created your first-ever IoT network with functioning devices and a solution backend!

Recap

We realize that it was a big chapter with a lot to grasp. But by the end, you were able to write IoT applications and create a network of your own. You learned how to:

- Get an Azure subscription required to use IoT Suite services

- Create an IoT Hub in Azure Portal

- Register devices in the hub via code and the Portal

- Create a simulated device using Azure IoT devices SDK that sends telemetry data to the hub

- Create a solution backend that receives device messages, analyzes them, and sends messages to another IoT device

- Send push notifications using the Azure Notification Hubs service

- Write applications for real IoT devices (Raspberry Pi Zero)

In the next chapter, you will learn about another key enabler of AI 2.0 applications—artificial intelligence.

CHAPTER 4

Understanding Cognitive APIs

By now, you are conversant with IoT and have a good understanding of creating a smart application using IoT. Chapter 1 started by introducing your journey to the world of artificial intelligence. As discussed in the previous chapters, we are presently in the first AI revolution, which marks the inception of "AI-as a service". What comes to your mind when you hear the term "artificial intelligence". Scary robots? A topic of sophisticated research? A future of machines that can do complex tasks with a blink of an eye? Normally, developers think of AI implementation as a tough task involving writing complex algorithms and writing hundreds of lines of code. Consider the following conversation:

User: How does my schedule look today?

Software: You have a meeting with your leadership today at 9 AM.

User: Thank you, let me leave by 8:30 AM then.

Software: There looks to be heavy traffic downtown; leave by 8 AM instead?

User: Should I go by metro then?

Software Absolutely, if you take the 8:20 AM metro, you should be in the office by 8:45.

User: Thanks. Please also mark my calendar booked, as I have a Tea meeting with a prospective client.

Software: I have already done it tentatively, based on your email interaction. Don't forget to come early today. Your favorite team, Barcelona, is in the finale with Real Madrid today."

User: Oh! I can't miss it! Please send me a reminder by 4 PM.

Software: Sure, will do.

© Nishith Pathak and Anurag Bhandari 2018
N. Pathak and A. Bhandari, *IoT, AI, and Blockchain for .NET*, https://doi.org/10.1007/978-1-4842-3709-0_4

Imagine creating software applications like this that can have human-like conversations and not only understand human jargon or its understated variations but also listen and speak with humans appropriately. To make it more interesting, imagine creating applications that can deeply understand and interpret content on the web or on a user's machine, intelligently react to direct user interaction through speech or text, or make smart recommendations about products or services that are tailored to each individual user. Wouldn't these capabilities make your software smart and intelligent? At the end of this chapter, you will have a good understanding about:

- Cognitive systems and types

- Why Microsoft Cognitive API

- Various Microsoft Cognitive API groups and their APIs

What Are Cognitive Systems?

Most of you may be coming from traditional programming systems, so before we really dive into Microsoft Cognitive API, it is important to understand what cognitive systems are. Figure 4-1 shows the general classification of the Cognitive API. Almost all the APIs released by Microsoft can be categorized into one of these groups.

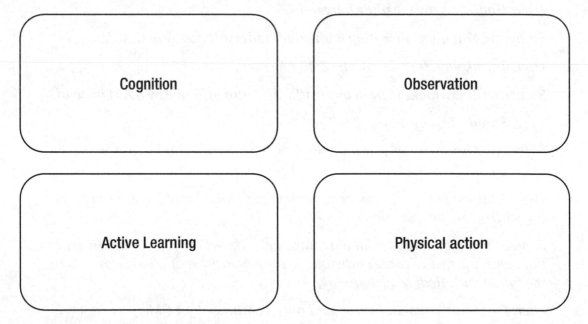

Figure 4-1. *Various categories of Cognitive APIs*

Cognition is the process of representing information and using that representation to reason. Observation enables machines to mimic human behavior. For example, interacting with speech, text, or vision the way humans do. Active learning is the process of improving automatically over time. A classic example of Active Learning is Microsoft Language Understanding Intelligent Service (LUIS), which we cover a little later in this chapter. Physical action requires using a combination of these three and devices to interact intelligently.

If you observe cognitive systems versus traditional computing programs, you will observe that cognitive systems differ in three ways:

- Cognitive systems understand like humans do. We have seen the era where AI led machines are defeating some of the champions of the game. Libratus, designed by a team from Carnegie-Mellon, has defeated several Poker champions. Poker, as you may know, requires information to be hidden until a point in time and it is very difficult to create a model to handle such a situation.

- Cognitive systems have a unique ability to understand ideas and concepts, form a proposition, disambiguate, infer, and generate insights, based on which they can reason and act. For example, you can create a cognitive web application that can recognize human beings by looking at their images and then conversing with them in slang.

- Unlike traditional computing programs, cognitive systems are always learning based on new data. In fact, each cognitive system gets cleverer day by day based on learning new information. Over a period, proficiency moves from novice to expert.

Why the Microsoft Cognitive API?

Now that we understand the essence of cognitive systems, you must have realized that creating a cognitive systems is not easy. It involves a great amount of research, understanding internals, understanding fuzzy algorithms, and much more. As an .NET developer you may have wondered, how can I make my software as smart as Microsoft's Cortana, Apple's Siri, or Google's Assistant? You probably did not know where to start.

Over the years, we have spent a good amount of time with software developers and architects at top IT companies. A common perception that we've found among all of them is that adding individual AI elements, such as natural language understanding, speech recognition, machine learning etc., to their software would require a deep understanding of neural networks, fuzzy logic, and mind-bending computer science theories. Various companies like Microsoft, Google, IBM, and others realized this and agreed that AI is not just about inventing new algorithms and research. The good news is this perception is not the case anymore. To get started, each of these companies has exposed their years of research in form of an SDK, mostly in the RESTful API that helps developers create a smarter application with very few lines of code. Together, these APIs are called the Cognitive API.

Built by Experts and Supported by Community

The Microsoft Cognitive API is a result of years of research done at Microsoft. This includes experts from various fields and teams like Microsoft research, Azure machine learning, and Bing, to name a few. Microsoft certainly did a great job of abstracting all the nuances of the deep neural network, which are complex algorithms that exposing easy-to-use REST APIs. This means that whenever you consume the Microsoft Cognitive API, you are getting the best functionality exposed in a RESTful manner. All the APIs have been thoroughly tested. We personally have been playing with Cognitive API since its inception and feel that each of these APIs, like all cognitive APIs, has been improving over time. What makes it more appealing is that entire functionality is supported by class documentation and has great community backing from GitHub, user voice, MSDN, and others along with sample code. In fact, the entire Microsoft cognitive documentation is being hosted on GitHub and individual developers can contribute to making it more effective.

Ease to Use

The Microsoft Cognitive API is easy to consume. You just need to get the subscription key for your respective API and then you can consume the APIs by passing this subscription key. The functionality is accomplished in a few lines of code. We will go into more detail about the subscription key later. For now, just understand that before you can start using Cognitive Services, you need a subscription key for each service you want to use in your application. Almost all Cognitive APIs have a free and paid tier. You can use the free API keys with a Microsoft account.

Language and Platform Independent

Microsoft has started supporting open source in a better and more seamless way. Previously, Microsoft functionality was limited through the use of Microsoft-specific tools and languages like VB.NET, C#, etc. We discussed Microsoft Cognitive API being available in RESTful. What makes Microsoft Cognitive API more appealing is that it's flexible. You can now integrate and consume Microsoft Cognitive API in any language or platform. This means it doesn't matter if you are a Windows, Android, or Mac developer, or if your preferred language ranges from Python to C# to Node.js—you can consume Microsoft Cognitive APIs with just a few lines of code. Exciting!

Note   The Microsoft cognitive space has been expanding at a steady pace. What started with four Cognitive APIs last year has risen to 29 while writing this book. Microsoft has suites of product offerings. They also have a suite with Cloud-based capability. While consuming these services, one may wonder why Microsoft created these services rather than creating specific solution and products. Well, the approach has been to emphasize platforms rather than creating individual systems. These platforms and services will eventually be used by other companies and developers to resolve domain-specific problems. The intent of the platform is to scale up and create more and more offerings in the cognitive space and give the immersive experience of consuming them to the end users. Don't be surprised if the cognitive list of APIs increases to 50+ in the next year or so.

Microsoft's Cognitive Services

Cognitive Services is a set of software-as-a-service (SaaS) commercial offerings from Microsoft related to artificial intelligence. Cognitive Services is the product of Microsoft's years of research into cognitive computing and artificial intelligence, and many of these services are being used by some of Microsoft's own popular products, such as Bing (search, maps), Translator, Bot Framework, etc.

Microsoft made these services available as easy-to-use REST APIs, directly consumable in a web or a mobile application. As of the writing of this book, there are 29 available Cognitive Services, broadly divided into five categories, as shown in Figure 4-2.

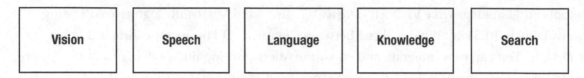

Figure 4-2. *The main categories of Cognitive APIs*

The rest of the chapter provides a good amount of overview of each of the APIs and their sub-APIs. Let's get a sneak preview of each of these APIs one by one in more detail.

Note   It requires a separate book to understand various Microsoft Cognitive APIs in more detail. If you are interested in getting a deeper understanding of Cognitive APIs, we recommend you read the Apress book entitled *Artificial Intelligence for.NET.*

Vision

The computer cannot deal with or understand images on its own. Image processing techniques combined with intelligent AI algorithms enables machines to see images and identify and recognize objects and people. These services deal with visual information, mostly in the form of images and videos. A scene or the photo being captured can comprise multiple objects. Image processing has been one of the core research areas of machine learning for decades. Various algorithm and new ways have been devised in the last few decades to process images and return valuable information about the image. This can certainly help in resolving some of the challenges. For example, think about using this solution to describe the scene to a blind person or capturing a photo of an object and then using it for verification, identification security, or even gathering more information about it. The ability of a machine to detect an object in the scene being captured is called *object detection,* as shown in Figure 4-3. Object detection is followed by recognition. The ability of a system to recognize and then label an object properly is called *object recognition.*

Figure 4-3. *A group of riders on a dirt road*

The accuracy of an image recognition system, like everything else in AI, depends heavily on the training data. Using machine learning techniques, the system is trained with hundreds of images to recognize objects of a specific class. The Microsoft Computer Vision API provides years of research done by Microsoft in the area of image processing combined with the latest algorithm and API to analyze images and provide information. Broadly, it has seven services, as shown in Figure 4-4.

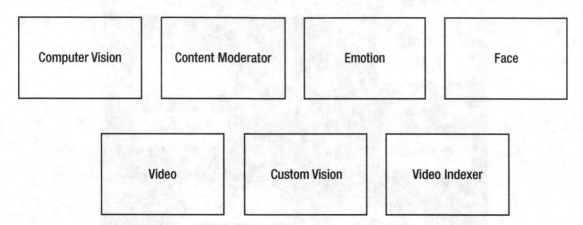

Figure 4-4. *Subcategories of the Microsoft Computer Vision API*

Face API

THE Face API helps detect human faces and compare similar ones (face detection). Using the same techniques, it is possible to detect faces in a photo and their related 27 attributes (age, gender, smile, etc.). If the system is pre-trained with the faces of a specific person, it can match and recognize that person's face in a photo, as shown in Figure 4-5. Face recognition could be used as a security authentication mechanism or to detect a dangerous criminal in a public place using CCTV cameras. It also helps in organizing people into groups according to visual similarity (face grouping) and identifies previously tagged people in images (face verification). Uber, one of the largest taxi service companies, is using face verification to verify Uber drivers. We delve more into face recognition in Chapters 5 and 6.

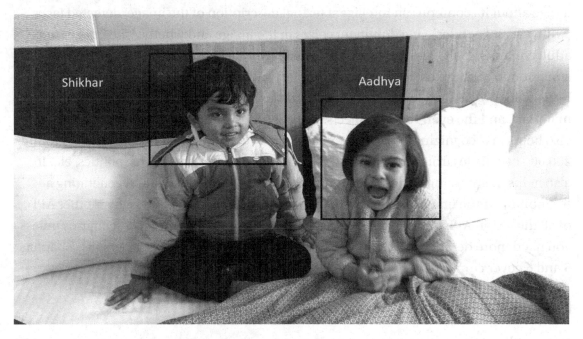

Figure 4-5. *Faces being identified in an image*

Emotions API

The Face API helps in detecting and recognizing faces. The Emotions API takes it to the next level by analyzing faces to detect a range of eight feelings—anger, happiness, sadness, fear, surprise, contempt, disgust, neutrality, etc. The Emotions API returns these emotions with a decreasing order of confidence for each face. The Emotions API also helps in recognizing emotions on a video. It helps in getting instant feedback. Think of a use case when the Emotions API can be applied to retail customers to evaluate their feedback instantaneously.

Computer Vision API

The Computer Vision API performs many tasks. It extracts rich information from an image about its contents: an intelligent textual description of the image, detected faces (with age and gender), and dominant colors in the image and whether the image has adult contents. It also provides an Optical Character Recognition (OCR) facility. OCR is a method to capture text in images and convert them into the stream that can eventually be used for processing. Image being captured can be handwritten notes, whiteboard materials, and the even various objects. Not only does computer vision do all these, it also helps in recognizing faces from their celebrity recognition model, which has around 200,000 celebrities from various fields, including entertainment, sports, politics, etc. It also helps in analyzing videos, providing information about videos, and generating a thumbnail for the images being captured. All in all, Computer Vision is the mother API of all the vision APIs. You will calling this API to get information in most scenarios unless you need more detailed information (such as the specific emotion of a person). Chapters 5 and 6 cover computer vision in more detail.

Content Moderation

Data, as discussed, is the new currency in any organization. Data and content are generated from various sources. Be it a social, messaging, or even peer platform, content is generated exponentially. There is always a need to moderate the content so it shouldn't affect the platform, people, ethics and core values and of course the business. Content moderations help in moderating the content. Whether the content source is text, image, or videos, the Content Moderation API serves content moderation with various scenarios and through three methods (manual, automated, and hybrid) for moderating content.

Video Indexer API

The Video indexer API allows you to use intelligent video processing for face detection, motion detection (useful in CCTV security systems), to generate thumbnails, and for near real-time video analysis (textual description for each frame). It starts getting insights on the video in almost real time. This helps make your video more engaging to the end user and helps more contents be discovered.

Custom Vision Service

So far we have seen our Microsoft Cognitive API doing image recognition on things like scenes, faces, and emotions. There are requirements wherein you need a custom image classifier, suited specifically for a domain. Consider a banking scenario where you need a classifier just to understand various types of currency and its denominations. This is where Microsoft Custom Vision Services come in. You must train the system with domain-specific images and then you can consume its REST API in any platform. In an order to use the custom vision service, you need to access at `https://www.customvision.ai/`. You then upload the domain-specific images, train them by labeling, and then exposing the REST API. You can evaluate custom vision service. With proper training, it works like a charm. Like LUIS, Custom Vision Service is also based on active machine learning, which means your custom image classifier keeps on improving over a period of time. More info about custom vision is found in later chapters.

Video Indexer

The Video Indexer API extracts insights from a video, such as a face recognition (names of people), speech sentiment analysis (positive, negative, neutral), and keywords.

Speech

Interaction with various devices has been transformed in the last decade. Every now and then, a new technique of interactions is introduced. Among those, speech has been a popular, natural, and inevitable choice. Many devices now have built-in speech functionalities. Think about some of the personal digital assistants like Cortana, Siri, or Alexa, which have changed the way we interact with our mobile applications. When you ask a question to Siri or Google (search by voice), it uses speech recognition to convert your voice into text. The converted text is then used to perform the search. Modern SR techniques can handle variations in accent and similar sounding words and phrases based on the context. Microsoft has been researching speech for more than two decades. In fact, the first version of the Speech API was part of Windows 95. Since then, one of the Microsoft research areas has been an incredible focus on speech and various versions of speech recognition have been released, with various OS having flavors of both speech-to-text and text-to-speech capabilities. With the advent of Speech API on the Cognitive API, Microsoft provides the best speech capabilities that are available on the Cloud and can be consumed in easy-to-use REST APIs. The Speech API provides the easiest way to enhance your application with speech-driven scenarios. The Speech API provides ease of use by abstracting all the complexity of the speech algorithms. Broadly speaking, functionalities of the Speech API are categorized into four main areas, as shown in Figure 4-6.

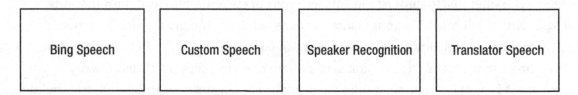

Figure 4-6.   *The subcategories of the Speech API*

Bing Speech API

The Bing Speech API converts speech to text, optionally, understands its intent, and converts the text back to speech. It has two main components—Speech Recognition and Speech Synthesis. Speech Recognition, also referred as Speech To Text (STT), allows you to handle spoken words from your users in your application using a recognition engine and translates the speech to text. This text transcription can be used for a variety of purposes, including for hands-free applications. These spoken words can come directly from a microphone, speaker, or even from an audio file. All this is possible without typing a single character.

Contract to STT, Speech Synthesis aka Text to Speech (TTS), allows you to speak words or phrases back to the users through a speech synthesis engine. Every Windows machine has an built-in Speech Synthesizer that converts text to speech. This built-in synthesizer is especially beneficial for all those folks who have difficulty or can't read text printed on the screen. This built-in synthesizer is good for simple scenarios. For enterprise scenarios, where performance, accuracy, and speed is important, the speech-based model should comply with the following prerequisites—ease of use, improves with time, upgrades continuously, handles complex computations, and is available on all platforms. The Bing Text to Speech API gives these features in an easy-to-consume REST API. Bing Text to Speech API supports Speech Synthesis Markup Language (SSML). SSML is a W3C specification and offers a uniform way of creating speech-based markup text. Check the official spec for the complete SSML syntax at `https://www.w3.org/TR/speech-synthesis`.

Custom Speech Services

The Custom Speech Service, previously known as CRIS, lets you build custom language models of the speech recognizer by tailoring them to the vocabulary of the application and the speaking style of your users. To understand the need of custom speech service, it is important to understand how the recognition engine works. At a high level, it takes audio input or speech from the user's microphone and processes it by trying to match audio signals to patterns in different databases. These signal patterns are then associated with known words and, if the engine finds a matching pattern in the database, it returns the associated word as text. Figure 4-7 shows the entire flow of speech recognition.

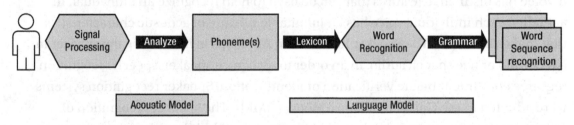

Figure 4-7. *The entire flow of speech recognition*

As you see Figure 4-7, audio signals are converted into individual sounds, known as *phonemes*. For example, the word Surabhi is made up of "Su" "ra" "bhi". These words are then mapped to the language model, which is a combination of lexicon and grammar. A catalog of language and words is called lexicon and the systems of rules combining these words are called grammar. This process of utilizing grammar is important, as some words and phrases sound the same but have different meanings (consider "stuffy nose" and "stuff he knows").

Training speech recognition is the key to success. The Microsoft Speech to Text engine is also been trained well with the enormous speech training, making it one of the best in class for generic scenarios. Sometimes you need speech recognition systems in a closed domain or for a specific environment. For example, there is a need for speech recognition in environments where speech recognition engines deal with background noise, specific jargon, or diverse accents that are not common. Such scenarios mandate customization on both the acoustic side as well as the language model, making them suitable for a specific environment. The Custom Speech Service enables you to customize your speech recognition system by creating custom language models and an acoustic model that are specific to your domain, environment, and accents. It also allows you to create your own custom speech-to-text endpoint that suits your specific requirements once your custom acoustic and language model is created.

Speaker Recognition

The term voice recognition or speaker identification refers to identifying the speaker, rather than what they are saying. Recognizing the speaker can simplify the task of translating speech in systems that have been trained on a specific person's voice. A voice has distinctive features that can be used to help recognize an individual. In actuality, each individual voice has an inimitable mixture of acoustic characteristics that makes it unique. The Speaker Recognition API helps in identifying the speaker in a recorded or live speech audio. In an order to recognize speaker, speech recognition requires enrollment before verification or identification. Speaker recognition systems were adapted to the Gaussian Mixture Model (GMM). The speaker recognition of Microsoft uses the most recent and advanced factor analysis based on the i-Vector speaker recognition system. Speaker recognition can be reliably used as an additional authentication mechanism for security scenarios.

Note   There is a clear distinction between speech recognition and speaker recognition. Speech recognition is the "what" part of the speech, whereas speaker recognition is the "who" part of the speech. In simple terms, speech recognition identifies what has been said. Speaker recognition recognizes who is speaking.

Speaker recognition has two main components:

- Speaker verification
- Speaker identification

Speaker verification, also known as speaker authentication, is the process that verifies the claim with one pattern or record in the repository. In speaker verification, the input voice and phrase is matched against the enrollment voice and phrase to identify whether they are the same or a different individual. You can assume speaker verification works on a 1:1 mapping. Speaker identification, on the other hand, is a mapping to verify the claim with all the possible records in the repository and is primarily used for identifying an unknown person from a series of individuals. Speaker identification works on a 1:N mapping. Before the Speaker Recognition API is used for verification or identification, it undergoes a process called enrollment.

Translator Speech API

The Microsoft Translator Speech API helps translates speech from one language to another in real time. The key to this translation is the real time component. Imagine a scenario in which a Chinese-speaking person wants to communicate with a Spanish-speaking person. Neither of them know a common language. To make it worse and a little more real, let's assume they are far apart in space. It would certainly be hard, if not impossible, for them to communicate. The Microsoft Translator Speech API helps resolve this barrier across languages in real time. As of the writing of this book, it supports 60 languages. It has various functionalities for both partial and final transcription, which can be used to handle various unique scenarios. The Translator Speech API internally uses the Microsoft Translator API, which is also used across various Microsoft products, including Skype, Bing, and translator apps, to name a few.

Language

Humans interact with each other and now with machines in one of three ways—verbally, using written language, and using gestures. The one common thing among these three ways is "language". A language is a set of rules to communicate that are the same for every individual. Although the same language can be used for written and spoken communication, there are usually subtle and visible variations, with written language being the more formal of the two. The most effort spent in AI research has been to enable machines to understand humans as naturally as humans do. As it is easier for machines to understand written text than speech, the Language category is one of the most important Cognitive APIs. These services deal with natural language understanding, translation, analysis, and more, as shown in Figure 4-8. Let's look at these areas one by one.

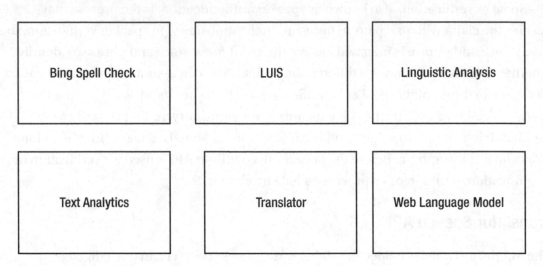

Figure 4-8. *The subcategories of the Language API*

Bing Spell Check API

Spelling mistakes are a common user behavior. Almost every user interaction, be it in form of search, filling in forms, or even now talking about conversational scenarios, requires handling spelling mistakes. Take for example a movie-based site where the user typed these movie names:

> Momento
>
> The Pursuit of Happiness
>
> Kick Ass

A search just based on the grammatical based text editor would result in a "No movies found" error. These are classic examples of spelling issues. "Momento" is a common misspelling of "Memento". In the second case, although the spelling was correct, the actual movie title was "The Pursuit of Happyness". In the last case, the movie name was hyphenated as "Kick-Ass" rather than separate words. The system should have the ability to handle such spelling mistakes. Otherwise, you could end up losing some of your loyal customers. Some of the popular search engines like Bing and Google handle this issue by handling spell checks with ease.

Bing Spell Check is an online API that not only helps to correct spelling errors but considers word breaks, slang, person, places, and even brand names. For each detected error, it also provides a suggestion in decreasing order of confidence. Bing was created with years and years of research, data, and of course using the machine learning model to optimize it. In fact, most applications, including Bing.com, use the Bing Spell Check API to resolve spelling mistakes.

Language Understanding Intelligent Service (LUIS)

LUIS, as its name suggests, helps in understanding the "what" question of the language. This helps in responding back to the users with a proper response. LUIS is Microsoft's Natural Language Understanding (NLU). NLU is an area of deep research. NLU helps machines understand humans through human language. Consider the following greeting scenarios:

> "Hi"
>
> "Howdy"
>
> "Hello"
>
> "Hey"

All of these words is the way to greet a user. There are more than hundred ways to greet a person in English alone. Unless you are aware of the real intent of the question being asked, it's imperative that you respond to the user correctly. Isn't it? LUIS helps the application understand the meaning of the sentence by breaking the sentence into entities and intents. In a simpler way, you can correlate intent as the verb and entities as the nouns. Once your application has a fair understanding of the context of the sentence, your application can respond to the user appropriately. Consider another scenario, shown in Figure 4-9, where a sentence is broken down in order to detect intent and entity.

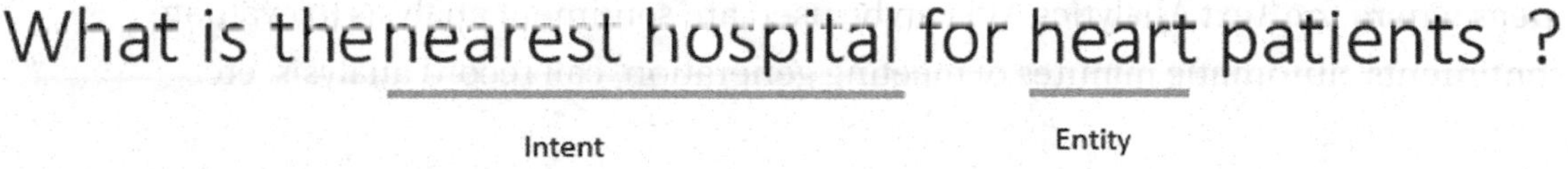

What is the nearest hospital for heart patients ?

Intent   Entity

Figure 4-9. *NLU analyzes each sentence for two things—intent and entity.*

As Figure 4-9 shows, NLU analyzes each sentence for two things—intent (the meaning or intended action) and entities. In the example, the nearest hospital information is the detected intent and the heart is the entity. A user may ask the same question in a hundred different ways. LUIS will always be able to extract the correct intent and entities from the user's sentence. The software can then use this extracted information to query an online API and show the user their requested info.

LUIS provides prebuilt entities. If you want to create a new one, you can easily create a simple, composite, or even hierarchical entity.

To create LUIS application, you need to visit `https://luis.ai`, create an application, add the intent and entities, train it, and then publish the app to get a RESTful API, which can then used by various applications. Like any machine learning based application, training is the key for LUIS. In fact, LUIS is based on active machine learning, which has the ability to continue to be trained. We discuss LUIS more in coming chapters.

Linguistic Analysis

The Linguistic Analysis API helps in parsing text for granular linguistic analysis, such as sentence separation and tokenization (breaking the text into sentences and tokens) and part-of-speech tagging. This eventually helps in understanding the meaning and the context of the text. Linguistic analysis has been used as a preliminary step in many NLP-related processing, including NLU, TTS, and machine translations, to name a few.

Text Analytics

Machine learning uses historical data to identify patterns. The more data there is, the easier it is to define the pattern. The rise of IoT and new devices fuels this evolution. The last two years have generated 90% of all data. A full 80% of this data is unstructured in nature. Text Analytics helps resolve some areas of unstructured data by detecting sentiments (positive or negative), key phrases, topics, and language from your text. Consider the case of the online retail bot. Being a global online retail bot, it can expect users from various geographies and queries in many languages. Language detection is one of the classic problems being resolved by the Microsoft Text Analytics API. Other areas where the Text Analytics API can be used are sentiment analysis to evaluate sentiments, automatic minutes of meeting generation, call record analysis, etc.

Translator Text API

The Microsoft Translator API detects the language of a given text and translates it from one language to another. Internally, it uses the Microsoft internal machine learning based translation engine, which has gone through tens of thousands of training sentences. It understands patterns and then translates the text as well as determines the rules of the language. Microsoft has been using the Translator Text API internally in all its applications where multilanguage support is required. You can also create your own customized translation system built on the existing system, which is suitable for specific domains and environments.

Web Language Model API

The success of a language model is solely dependent on the data used for training. The Web contains an enormous amount of data in the textual format under millions of images. Although this data has several anomalies like grammatical errors, slang, profanity, lack of punctuation, etc., it can certainly help in understanding patterns, word prediction, or even breaking a word without spaces to understand it better. The Web Language Model or WebLM is the process of creating a language model using this method.

WebLM provides a variety of natural language processing tasks not covered under other Language APIs—word breaking (inserting spaces into a string of words lacking spaces), joint probabilities (calculating how often a particular sequence of words appear together), conditional probabilities (calculating how often a particular word tends to follow), and next word completions (getting the list of words most likely to follow).

Knowledge

These services deal with searching large knowledgebases to identify entities, provide search suggestions, and give product recommendations. Figure 4-10 shows you the sub-APIs available under the Knowledge API. Let's look at each of them briefly.

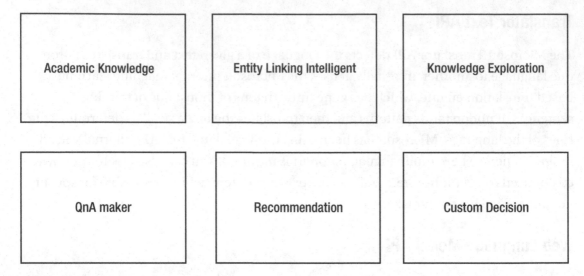

Figure 4-10. *The subcategories of the Knowledge service*

Academic Knowledge API

As the name implies, the Academic Knowledge API allows you to retrieve information from Microsoft Academic Graph, a proprietary knowledgebase of scientific/scholarly research papers and their entities. Using this API, you can easily find papers by authors, institutes, events, etc. It is also possible to find similar papers, check for plagiarism, and retrieve citation stats. It allows you to interpret and evaluate knowledge entity results. It also provides an option to calculate the histogram of the distribution of academic entities, thereby giving you a rich semantic experience by understanding the intent and context of the query being searched.

QnA Maker

QnA Maker creates FAQ-style questions and answers from the provided data. Data can include any file or links. QnA Maker offers a combination of a website and an API. Use the website to create a knowledgebase using your existing FAQs website, PDF, DOC, or text file. QnA Maker will automatically extract questions and answers from your documents and train itself to answer natural language user queries based on your data. You can think of it as an automated version of LUIS. You do not have to train the system, but you do get an option to do custom re-training. QnA Maker's API is the endpoint that accepts user queries and sends answers for your knowledgebase. Optionally, QnA Maker can be combined with Microsoft's Bot Framework to create out-of-the-box bots for Facebook, Skype, Slack, and more.

Entity Linking Intelligence Service

Words have different meanings based on the context of a sentence. Consider the following sentences in Figure 4-11.

"The bird in the pic is a <u>crane</u>"
"Finally, they had to use a <u>crane</u> to lift the car"
"She had to <u>crane</u> her neck to see the entire tower"

Figure 4-11. *The use of the word "crane" in three different contexts*

In these sentences, "crane" is being used to denote a bird, a large lift, or even the movement of a body. It requires considering the context of the sentence to identify the real meaning of the words being used. The Entity Linking Intelligence service allows you to determine keywords (named entities, events, locations, etc.) in the text based on its context.

Knowledge Exploration Service

KES, aka the Knowledge Exploration Service, adds support for natural language queries auto-completion search suggestions and more to your own data. You can make your search more interactive with autosuggestion in a fast and effective manner.

Recommendation API

Recommendations are everywhere in the digital world. A more powerful recommendation system means better user traction and of course great ROI. The power of recommendations has been a tremendous boost for many companies. Consider a few examples:

- YouTube uses a recommender system to recommend videos
- Netflix uses a recommender system to recommend interesting videos/stories

- Amazon is not just using recommendations for showing product results but also for recommending products to sell to their end users

- Google is not just using recommendation systems to rank web links but is also suggesting web and news links for you

- News sites like *The New York Times* are providing recommendations for news you should watch

Many successful companies continue to invest in, research, and re-innovate their recommendation systems to improve them and to provide more personalized user experiences to their end users. Creating a recommendation system is not easy. It requires deep expertise on data, having exemplary research and analytics wings, and of course lots of money.

There are various types of recommendation systems available in the market. The Microsoft Recommendations API helps you deal with transaction-based recommendations. This is particularly useful to retail store—both online and offline—in helping them increase sales by offering their customers recommendations, such as items that are frequently bought together, personalized item recommendations for users based on their transaction history, etc. Like QnA Maker, you use the Recommendations UI website with your existing data to create product catalog and usage data.

At a high level, it supports three types of recommendations:

- Frequently brought together (FBT)

- Item to item recommendations

- Recommendations based on past user activity

The FBT Recommendations API recommends items that are frequently bought or used in combination with each other. For example, you might likely want to buy an iPhone protector glass when you buy a new iPhone app, as shown in Figure 4-12. Such recommendations are called FBT. Item-to-item recommendations, on the other hand, are collaborative filtering based recommendations. You often have seen the site mentioning products as "customers who bought this also bought" section, which is from the item to item recommendation. Recommendations based on past user activity simply provide recommendations based on historical transactions by the user. This type of recommendation is also called a "customer to item recommendation".

Frequently bought together

Total price: $387.98

Add both to Cart

Add both to List

ℹ These items are shipped from and sold by different sellers. Show details

☑ **This item:** Apple iPhone 7-32GB - GSM Unlocked - Black (Certified Refurbished) $379.99

☑ amFilm iPhone 8, 7, 6S, 6 Screen Protector Glass, amFilm Tempered Glass Screen Protector for Apple... $7.99

Figure 4-12. *The FBT use case while buying an iPhone*

Custom Decision Service

The Custom Decision Service helps you create intelligent systems by providing decision API that use feedback-based reinforcement learning to improve over time. Reinforcement learning is when a machine is not explicitly supplied the training data. It must interact with the environment in order to achieve a goal. Due to a lack of training data, it must learn by itself from scratch and rely on the trial-and-error technique to make decisions and discover the best paths. For each action the machine takes, there's a consequence, and for each consequence, it is given a numerical reward. So if an action produces a desirable result, it receives "good" remarks. And if the result is disastrous, it receives "very, very bad" remarks. The machine strives to maximize its total numerical reward—that is, get as many "good" and "very good" remarks as possible by not repeating its mistakes. This technique of machine learning is especially useful when the machine has to deal with very dynamic environments, where creating and supplying training data is just not feasible. For example, when driving a car, flying drones (see Figure 4-13), playing a video game, and so on.

Figure 4-13. *Flying drones that do not require a human to operate them uses reinforcement learning to learn from the dynamic and challenging environment to improve their skills over time*

You can use Custom Decision Service in pool or application-specific mode. Pool mode uses a single model for all applications and is suited for low traffic applications. Applications that have heavy traffic require application-specific mode.

Search

Search has been ubiquitously available, from the desktop, mobile search, web search, and even routine stuff in our daily lives. In the latest report, 50 billion connected devices are expected to be available by the end of 2020 and each of them requires a connected search. Microsoft also has certainly made great progress on search in bringing Bing in the platform. Microsoft search, which is based on Bing, provides an alternative option to Google search. One of the missions of Bing search API was to go against the Google monopoly and try to give an alternative option to search. Bing currently is the second most powerful search engine after Google. The Bing Search APIs allow you to implement the capabilities of Google or Microsoft Bing into your enterprise application with a few lines of code.

Microsoft recently revised their mission as "Empowering every person and every organization on the planet to achieve more". This mission is more human-centric. This mission has a lot of caveats to provide a lot of services anywhere and everywhere. Bringing Search Bings API to common people and making some of the services available in terms of RESTful APIs is one of the ways to achieve this new Microsoft mission. The Microsoft Bing Search APIs have been driven on three Ps, namely pervasive, predictive, and proactive. This makes the Bing Search API available, anywhere, anytime, and on any device proactively with just a few lines of code. The Bing Search APIs allows you to leverage the power of Bing by calling different APIs, as shown in Figure 4-14. Let's take a look at each of these APIs.

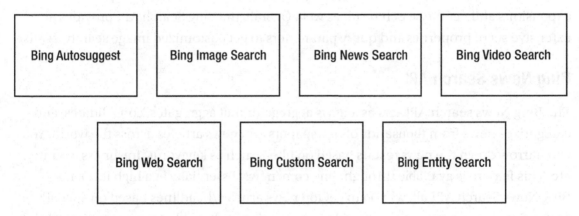

Figure 4-14. *The subcategories of Search*

Bing Autosuggest API

As the name suggests, the Bing Autosuggest API provides intelligent type-ahead and search suggestions, directly from the Bing search, when a user is typing inside the search box. As the user types in the search textbox, your application calls the API to show a list of options for the user to select. Based on each character entered, the Bing Autosuggest API shows distinctive relevant search results. Internally, this is achieved by passing partial search queries to Bing. This result is a combination of contextual search based on what other users have searched for in the past. All Bing APIs, including BingAutosuggest, provide customization of search results using query parameters and headers being passing while consuming APIs.

Bing Image Search API

Images are more expressive than textual content. The Bing Image Search API provides developers an opportunity to get an analogous experience of Bing.com/images in their applications. One thing to note here is that you should only use Bing Image Search API when the results are just images. It allows you to return images based on filters such as keywords, color, country, size, license, etc. As an added bonus, the Bing Image Search API breaks the query into various segments and provides suggestions to narrow down the search options. For example, if you search for the keyword "Microsoft search," Bing smartly breaks it into various options like "Microsoft Desktop search," "Microsoft Windows Search," and "Microsoft Search 4.0". You can choose one of the query expansions and get the search result as well. Overall, the Bing Search API provides an extensive set of properties and query parameters to get customized image search results.

Bing News Search API

The Bing News search API acts as a news aggregator that aggregates, consolidates, and categorizes news from thousands of newspapers and news articles across the world. You can narrow down the news results based on filters such as keywords, freshness, country, etc. This feature is available through Bing.com/news. Essentially at a high level, the Bing News Search API allows you to get top news articles/headlines based on specific categories, return news articles based on the user's search, or allows news topics to be returned that are trending in social media.

Bing Video Search API

The Bing Video search API allows you to get videos based on various filters, such as keywords, resolutions, video length, country, etc., return more insight about a particular video, or show videos to be returned that are trending in social media. The Bing News Videos API provides immersive video searching capabilities and are the easiest way to create a video-based portal experience with just a few API calls. The Bing Video Search API has free and paid tiers, like Bing image search.

Bing Web Search API

By now, you got a fair idea about Bing API services. Each of these API gives specific information. For example, you use Bing Image API if you only need image results. Similarly, you would use the News API if you need news results. There are quite a lot of scenarios in which you need a combination of results, such as needing images and videos together in the result set. This is similar to Bing.com/search, where you get results that include image, videos, and more. The Bing Web search API provides solutions to these scenarios.

Bing Custom Search

The Bing Custom Search allows a search based on custom intents and topics. So instead of searching the entire web, Bing will search websites based on topics. It can also be used to implement site-specific searches on a single or a specified set of websites. Internally, custom search first identifies on-topic sites, applies Bing rankings, and returns the results. You also have an option to adjust the result by applying boost, pin, demote, or even blocking the site. In an order to customize the view and use custom search, visit `https://www.customsearch.ai/`. Once you have created the instance, modified it as per the convenience, and are satisfied with the result, use the custom search API to consume it in any platform.

Bing Entity Search API

The Bing Entity Search API allows you to get search results that include entities (people and objects) and places (cinema hall, hotels, local business, etc.). This provides a great immersive experience for the end user by providing primary details about the entity being searched. For example, if you are searching for a famous person, you would certainly get the wiki link and a brief description of the person being searched.

All Cognitive Services APIs are available in free and pay-as-you-go pricing tiers. You can choose a tier based on your application's usage volume. Although we would love to cover each of these in great detail, we are limited by the scope of this book. We will cover enough services from the speech, language, and search categories to launch you into building smart applications in little time.

You can learn more about these services (and possibly more that may have been added recently) by visiting `www.microsoft.com/cognitive-services/en-us/apis`.

Recap

This chapter serves as an introduction to Cognitive Services. As you understand by now, these APIs are a tremendous boost to resolve some of the complex problems that were not possible to resolve earlier. Another reason for this API-driven model is that it abstracts thousands of processor and VMs running behind the API. With the rise of technologies like IoT and sensors, there are unbelievable opportunities to automate and analyze data. You also learned about Cognitive Services and how are they different from the traditional programming model. The chapter then had a quick overview of the various commercial AI offerings by Microsoft in the form of their Cognitive Services REST APIs.

In the next chapter, you learn to install all the prerequisites for building AI-enabled software and build your first cognitive application using Visual Studio.

CHAPTER 5

Consuming Microsoft Cognitive APIs

By now, you have a fair understanding of Microsoft Cognitive technologies, its various offerings in terms of service, and a sneak preview of understanding their concepts. Microsoft has done a fantastic job in abstracting the research on AI and machine learning, hiding all complex processing nuances by giving easy-to-consume REST based services, sitting on its Azure Cloud solution. In fact, the entire suite of Microsoft Cognitive Services is exposed as REST APIs. Since the REST API has an API endpoint, you really don't need any specific platform or programming language to consume it. Another advantage of the REST API is that it can accept input in JSON or XML format and give output in the same formats. This gives you great flexibility to consume REST API directly in all major programming languages, such as C#, Java, PHP, Ruby, Python, JavaScript, and so on. As this book targets .NET developers, we will restrict ourselves to using C# throughout the book. But, really, the fundamentals of consuming Microsoft Cognitive Services remain the same for any language.

Like any enterprise service, every call to Microsoft Cognitive Services needs to be authenticated and authorized before being used. This is achieved through the use of a subscription key. Once you get a subscription key (we are going to discuss later how to do that), it is passed as a query string parameter or in a header while calling the REST endpoint of cognitive services. At the end of this chapter, you will learn

- Prerequisites for consuming Cognitive Services

- Obtaining a subscription key for Cognitive Services

- Calling the Microsoft Cognitive Vision API

- Consuming the Cognitive Vision API using Visual Studio

- Interesting uses of the Computer Vision API

© Nishith Pathak and Anurag Bhandari 2018
N. Pathak and A. Bhandari, *IoT, AI, and Blockchain for .NET*, https://doi.org/10.1007/978-1-4842-3709-0_5

Free Tier and Pay Per Use Model

When people get to know the Microsoft Cognitive API, the first thing that strikes them are the following questions:

- What's the cost of calling Microsoft Cognitive Services?

- Are there some free services available for personal use?

- What happens if I provide my credit card details?

- Can I put a limit on the use of APIs?

- What are the SLAs for Cognitive APIs being available in enterprise scenarios?

Before we delve into more details, let's answer these questions. Microsoft Cognitive Services come with two types of models for consuming cognitive services, namely free tier and paid tier (some of the services only have a paid tier). Free tier, as the name suggests, provides an opportunity to consume Microsoft Cognitive Services without paying anything to Microsoft. Free tier is mostly useful for the end user to give a try with personal or low-volume applications. If your requirement fulfills any of these requisites, we certainly encourage you to use free tier. As you can expect, a free tier for each service also have some restrictions. As it doesn't support SLA for services provided by Microsoft, free tier is often called as a restricted tier.

Cognitive Services also has the paid tier for service, which is based on pay per use model and is a model that should be used for any non-personal consumption of the cognitive services including enterprise applications. The pay per use model has a different pricing model for different services. For example, the pay per use model used by the Emotions API differ from the Speech API. Some of the Cognitive Services pay per use models have different payment consumption models. Figure 5-1 shows the pricing model for the Emotions API. Some of the Cognitive Services also provide services on a standard tier that ensure Cognitive Service SLA availability at least 99 percent of the time.

Tier	Description	Restriction	Price	SLA Support
Free Tier	30K image transaction free per month	5 status queries per min	Free	No
Basic Tier	10 image transaction per second	No restriction	$0.10 per 1000 transaction	No
Standard Tier	10 image transaction per second	No restriction	$0.25 per 1,000 transactions	Yes

Figure 5-1. Various pricing tiers for the Emotions API

> **Note**   While writing this book, if your free tier session or usage expires, Microsoft Cognitive Services does not automatically move from free tier to paid tier. Rather, your services don't yield a response. We encourage you to go ahead and use free tier with ease but do check the Microsoft Cognitive Service policy, as it can change over time.

Understanding the Prerequisites

Each cognitive API is unique and so is its usage and applicability. It is important first to understand which Cognitive API needs to be consumed. Chapter 4 introduced the various APIs. Apart from knowing which cognitive API to consume, you need to have its subscription key and programming language of choice. Each subscription key for any cognitive service is unique and exclusive, i.e. the subscription key is unique for that user and for that specific service. You can't use the same subscription key to call two different cognitive services—the subscription key for the Emotions API is not valid for calling the Speech API.

In previous chapters, we discussed that consuming cognitive services through REST API is language and platform independent. This means you are free to consume in any of your favorite languages. Since we are targeting .NET developers in this book, we use Visual Studio as our development IDE. Visual Studio 2017, as you may know, is a perfect development environment and default industry-wide code editor for creating an application for the .NET developer. Installing Visual Studio by default installs your .NET Framework, language support, template, and compiler. All versions of Visual Studio come with several editions (community, professional, enterprise, etc.)—we use the Visual studio 2017 professional edition.

> **Note**   We don't cover the installation of Visual Studio 2017 professional edition. If you don't have Visual Studio, visit the download section of `https://www.visualstudio.com` to install it.

Although we use C# as our preferred language for creating examples, concepts of consuming REST services don't really change even if you are consuming it in a non-.Net environment. We further extend our smart hospital use case to consume some cognitive services. Flip back to the end of Chapter 1 if you need to review the smart hospital use case. Throughout this book, our examples and code are entirely focused on building the smart hospital.

Just to recap, here are the prerequisites required for consuming the Cognitive API:

- Subscription key

- Visual Studio 2017

- Your passion and enthusiasm

You already have the passion and enthusiasm for creating a smart AI application, that's why you are reading this book. Assuming you have installed Visual Studio 2017, you now just need to grab your subscription key for the Cognitive API and get started.

How to Get the Subscription Key for Cognitive Services

All Microsoft Cognitive Services API require a subscription key to be passed either as a header or query parameter. All you need in order to get a subscription key for your cognitive services is a Hotmail account. You can go through any of the Microsoft Cognitive APIs and click on the Get an API key option, which requires signing it, and you are done. But wait!! You also need more quota for consuming the key. Thinking of longer-term perspective, we recommend you get it through a free subscription, which requires you to have an Azure account. If you already have an Azure account, you can directly go to the next section or create the account here.

Creating the Azure Account

Go to `https://azure.microsoft.com/en-in/free` and click on the Start Free button, as shown in Figure 5-2.

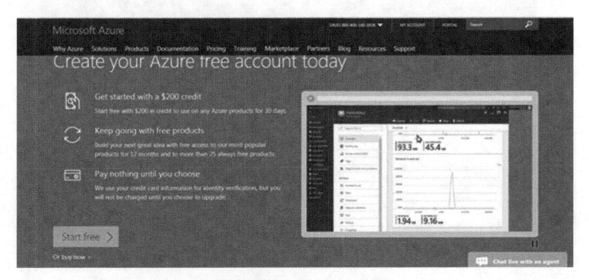

Figure 5-2. *The screen for Azure portal free subscription*

Microsoft wants to encourage new developers and architects such as you to play with an Azure account. As soon as you create the Azure account, you are entitled with $200 of credit which you can eventually use during your trial period of 30 days to explore other Azure products, such as testing and deploying apps on Azure VMs, getting insightful information about your data, to name a few. In addition to $200, you will get $50 every month for using professional Visual Studio 2017 edition.

Tip   These bonus freebies are certainly useful to consume other Azure services and make your application more interesting. In due course of the book, we use this money to consume other IOT services as well.

Clicking on Start Free redirects you to the form shown in Figure 5-3. Fill in the details for getting the Azure account.

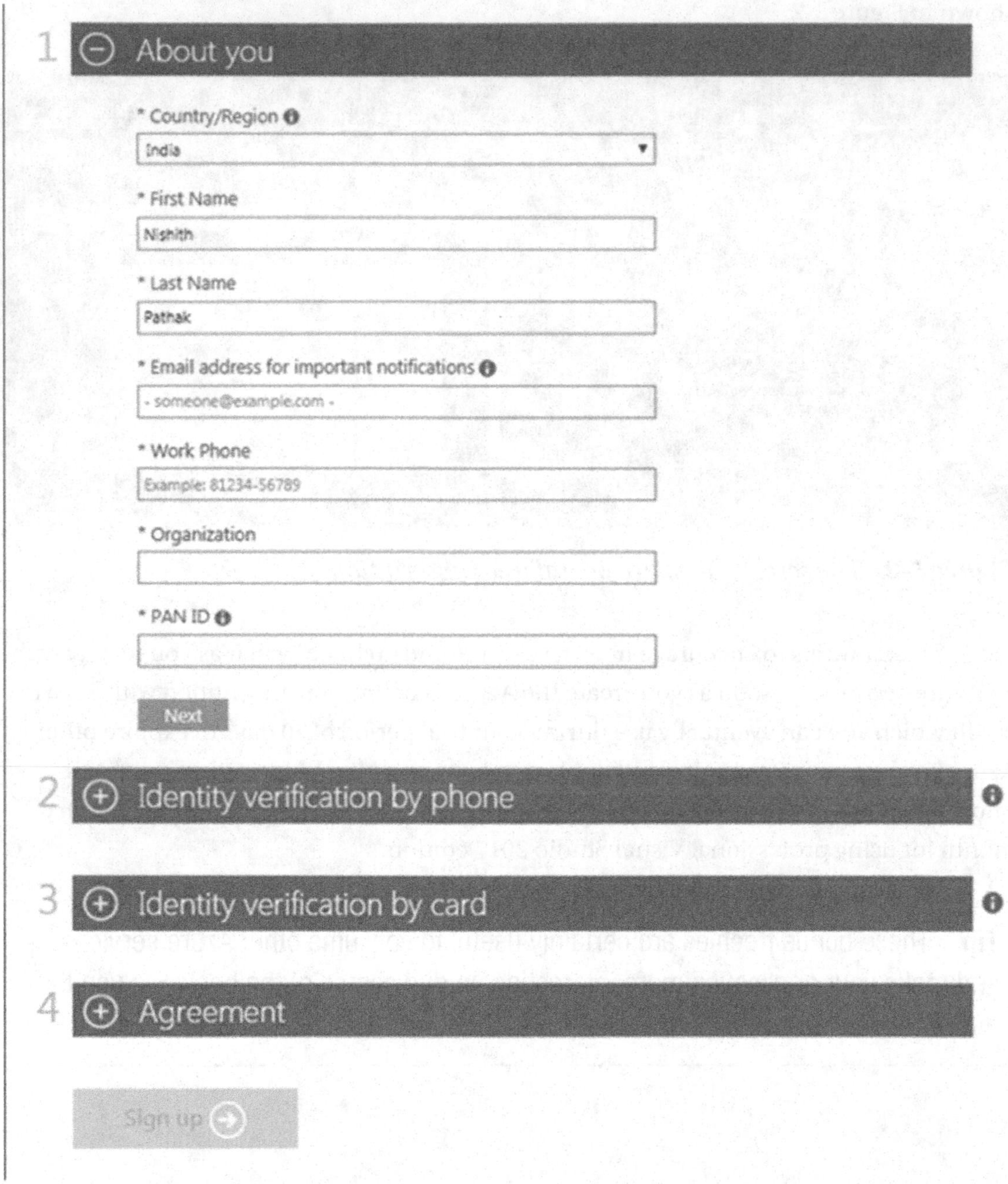

Figure 5-3. *The form for signing up for the free Azure subscription*

Fill in the form by entering your personal details, phone, and credit card details before clicking on Sign Up. It is important to note that phone and card details are just for verification of your identity. There won't be any charges levied on the card. It is also important to know that Azure doesn't upgrade your tier (from free to paid) by default. Instead, once the trial period is over, the service stops but your accounts still stays. You have the option anytime to go back again, access your account, and access the service. You can also use the credits that you have received by creating your free account along with using the professional edition of VS 2017.

Once your identity is verified, you need to accept the subscription agreement to complete your application. At this point, it's a good idea to spend a few minutes quickly scanning through the agreement terms and offer details, links to both of which are given in the Agreement section of the application form. Once you've accepted the agreement and clicked the Sign Up button, you will be redirected to the subscriber's page. Here, click the Start Managing My Service button to go to the Azure portal. First-time users of the Azure portal are encouraged to get a little tour, as shown in Figure 5-4. It is a good idea to take a tour and become familiar with the dashboard.

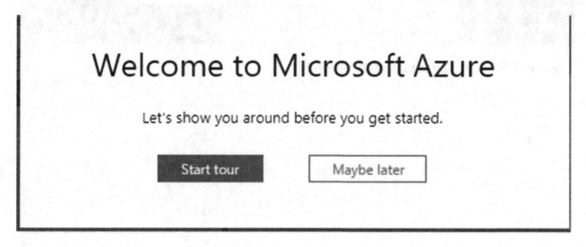

Figure 5-4. *The options for first-time users to take a tour of the Azure portal. If it is your first time on Azure portal, it is highly recommended to take a quick short tour of the portal.*

You are then redirected to the dashboard, as shown in Figure 5-5, which gives you the step-by-step process in a wizard-like interface to create new resources.

Getting the Subscription Key from Azure Portal

Creating the Azure account is a one-time activity. If you already have an Azure account, you can directly access the Azure portal to get the subscription keys.

Figure 5-5. *The Azure portal dashboard*

Search for Cognitive Services at the top and you are redirected to the Cognitive Service page, as shown in Figure 5-6. If this is your first time on the page, no cognitive service have been created.

Figure 5-6. *No keys and subscription associated for the first-time users*

Click Add and the search for the Computer Vision API. Then fill in the details shown in Figure 5-7.

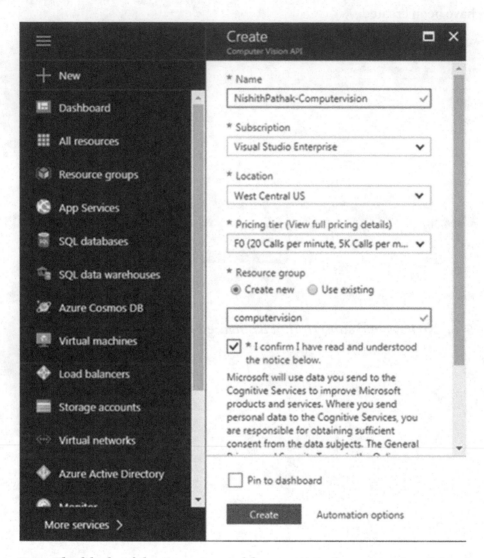

Figure 5-7. *The blade of the Azure portal for creating the computer vision subscription key*

Once all the fields are filled in, click the Create button as shown in Figure 5-7. It will take a few seconds to a minute for your new account to be created and deployed to the selected resource group. You can track the deployment status in the Alerts menu in the top-right corner of the portal. Once it's done, the Alert menu shows a confirmation, as shown in Figure 5-8.

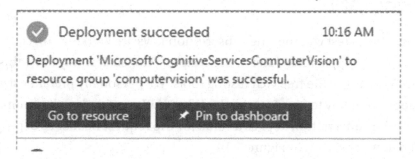

Figure 5-8. *The notification of successful creation of the computer vision in Azure portal*

This confirms the one-time process of creating the keys. You can now click the Go the Resource link and select Computer Vision to get the keys. Scroll down a bit to find the Keys option under Resource Management. Clicking this option will reveal two subscription keys created especially for you, as shown in Figure 5-9. Copy one of the two keys and keep it handy. You are going to need it soon.

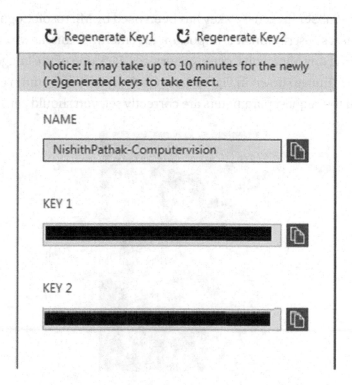

Figure 5-9. *The computer vision keys generated in the Azure account*

Testing the API

It is now important to test whether the subscription keys are working correctly before you use them in your application later in the chapter. The easiest way to do this is to validate them with any of the free GUI testing tools. We personally prefer Postman, which is easier and handy to use. Just call the HTTP API provided by the computer vision and use one of the subscription keys as a value for the request header as `Ocp-Apim-Subscription-Key`, as shown in Figure 5-10.

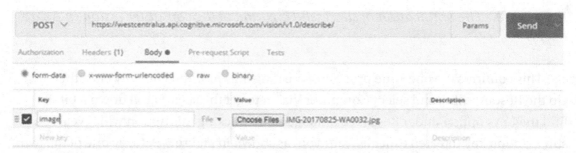

Figure 5-10. *The Postman tool for testing the computer vision API*

The `Ocp-Apim-Subscription-Key` key has been used by Microsoft Cognitive Services to assume its value as a subscription. It is important to remember this, as we are going to use this key while calling any Microsoft Cognitive Services. Pick one of the images from your desktop; I chose the image shown in Figure 5-11. Click on the Send button on Postman to call your API. If all the request parameters are correctly set, you should get a 200 status.

Figure 5-11. *Image used in Postman to test the subscription key*

The JSON response for this image should be:

```
{"description":{"tags":["person","indoor","boy","young","child","little",
"standing","small","man","front","holding","shirt","wearing","table","ro
om","girl","playing","suitcase","luggage","red","video","living","remote","
people"],"captions":[{"text":"a young boy standing in a room","confidence":
0.74894680759015353}]},"requestId":"f1f9b0fa-d0cf-4e17-9cd2-9d87b8c1c53c","
metadata":{"width":441,"height":662,"format":"Jpeg"}}
```

As you see, the text caption shows "a young boy standing in a room". Isn't this really accurate! Think about how useful this is, in just a single call. These insights can be tremendously beneficial in quite a number of use cases, such as security, creating a visual impaired solution for the blind, and so on. Now you are all set to use the same cognitive services to do more interesting work. The first thing we should do is get familiar with calling these cognitive services in Visual Studio.

Creating Your First Smart Cognitive Application

(This section assumes you already have VS 2017 installed.) Open Visual Studio 2017. From the File menu, point to New and then click Project. In the New Project dialog box, expand the Visual C# node in the Project Types tree. You'll see various templates under it. As we want to quickly create our first cognitive application, select Windows Classic Desktop under Visual C#. Select the Console App (.NET Framework). Give your project a name, such as myFirstCognitiveApp, as shown in Figure 5-12, and click OK to create a new console-based project in Visual Studio 2017.

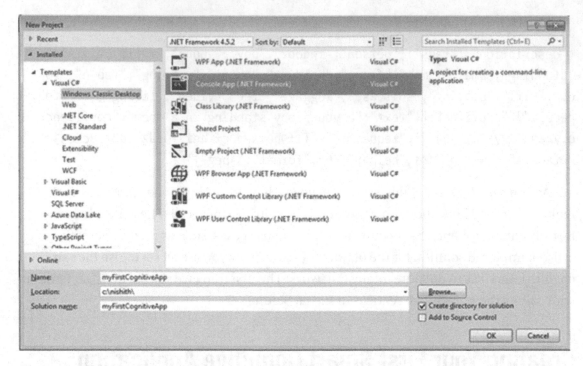

Figure 5-12. *The VS 2017 new project template*

Note   From here on, we assume that you understand how to create a new project using Visual Studio 2017. Going forward, we will simply ask you to create a new project in VS, specifying the template and any specific project name (if required).

Open the Solution Explorer and rename the `Program.cs` file to `CognitiveApp.cs`. In the Project menu, click Add Reference. In the Add Reference dialog box, click the Framework tab and add references to the following assemblies, as shown in Figure 5-13.

- `System.Web`

- `System.Configuration`

- `System.Net.Http`

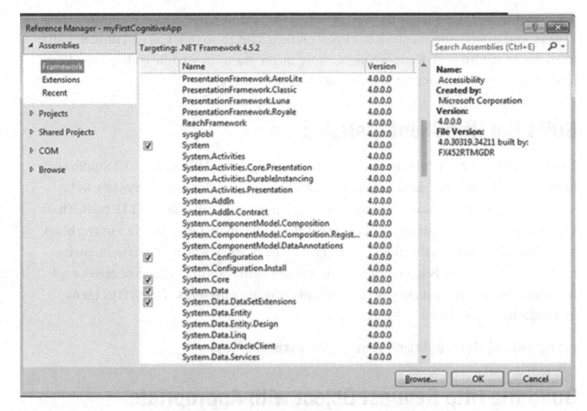

Figure 5-13. *The Add Reference dialog box in Visual Studio 2017*

Steps for Consuming the Cognitive API

Create a new function called DescribeImage that takes images, calls our cognitive API, and returns the result from the API as a string. In order to do this, your function would follow these series of steps:

Step 1. Create the HTTP client to make HTTP calls.

Step 2. Build the HTTP request object with appropriate parameters.

Step 3. Call the Computer Vision API by passing the HTTP request created in Step 2 and getting the response back from the API.

Your function signature should look like the following:

```
public static async Task<string> DescribeImage(string imageFilePath)
```

If you look at this signature, you'll observe that the function has been marked as `static` and `async`. The function has been marked `static` so that you can directly call it from the `main` function. Here, we use C#'s async programming while calling the API to make the user experience smoother and more responsive.

Build the HttpClient Instance

The first and most important step for calling the Cognitive API from Visual Studio is to build the `httpClient` instance. The `HttpClient` class resides in the `System.Net.Http` namespace. Its instance is required to get, post, put, and delete HTTP calls. There are multiple ways to instantiate `httpclient`. Creating an instance inside a `using` block automatically disposes the object at the end of the block. Disposing of I/O-intensive objects appropriately is important because the system resources they use aren't kept reserved and are immediately made available to other programs. Your `httpclient` instantiation should look like this:

```
using (HttpClient myhttpClient = new HttpClient())
```

Build the Http Request Object with Appropriate Parameters

Now that you have created the `httpClient` instance, the next step is to pass the subscription key in the header and the image as multipart form data content. In order to pass the subscription key as a header, you need a unique header key named *Ocp-Apim-Subscription-Key*, which is used across all cognitive services to recognize its value as a subscription key. You can create the key-value pair or hard code it. Instead, we recommend storing the subscription key in the configuration file, which will prevent any recompilation due to a change in the subscription key. You can add it to `httpclient` instance created in the previous steps. Your code should look like this:

```
myHttpClient.DefaultRequestHeaders.Add("Ocp-Apim-Subscription-Key",
ConfigurationManager.AppSettings["AzureSubscriptionKeyVision"]);
```

The next step is to pass the image as multipart form data content to the `httpclient`. The .NET Framework provides the container class `MultipartFormDataContent`, which resides in the `System.net.http` namespace, to do the honors.

```
using (MultipartFormDataContent reqContent = new
MultipartFormDataContent())
```

It's better to instantiate these objects using `using` to get them automatically disposed of. Once the container class is created, you can read the entire image in the body in the byte format and add it to the `multipartFormDataContent` instance, as shown here. The `File.ReadAllBytes()` method takes in the absolute path of a file and returns its byte sequence.

```
var imgContent = new ByteArrayContent(System.IO.File.
ReadAllBytes(imageFilePath));
                        reqContent.Add(imgContent);
```

Calling Microsoft Cognitive Vision API

Now you are all set to call the Cognitive Vision API. For the `httpclient` to make a POST call to the Cognitive Vision API, you need to provide it the correct HTTP address of the Cognitive API and the API in the `multipartFormDataContent` object. Specify the address as shown here by setting `maxCandidates` as 1, which ensures that only one description is returned from the API.

```
var queryString = HttpUtility.ParseQueryString(string.Empty);
                queryString["maxCandidates"] = "1";
var uri = "https://westcentralus.api.cognitive.microsoft.com/vision/v1.0/
describe/?" + queryString;
```

The next step is to call the Microsoft Cognitive API in an asynchronous manner, passing the address and the multiform data content, as shown in this code:

```
HttpResponseMessage  respMessage = await myHttpClient.PostAsync(uri,
reqContent);
string finalJson = await respMessage.Content.ReadAsStringAsync();
                        return finalJson;
```

The previous code uses the asynchronous operation while calling the API. It is always a best practice to call all your APIs in an asynchronous way to ensure your application is not unresponsive until you hear back from the API. The entire code of your console application should now look something like this:

```
using System;
using System.Collections.Generic;
using System.Configuration;
using System.Linq;
using System.Net.Http;
using System.Text;
using System.Threading.Tasks;
using System.Web;

namespace myFirstCognitiveApp
{
    class CognitiveApp
    {
        static void Main(string[] args)
        {
            Task<string> result = DescribeImage(@"C:\nishith\image.jpg");
            Console.WriteLine(result.Result);
            Console.ReadLine();
        }

        public static async Task<string> DescribeImage(string imageFilePath)
        {
            using (HttpClient myHttpClient = new HttpClient())
            {
                myHttpClient.DefaultRequestHeaders.Add("Ocp-Apim-
                Subscription-Key", ConfigurationManager.AppSettings
                ["AzureSubscriptionKeyVision"]);

                using (MultipartFormDataContent reqContent = new
                MultipartFormDataContent())
                {
```

```csharp
var queryString = HttpUtility.ParseQueryString
(string.Empty);
queryString["maxCandidates"] = "1";
var uri = "https://westcentralus.api.cognitive.
microsoft.com/vision/v1.0/describe/?" + queryString;

try
{
    var imgContent = new ByteArrayContent(System.
    IO.File.ReadAllBytes(imageFilePath));
    reqContent.Add(imgContent);

    HttpResponseMessage  respMessage = await
    myHttpClient.PostAsync(uri, reqContent);
    string finalJson = await respMessage.Content.
    ReadAsStringAsync();
    return finalJson;
}
catch (System.IO.FileNotFoundException ex)
{
    return "The specified image file path is invalid.";
}
catch (ArgumentException ex)
{
    return "The HTTP request object does not seem to be
    correctly formed.";
}
            }
        }
    }
}
```

The Result of Your Code

Build the project and correct any syntax errors if necessary. In Visual Studio, pressing F5 or Ctrl+F5 will run your program. This program, being part of a console application, will open and run inside the command prompt. Figure 5-14 shows the same result in a console window against the child image that we used in the Postman example.

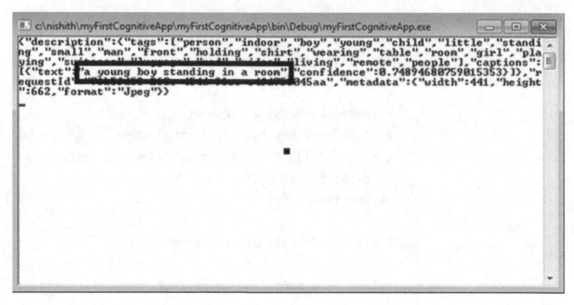

Figure 5-14.   *The output in the console window*

Congratulations! You are finally not just able to call cognitive applications but have a clear understanding of the steps required to call the Cognitive API. Similar steps need to be performed in the next chapters for consuming cognitive services, so it's better to revise the steps once again before marching ahead in our journey of creating smarter applications.

Let's Do Something a Little More Interesting

Go back to your Console application and replace

```
Task<string> result = DescribeImage(@"C:\nishith\image.jpg");
```

With

```
Task<string> result = DescribeImage(@"C:\nishith\mahatma.jpg");
```

Then run the application. What we did in this code was replace the image of the child with the father of a nation, Mahatma Gandhi, as shown in Figure 5-15.

Figure 5-15. *The image of Mahatma Gandhi, which now we are passing to the console application*

The Output

As you see in Figure 5-16, the caption returned is "Mahatma Gandhi wearing glasses posing for the camera".

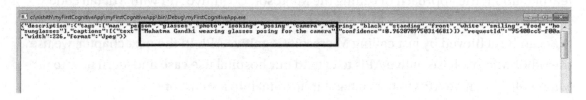

Figure 5-16. *The output of passing the Mahatma Gandhi image*

This same cognitive service API that could describe the image is able to recognize Steve Jobs. Isn't this amazing? What's the trick? Under the covers, Microsoft has a celebrity recognition image classification model that spans more than 200,000 celebrities from various verticals like industry, politics, sports, and entertainment. Whenever any call is made to Microsoft Cognitive Vision API, a check is performed to see if the person detected is part of this classification model or not.

Your Next Tasks

Each of the 29 cognitive APIs is very powerful. Some of these APIs are multitaskers and do more than one task. Our Computer Vision API, for example, is one of the most powerful APIs under the Vision category. As you have seen in the previous simple examples, the computer vision API is not just able to describe the scene for us, but it can also identify the celebrities. Give it a try with some landmarks in your city/country and see if the Computer Vision API can recognize things. Apart from scene recognition and identifying celebrities, it can be used to accomplish the following tasks

- Provide an image and generate thumbnails

- Extract a printed or handwritten text from an image

- Analyze a video in real time, frame by frame

We suggest that you modify this program and try it with various images and test functionalities by tweaking the code a bit. You will be amazed to see how the Microsoft Cognitive Vision API can do all these tasks with great finesse.

Recap

In this chapter, you learned about the prerequisites required to consume the Cognitive API. This was followed by a stepwise approach to getting your subscription key. You then learned about the approach of calling the Microsoft Cognitive API with a detail code walkthrough in Visual Studio. You also got an idea about the various possibilities of tasks that can be achieved by just calling Microsoft Cognitive API. In the next chapter, we use the other Microsoft Cognitive APIs to extend our hospital use case and learn how to use Microsoft Cognitive APIs to turn a regular hospital into a smart one.

CHAPTER 6

Building Smarter Applications Using Cognitive APIs

The famous saying "Rome wasn't built in a day" is so true about Microsoft cognitive services. Each service is exposed as a RESTful API by abstracting years and decades of experience, complex algorithms, deep neural networks, fuzzy logic, and research from the Microsoft research team. In Chapter 4, you were introduced to Microsoft Cognitive Services. You also learned how cognitive services are different from traditional programming systems. Later in Chapter 4, you got a sneak preview of all the Microsoft Cognitive Services API that Microsoft has produced.

Chapter 5 continued the journey of cognitive services by covering the prerequisites of creating Cognitive Services and setting up a development environment. You also got familiar with using your first cognitive applications in Visual Studio and recognized the power of the Computer Vision API.

Welcome to this chapter. In this chapter, we extend Cognitive Services by applying them to the smart hospital use case that we introduced in Chapter 1. As you now know, Microsoft Cognitive Services are broadly classified into six main categories, and each of them has 4-5 services, which leads to about 29 services while writing these books. Each of the Cognitive Services can be used in our smart hospital Asclepius Consortium. We will go through some of the most powerful ways of using cognitive services, especially around NLU, speech, and using the Face API, and apply them to the Asclepius hospital example.

© Nishith Pathak and Anurag Bhandari 2018
N. Pathak and A. Bhandari, *IoT, AI, and Blockchain for .NET*, https://doi.org/10.1007/978-1-4842-3709-0_6

At the end of chapter, you'll:

- Understand some of the powerful ways to apply cognitive services

- Understand natural language understanding (NLU) and LUIS

- Develop, test, host, and manage the LUIS application for the smart hospital

- Interact with the Speech API

- Use the Speech API to convert speech to text and text to speech

- Use face detection and recognition in hospital scenarios

The Asclepius Consortium is a chain of hospitals that deal with almost every kind of disease. As part of their offering, they have the Dr. Checkup mobile application that provides natural language functionality in series of applications. This includes a mobile application that serves not only to maintain history, records, and payment transfers, but also helps user perform basic diagnosis by providing symptoms. This helps patients not only take quick action but understand the complexity of diseases, as shown in Figure 6-1.

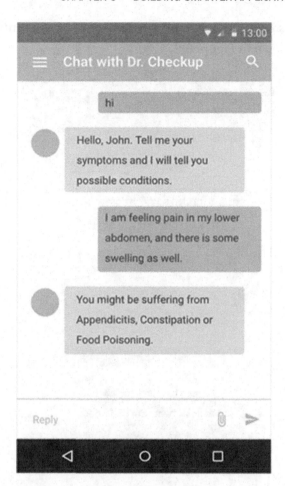

Figure 6-1. *The Dr. Checkup app provides a basic diagnosis*

Once the disease is identified, patients can schedule an appointment with a specific specialist/doctor, as shown in Figure 6-2.

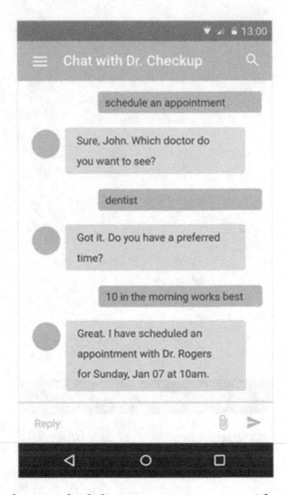

Figure 6-2. *Dr. Checkup is scheduling an appointment with a doctor after chatting with a patient*

Asclepius Consortium also uses the same NLU techniques of scheduling appointments in their frontend teller machines.

Microsoft's Mission and NLU

Microsoft's earlier mission was to have desktop computers in every home. Microsoft has been very successful in achieving that in most of the Western world. Recently Microsoft revised their mission to "Empowering every person and every organization on the planet to achieve more". This new mission from Microsoft is more human in nature compared to previously being more technological. The supreme goal of artificial intelligence has always been to serve humanity. In order for AI to serve humanity, it should be able to understand humans. As a first step, AI should understand and process the languages that humans speak.

As more and more intelligent systems are devised, it is important for these systems to understand human languages, interpret the meanings, and then take appropriate actions wherever necessary. This domain of interpreting human languages is called Natural Language Understanding (NLU). NLU is the ability of a machine to convert natural language text to a form that the computer can understand. In other words, it's the ability to extract the meaning from the sentence. This enables the system to understand the "what" question of the language.

Take the use case in Chapter 4 where a person is asking an intelligent system questions like the following:

"How does my schedule look today?

Now this question can be asked in a variety of ways. Some of them
What's my schedule for the day?
Are there a lot of meetings in the office?
How busy is my calendar for today?
To humans, it is immediately clear that these sentences are a person's way of inquiring about her schedule for the day. For a machine, it may not be clear. In fact, creating an NLU engine has been one of the more complex problems to solve. There is variety of factors, but the main issues is that there is no one algorithm to resolve it. Moreover, training a machine to understand grammar, rules, and slang is difficult. Thanks to the advent of deep learning, we can now achieve great precision of language understanding by training the engine with thousands of utterances, create a pattern recognition based on those examples, and then constantly improve on it to identify formal and informal rules of language understanding.

Based on this NLU theory, various commercial offerings exist and are based on the intent-entity schema that we briefly discussed in Chapter 4. Intent helps in understanding the intention of the user behind the question being asked. If you look at these examples, there were multiple ways of asking same questions, but the intention was the same—get me the schedule for that day. Once we know the right intent, it is then straightforward for the system to respond with a correct answer.

To identify the right intention, NLU systems are also trained to recognize certain keywords. These keywords are called *entities*. In our previous examples, to get a schedule from a calendar, you often need require person's name and date. Each of these can be marked as entities. It is important to understand that entities are optional and not all sentences may be accompanied by them. There is also a good chance that a sentence may have more than one entity as well. We are going to discuss identifying intents and entities later in the chapter.

Language Understanding Intelligent Service (LUIS)

The Language Understanding Intelligent Service aka LUIS is Microsoft's NLU cloud service and is part of the cognitive suite discussed in Chapter 4. It is important to understand that LUIS shouldn't be treated as a full-fledged software application for your end user. LUIS only replaces the NLU component from the overall stack. It's an NLU engine that handles NLU implementation by abstracting the inner machine learning model's complexity. Your frontend still can be a website, chatbot, or any application ranging from a graphical to conversational user interface. In our Asclepius use case, the frontend is mobile application (Dr. Checkup). Before we open LUIS and start working, it is important to understand the underpinnings of LUIS that require deep expertise in design. Let's look at the behind the scenes aspects of LUIS.

Designing on LUIS

The LUIS framework is just like a clean slate that's been trained on a few built-in entities. As a first step, it is important to design the LUIS application in an effective manner. Designing a LUIS application requires a profound understanding of the problems that your software is trying to solve. For example, our use case of the smart hospital requires LUIS to be used to converse with patients to book an appointment with a doctor or to talk with the hospital chatbot to detect whether a doctor's attention is really required.

There are no strict guidelines or rules to follow while implementing LUIS. However, based on our experiences while interacting with LUIS and another NLU system, we came up with some high-level guidelines.

Design Guidelines for Using LUIS

The LUIS application should have the right intent and entities for this smart healthcare use case. There are many ways to identify the right intent and entities. We propose the following design principles for achieving effective identification:

- **Plan your scope first**. It is very important to plan the scope and narrow it down to what's inside the scope of LUIS. Clear identification of the scope is the first step in successfully achieving delivery of LUIS implementation. We recommend you keep the scope of applying LUIS limited to a few tasks or goals.

- **Use a prebuilt domain (if possible)**. Once the scope is finalized, you are aware now of the use case or domain that LUIS is going to solve. LUIS also comes with some prebuilt domains that have a set of entities and intents previously defined. These prebuilt domains are also pre-trained and are ready to use. Use prebuilt domain whenever you can. If your requirement is achieved with prebuilt intents or entities, choose them before creating a new one. You can always customize the prebuilt domains. You should always try to pick at least one of the prebuilt domains and entities along, even if you also have to create a few new ones to suit your requirements.

- **Identify the tasks that your application is going to perform**. Once a domain is identified, list the tasks that your application is going to perform. These tasks identify the intention of the end user to access your application. As you may have guessed, create each task as an intent. It is important to break tasks appropriately so that you don't have tasks that are non-specific. The more tasks you have, the more rigorous the training is.

- **Identify additional information required for tasks**. Not all tasks are straightforward. Most of them require some additional information. This additional information are called entities. Entities complement the intents for identifying specific tasks. You can think of entities as variables of your application that are required to store and pass information to your client application.

- **Training is a key**. At the core, LUIS accepts textual inputs. These inputs are called *utterances*. LUIS needs to be trained extensively on these utterances before the LUIS model will really understand future utterances. The more example utterances you have, the better the model. In order to identify various utterances, it's better to collect phrases that you expect the user would type and identify different ways through which the same questions can be asked. If your application must deal with multiple similar use cases, there's a good chance LUIS will get confused with the lack of sufficient training for each of the similar use cases. Despite your training, it is not safe to assume that LUIS will respond with absolute accuracy. LUIS is based on the active machine learning model, which ensures that the LUIS model keeps on learning and enhancing the model in time. In fact, LUIS keeps track of all utterances for which it was unable to predict an intent with high confidence. You will find such utterances under the "Suggested Utterances" section on an intent's page. Use this option to appropriately label utterances and confirm to LUIS whether it was right or wrong. LUIS training is a continuous process, until you find suggested utterances sections showing no suggestions.

Plan Your Scope First

The high-level sequence diagram for this mobile application and frontend teller is shown in Figure 6-3.

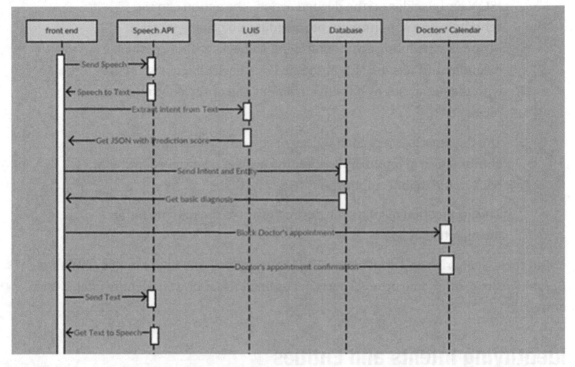

Figure 6-3. *The high-level interactions between various actors while booking appointments or during initial diagnosis*

Here are the stepwise interactions as well.

1. The patient asks, either through a mobile application or the frontend teller machine (either through message or voice), to talk with Dr. Checkup.

2. If the patient submits the query through voice, the mobile app/ frontend teller machine uses the Microsoft Speech API to convert the voice into text.

3. The application then passes the text to the LUIS app to determine the intent of the question asked.

155

4. LUIS performs its NLU analysis and returns its predictions for intent and entity. The result is returned as JSON back to the application.

5. The application checks for top scoring intents in the returned JSON and decides on the desired action. The action can be scheduling an appointment or providing a basic diagnosis. If action is scheduling an appointment, it checks with a doctor's calendar and sets the appointment. For a basic diagnosis, it talks with the databases by passing the intent and entity combination received.

6. The database has a predefined set of answers stored for the combination of intent and entity. The answer is retrieved and sent back to the mobile application.

7. The application displays the desired result to the patient, either through text or voice.

In these scenarios and applications, NLU plays a vital role in the implementation. Before we delve more into other aspects, let us first look at how to identify intents and entities.

Identifying Intents and Entities

Once the scope is finalized, the next step is to identify the intents and entities. Let's take the case of early diagnosis. What do you expect from the end user? Apart from the name, age, and gender details, you expect the user to list his symptoms so that, based on some general set of rules, an early diagnosis can be provided. Now the user can provide these symptoms in a simple sentence or in a couple of sentences. Figure 6-4 shows some of the examples of how someone can provide symptoms.

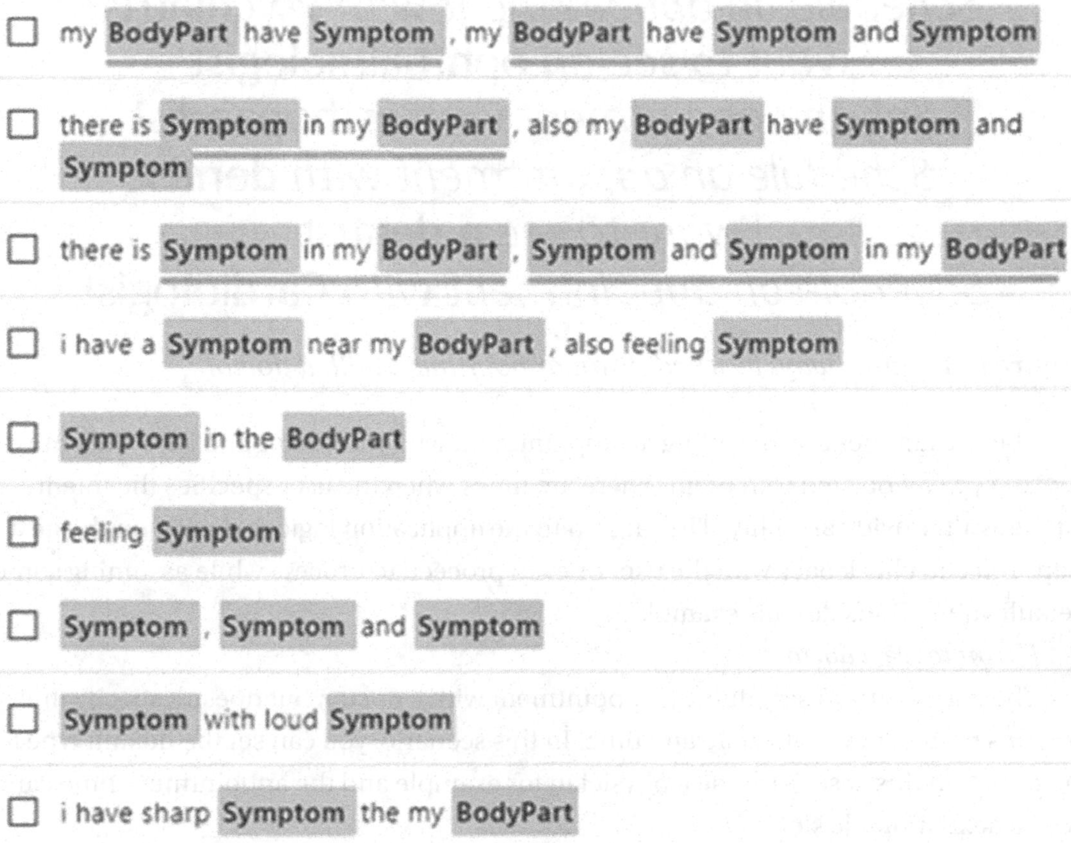

☐ my **BodyPart** have **Symptom** , my **BodyPart** have **Symptom** and **Symptom**

☐ there is **Symptom** in my **BodyPart** , also my **BodyPart** have **Symptom** and **Symptom**

☐ there is **Symptom** in my **BodyPart** , **Symptom** and **Symptom** in my **BodyPart**

☐ i have a **Symptom** near my **BodyPart** , also feeling **Symptom**

☐ **Symptom** in the **BodyPart**

☐ feeling **Symptom**

☐ **Symptom** , **Symptom** and **Symptom**

☐ **Symptom** with loud **Symptom**

☐ i have sharp **Symptom** the my **BodyPart**

Figure 6-4. *Some of the ways that users can share their symptoms*

If you look these examples, they all are being requested for the early diagnosis intent. Most of these early diagnosis sentences are matched with various entities, like body part and symptom. Each body part and symptom can be replaced with some body parts or with symptoms. For the first example, you can have the following:

My ankles have pain, my knees have swelling and stiffness

Of course, this list is not exhaustive and you may need to work on creating a more complete list. Let's take another use case of scheduling an appointment with the doctor. What do you need to schedule a doctor appointment? Essentially, you need the type of doctor (gynecologist, dentist, cardiologist, and so on), the potential date, and optionally a specific time range, before blocking the time of the doctor. Figure 6-5 shows some of the ways you can schedule your appointment.

157

Schedule an appointment with **Psychiatrist**
I want to see an **ophthalmologist**
Set an appointment with **orthopaedist**
Schedule an appointment with **dentist**
I want to see a **dentist**
Schedule an appointment with **Cardiologist**

Figure 6-5. *Some ways to schedule an appointment with a doctor*

These examples are for setting an appointment with the doctor and have the entity
`doctortype` associated with them. There are times when the user specifies the intent
but doesn't provide an entity. Then it's up to the application logic to decide on the next
step. You can check back with the user or even proceed to process while assuming some
default value. Consider this example:

I want to see a doctor

The user wants to schedule an appointment with a doctor, but doesn't specify the
doctor's name or even the date and time. In this scenario, you can set the default type for
the entity. In this case, it can be a physician for example and the appointment time can
be the next available slot.

Creating a Data Dictionary for LUIS

As you know by now, LUIS doesn't perform any calculations or logic. It only extract
meaning from utterances by extracting intents and entities from them. As a good design
process, it helps to create a data dictionary before you open LUIS and start working on it.
The data dictionary is more like a bible of metadata that stores utterances, along with its
associated intents and entities. You can use it as a design document for your NLU. This
is also helpful, as through this dictionary, you can determine the count of intents and
entities to be created. Table 6-1 shows a good way to create three columns of a data
dictionary for the LUIS application.

Table 6-1. *The Data Dictionary Sample for Dr. Checkup*

Utterances	Intent	Entity

Schedule an appointment with the physician tomorrow before 5 PM	`scheduleAppointment`	`DoctorType = physician,`
		`datetime = tomorrow,`
		`AppointmentTime::StartTime =`
		`AppointmentTime::EndTime = 5 PM`

Pain in abdomen	`checkCondition`	`Symptom = Pain` `Body part = abdomen`
Feverish with loud cough	`checkCondition`	`Symptom = feverish` `Body Part = Loud Cough`
Set an appointment with orthopedist	`scheduleAppointment`	`Doctor type = orthopedist`

This table is just an example, but it would be wise to create it as Excel sheet and use it as a design document for your LUIS application.

Tip   The data dictionary shown in Table 6-1 is a basic dictionary to get started. You can extend it and make it more usable. For instance, add an Answer column that provides a message about what answer would be returned to the user. You can also use this data dictionary to create test use cases.

Identifying intent and entities is the one of the most important tasks. Once the intents and entities are identified, the next task is to create these entities and intents on LUIS. Before you create entities in LUIS, you need to grab a subscription key for LUIS.

Getting a Subscription Key for LUIS

Chapter 5 described in detail how to create an account in Azure Portal and get the subscription key for the Vision API. You can use the same account to get a subscription key for LUIS. Open Azure Portal and, from the left side menu, choose New ➤ AI + Cognitive Services. Click on Language Understanding, as shown in Figure 6-6.

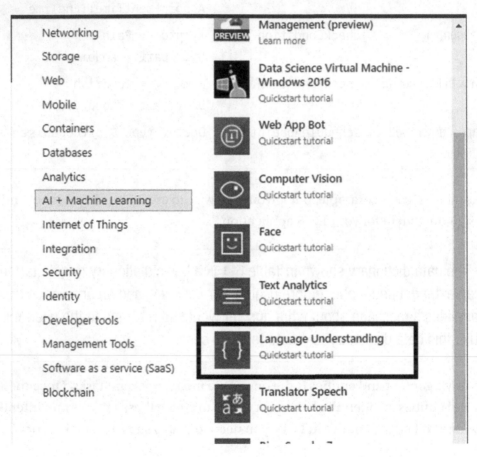

Figure 6-6. *A screenshot of the Azure Service Portal after selecting the new option from the menu*

Fill out the form with an appropriate subscription, pricing tier, and resource, as shown in Figure 6-7. You may want to get started with the free tier (F0), as we discussed in the previous chapter. Click on Create.

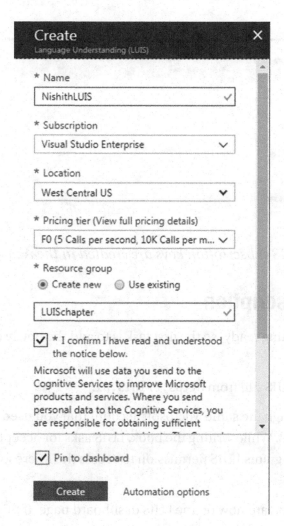

Figure 6-7. *Filling in the form for creating a LUIS subscription key*

Once this is submitted, it will take some time to get the account validated and then created. You can then go back to the dashboard after receiving notification on it. Click on your LUIS account in the dashboard and get the keys to take it forward, as shown Figure 6-8.

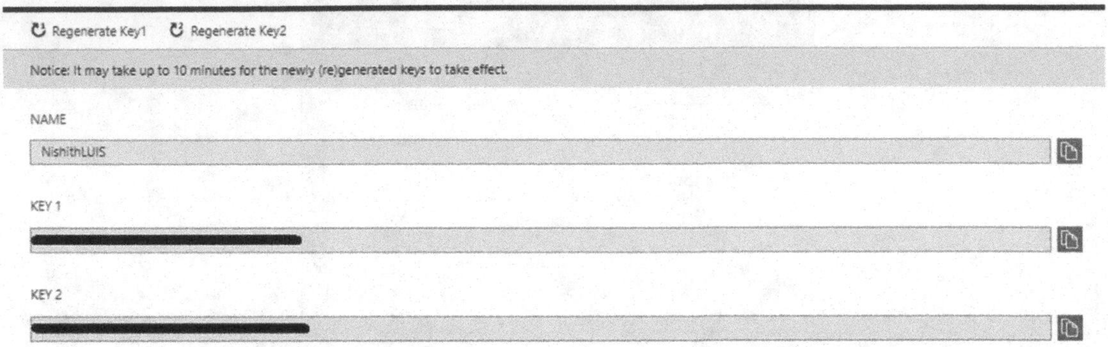

Figure 6-8. *The LUIS subscription keys are created in the Azure Portal*

Apply the Subscription

Now you have everything ready, so the first task is to add the newly created subscription keys to LUIS.

1. Open the LUIS site from `https://luis.ai`.

2. Log in through the same Microsoft account that you used in the Azure Portal. While writing the book, LUIS asks for accepting license and grants LUIS permission to access the Microsoft account.

3. Click OK. You are now on the LUIS dashboard page. If this is the first time you have logged in, you will see the MyApps section empty.

4. Click on Create New App to create a new app and specify name, culture, and optional description, as shown in Figure 6-9. Click Done. You can provide your own name and culture as per your logic.

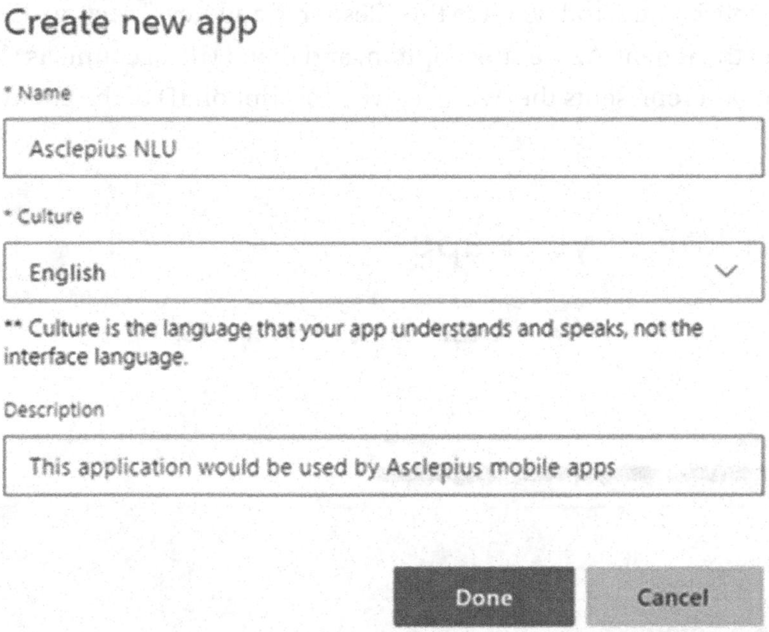

Create new app

* Name

Asclepius NLU

* Culture

English ⌄

** Culture is the language that your app understands and speaks, not the interface language.

Description

This application would be used by Asclepius mobile apps

[Done] [Cancel]

Figure 6-9. *Creating a new application in LUIS*

Congratulations, you have quickly created an application. Now it's time to add your subscription keys to the application before creating intents and entities.

Applying the Subscription Key in LUIS

As you click Done previously, you are redirected to the application's page. If not, click on Asclepius NLU from the MyApps section.

Click on Publish and scroll down to the "Resource and Keys" section. Click on Add Keys and select the tenant, Azure subscription, and then LUIS account, as shown in Figure 6-10. Tenant represents the Azure active subscription ID of the client or of your organization.

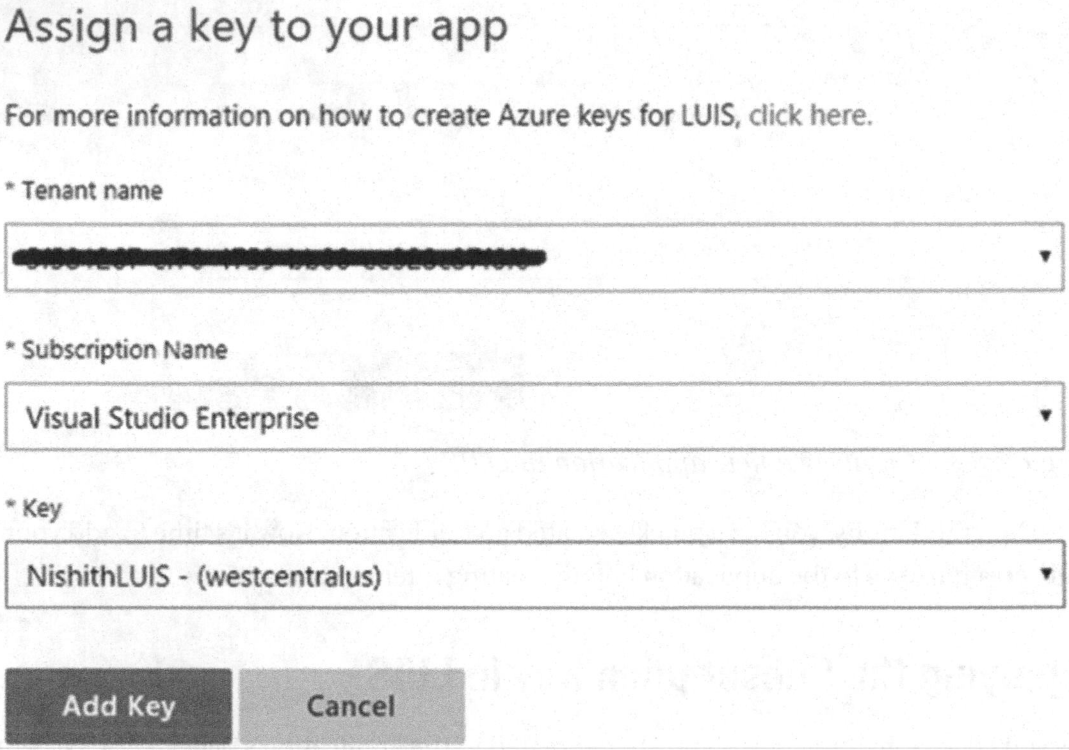

Assign a key to your app

For more information on how to create Azure keys for LUIS, click here.

* Tenant name

[redacted]   ▼

* Subscription Name

Visual Studio Enterprise   ▼

* Key

NishithLUIS - (westcentralus)   ▼

[Add Key]   [Cancel]

Figure 6-10. *Assigning a LUIS key to the app*

It's time now to add intents and entities.

Adding Intent and Entities

Adding intents and entities is very straightforward. To add a new intent, from the left sidebar go to the Intents page. If this is the first time you have been on this page, you won't have any intents created. Keep your data dictionary handy. Now click on Create New Intent, specify the first entry of the intent from the data dictionary as the intent name, and click Done. The first column of your data dictionary also lists the sample utterances. Start adding sample utterances as shown previously. After adding the initial utterances, click the Save button to save your changes. Hover over the word Psychiatrist in the Just Added utterance to see it surrounded by square brackets. Clicking on the word will give you the option to either label it as an existing entity or as a new entity. Create an entity called *Doctor type*. Figure 6-11 shows how the `scheduleAppointment` intent will look once you have committed the initial utterances.

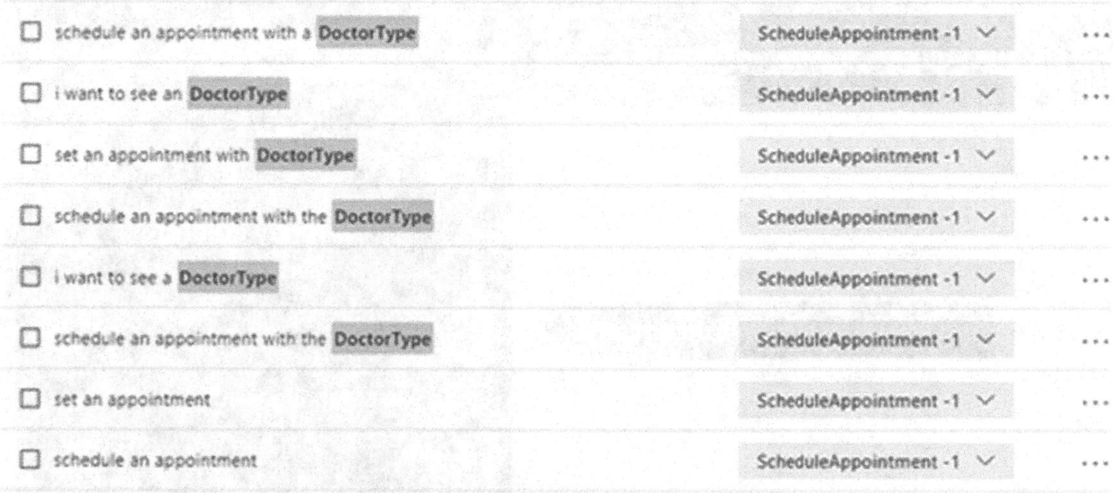

☐ schedule an appointment with a **DoctorType**	ScheduleAppointment -1 ∨	...
☐ i want to see an **DoctorType**	ScheduleAppointment -1 ∨	...
☐ set an appointment with **DoctorType**	ScheduleAppointment -1 ∨	...
☐ schedule an appointment with the **DoctorType**	ScheduleAppointment -1 ∨	...
☐ i want to see a **DoctorType**	ScheduleAppointment -1 ∨	...
☐ schedule an appointment with the **DoctorType**	ScheduleAppointment -1 ∨	...
☐ set an appointment	ScheduleAppointment -1 ∨	...
☐ schedule an appointment	ScheduleAppointment -1 ∨	...

Figure 6-11. *The ScheduleAppointment intent screenshot with a few utterances*

Repeat this process for all the intents, entities, and utterances created in the data dictionary. You should now train, test, and publish the LUIS as an endpoint, which can be used by the mobile application.

Training and Testing LUIS

One of the reasons we followed this process was to ensure that all the intents have some sample utterances. If an intent doesn't have an utterance, you can't train the application. Hover over the Train button. You will see the message "App has untrained changes". Click Train on the top right to train the app. By training, you ensure that LUIS is creating a generalized model with utterances and will be able to identify intents and entities. Once the training process is successfully complete, your Train button should have a green notification bar mentioning this fact. You can now hover the Train button. You will get the message "App up to date".

LUIS also provides a testing interface so the user can test the application. Click on the Test button to open the Test slide-out page and start interactive testing. Provide some utterances other than what you have used in training to see whether the results come in as expected or not. Your testing slide also contains the inspect panel to inspect LUIS results and change the top scoring intent, as shown in Figure 6-12.

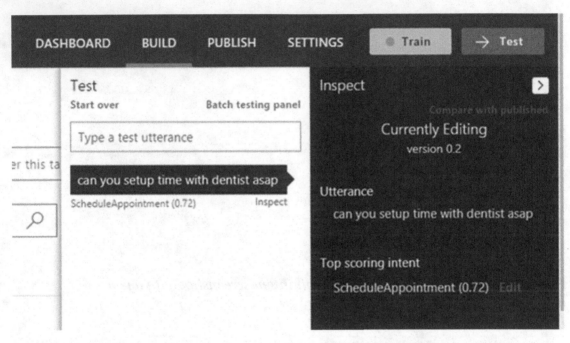

Figure 6-12. *The LUIS test and inspect screen to inspect the LUIS result and change the top scoring intent*

You will realize soon that not all tests yield the desired result. Initially, apart from getting a positive output from LUIS, you may also end up getting different intents for your test utterances, or even getting the right intent without an entity. Both require rigorous training. It can come through either through your training utterance or through the production application. For your application to use it, you need to push it to the production endpoint so you can get an HTTP endpoint, which can be used to call your LUIS app.

Publishing LUIS App

The endpoint is nothing but a web service to access a LUIS app. The endpoint receives an utterance via a query string parameter and returns a JSON output with a corresponding intent-entities breakdown. When you are publishing for the first time, an endpoint URL is generated for you based on your application's ID and the subscription key. This URL remains constant throughout the lifetime of your LUIS app.

For creating a production endpoint, click on Publish on the top left. Select Production from the Publish to dropdown. If you want your JSON endpoint to include all predicted scores, check the Include All Predicted Intent Scores option. Click on Publish to Production Slot as shown in Figure 6-13. After publishing, you will get the endpoint.

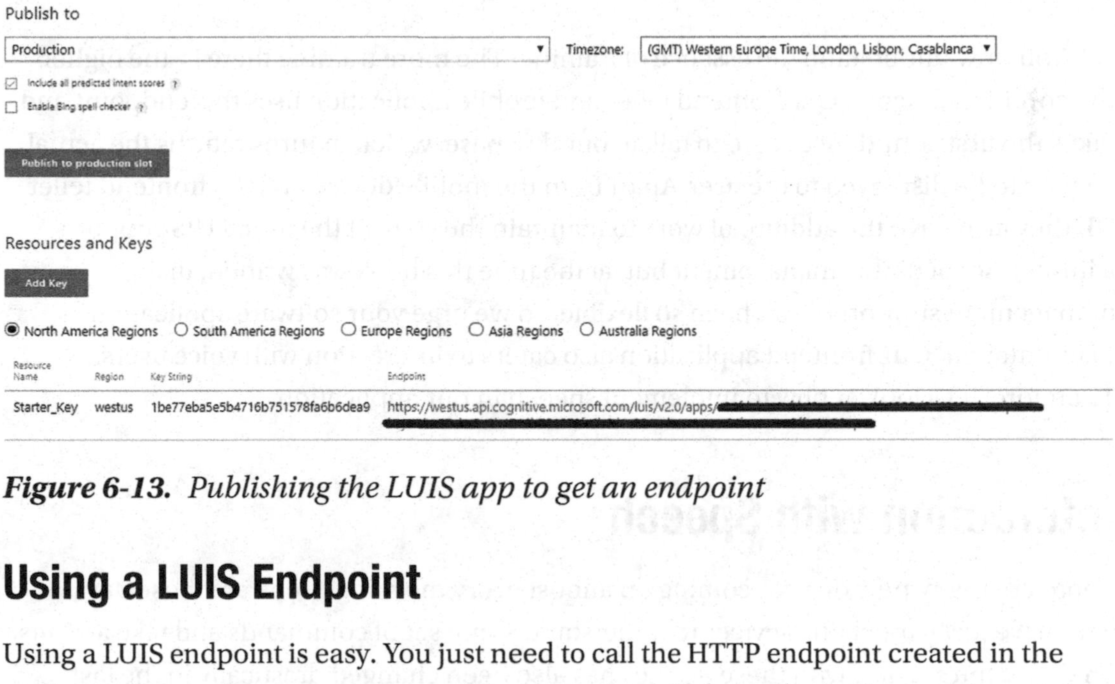

Publish to

| Production ▼ | Timezone: | (GMT) Western Europe Time, London, Lisbon, Casablanca ▼ |

☑ Include all predicted intent scores ?
☐ Enable Bing spell checker ?

[Publish to production slot]

Resources and Keys

[Add Key]

◉ North America Regions   ○ South America Regions   ○ Europe Regions   ○ Asia Regions   ○ Australia Regions

Resource Name	Region	Key String	Endpoint
Starter_Key	westus	1be77eba5e5b4716b751578fa6b6dea9	https://westus.api.cognitive.microsoft.com/luis/v2.0/apps/

Figure 6-13. *Publishing the LUIS app to get an endpoint*

Using a LUIS Endpoint

Using a LUIS endpoint is easy. You just need to call the HTTP endpoint created in the earlier section and pass your query with parameter q. If the endpoint is correct, you start getting the response in JSON, as shown in the following code:

```
{
  "query": "can you set appointment for dentist",
  "topScoringIntent": {
    "intent": "ScheduleAppointment",
    "score": 0.999998569
  },
```

```
"intents": [
  {
    "intent": "ScheduleAppointment",
    "score": 0.999998569
  },
  {
    "intent": "GetCondition",
    "score": 0.0250619985
  }
],
  "entities": []
}
```

You now understand the essence of training. The more training there is, the higher the confidence score. Our frontend teller and mobile application uses this endpoint and takes the first confidence score to talk to our database, which in turns returns the actual answer to be displayed to the user. Apart from the mobile device and the frontend teller UI, they also have the additional work to maintain the state of the user. LUIS supports a limited set of dialog management but, at the time this book was written, dialog management support hasn't been so flexible, so we urge your software application to maintain it. Our frontend application also caters to interaction with voice users. Therefore, let's look at how to implement speech in our application.

Interaction with Speech

There are many new devices coming up almost every morning. Gone are those days where we just expect our devices to understand some set of commands and take actions on them. Interaction with these devices has also been changed drastically in the last decade. Among all of them, speech has been one of the most powerful, and it is of course a natural way for interaction with the users. Consider the personal assistants like Cortana, Siri, or even smart voices controlling cars—almost all of them have the natural interaction of speech. The Asclepius chains of hospitals have patients coming from various fields and they also want their frontend teller machine, along with mobile devices, to have speech interaction capabilities.

Broadly speaking, speech interactions used in the Asclepius mobile and frontend teller applications must convert speech into text or vice versa. Traditionally, implementing speech in the application has been always been a difficult job. Thanks to the Microsoft Cognitive Bing Speech API, which provides the easiest way to enhance your application with speech-driven scenarios. The Speech API provides ease of use by abstracting all the complexity of speech algorithms and presenting an easy-to-use REST API.

Getting Started with Bing Speech API

The Bing Speech API has various implementations of the Speech API to suit customer requirements. Requirements are accomplished by using Speech Recognition and Speech Synthesis. Speech recognition, aka speech to text, allows you to handle spoken words from your users in your application using a recognition engine and convert the words to text. Speak Synthesis, also known as Text to Speech (TTS), allows you to speak words or phrases back to the users through a speech synthesis engine.

Speech to Text

The Bing Text to Speech API provides these features in an easy-to-use REST API. Like all other Microsoft Cognitive APIs, all interactions are done through HTTP POST. All calls go through these APIs, which are hosted on a Azure Cloud server. You need to follow these steps to use the Bing Speech API for text to speech.

1. Get a JSON Web Token (JWT) by calling the token service.

2. Put the JWT token in the header and call the Bing Speech API.

3. Parse the text.

Getting the JWT Token

All calls to the Microsoft Cognitive Services API require authentication before actually using the service. Unlike other Cognitive Services, which just require a subscription key to be passed, the Bing Speech API also requires an access token, also called a JWT token, before it's called. `access_token` is the JWT token passed as a base64 string in the speech request header. To obtain the JWT token, users need to send a POST message to the token service and pass the subscription key as shown here:

```
POST https://api.cognitive.microsoft.com/sts/v1.0/issueToken HTTP/1.1
Host: api.cognitive.microsoft.com
Ocp-Apim-Subscription-Key: 00000000000000000000000000000000
```

The following code shows you how to use this in the frontend teller ASP.NET application:

```
private GUID instanceID;
public async Task<string> GetTextFromAudio (Stream audiostream)
        {
            var requestUri = @"https://speech.platform.bing.com/re
            cognize?scenarios=smd&appid=D4D52672-91D7-4C74-8AD8-
            42B1D98141A5&locale=en-US&device.os= WindowsOS&version=3.0&
            format=json&instanceid=instanceID3&requestid=" + Guid.
            NewGuid();

            using (var client = new HttpClient())
            {
                var token = this.getValidToken();
                client.DefaultRequestHeaders.Add("Authorization", "Bearer"
                + token);

                using (var binaryContent = new ByteArrayContent(StreamToByt
                es(audiostream)))
                {
                    binaryContent.Headers.TryAddWithoutValidation("content-
                    type", "audio/wav; codec=\"audio/pcm\";
                    samplerate=18000");

                    var response = await client.PostAsync(requestUri,
                    binaryContent);
                    var responseString = await response.Content.
                    ReadAsStringAsync();
                    dynamic data = JsonConvert.DeserializeObject(responseS
                    tring);
```

```
                return data.header.name;
            }
        }
private const int TokenExpiryInSeconds = 600;
private string Token;
private void getValidToken()
        {
            this.token = GetNewToken();
            this.timer?.Dispose();
            this.timer = new Timer(
                x => this. getValidToken(),
                null,
//Specify that token should run after 9 mins              TimeSpan.FromSe
conds(TokenExpiryInSeconds).Subtract(TimeSpan.FromMinutes(1)),
        TimeSpan.FromMilliseconds(-1));  // Indicates that this function
                                           will only run once
        }
private static string GetNewToken ()
        {
            using (var client = new HttpClient())
            {
                client.DefaultRequestHeaders.Add("Ocp-Apim-Subscription-
                Key", ApiKey);

                var response = client.PostAsync("https://api.cognitive.
                microsoft.com/sts/v1.0/issueToken", null).Result;

                return response.Content.ReadAsStringAsync().Result;
            }
        }
```

Code Walkthrough

As an experienced developer, you might have immediately observed that the essence of the code for calling speech to text lies in the GetTextFromAudio method. Here is the step-by-step procedure for this code:

1. Create a URL pointing to the speech endpoint with a necessary parameter. Ensure each parameter is been used once, otherwise, you end up getting an HTTP 400 error.

2. Call the getValidToken method to get the JWT token. In order to ensure utmost security, each JWT token is valid for only 10 minutes. Therefore, tokens need to be refreshed on or before 10 minutes to ensure they are always valid. Calling the Speech API with an invalid token results in an error. GetValidToken shows a mechanism to achieve it. You are also free to use your own method. Internally, the GetValidToken method calls the getNewToken method to get the JWT token.

3. Pass the valid JWT token as an authorization header prefixed with the string Bearer.

4. Convert the audio being passed from analog to digital by using codecs.

5. Call the Speech API asynchronously and get the JSON data.

6. Deserialize JSON to a .NET object for further use.

Congratulations! You now know how to convert any speech to text with just a few lines of code. Let's also learn how to convert text to speech as well.

Text to Speech

Text-to-speech conversion follows nearly the same pattern of speech-to-text conversion. Let's look at the code first before going through the code walkthrough:

```
private string GenerateSsml(string locale, string gender, string name,
string text)
{
    var ssmlDoc = new XDocument(
```

```
                new XElement("speak",
                    new XAttribute("version", "1.0"),
                    new XAttribute(XNamespace.Xml + "lang", "en-US"),
                    new XElement("voice",
                        new XAttribute(XNamespace.Xml + "lang",
                        locale),
                        new XAttribute(XNamespace.Xml + "gender",
                        gender),
                        new XAttribute("name", name),
                        text)));
    return ssmlDoc.ToString();
}

Public void ConvertTexttoSpeech(string text)
{
String ssml = this. GenerateSsml("en-US"," Female","TexttoSpeech",text)
byte[] TTSAudio = this.convertTextToSpeech(ssml);
SoundPlayer player = new SoundPlayer(new MemoryStream(TTSAudio));
player.PlaySync();
}
private byte[] convertTextToSpeech(string ssml)
{
    var token = this.getValidToken();
    var client = new RestClient("https://speech.platform.bing.com/
    synthesize");
    var request = new RestRequest(Method.POST);
    request.AddHeader("authorization", "Bearer" + token);
    request.AddHeader("x-search-clientid",
    "8ae9b9546ebb49c98c1b8816b85779a1");
    request.AddHeader("x-search-appid",
    "1d51d9fa3c1d4aa7bd4421a5d974aff9");
    request.AddHeader("x-microsoft-outputformat", "riff-16khz-16bit-mono-pcm");
    request.AddHeader("user-agent", "MyCoolApp");
```

```
request.AddHeader("content-type", "application/ssml+xml");
request.AddParameter("application/ssml+xml", ssml, ParameterType.
RequestBody);
IRestResponse response = client.Execute(request);
return response.RawBytes;
}
```

Code Walkthrough

Here are the steps to convert text to speech:

1. Create a SSML markup for the text to be converted into speech by
    calling the generateSSML method.

Note   Speech Synthesis Markup Language (SSML) is a common standard way
to represent speech in XML format . It is part of W3C specification. SSML provides
a uniform way of creating speech-based markup text. Check the official spec for
complete SSML syntax at `https://www.w3.org/TR/speech-synthesis`.

---

2. Call the Text to Speech API. You first need to get a valid token. For
    that, you can reuse the getValidToken() method shown in the
    speech-to-text code.

3. Make a POST request to `https://speech.platform.bing.com/`
    `synthesize` to get a byte array of the audio sent back as a response
    by the Text to Speech API. There are various ways to make POST
    requests. We use a popular third-party HTTP library called
    RestSharp. Easy installation of RestSharp in Visual Studio is
    supported via NuGet.

4. Use a SoundPlayer class, a built-in .NET class, to play audio
    files and streams, in order to convert a byte array into speech.
    SoundPlayer is a built-in .NET class that plays audio files and
    streams. The format of this audio file is determined by the value
    of the x-Microsoft-outputformat header. As SoundPlayer only
    supports WAV audio files, use riff-16khz-16bit-mono-pcm as the
    value for the outputformat header.

Identifying and Recognizing Faces

Like any smart hospital, Asclepius has a very tight surveillance system. Asclepius consortium is also very careful about the number of people visiting patients. The Asclepius surveillance system monitors inventory warehouse, restricts only a limited set of doctors and nurses into security and warehouse zones, and even with the attending patients. This smart digital action helps restrict unwanted people from entering buy raising the alarm when a security breach is attempted. Asclepius also has an automated attendance system, which doesn't require the user to carry an identity card or any device. As soon as the employee enters the hospital, she is identified from the CCTV camera and her attendance is registered. Her time in and out of the system is also being monitored. All rooms and bays have digital identification mechanism for allowing only authorized people to enter rooms. This all has been achieved through the use of various cognitive technologies, especially the Face API.

What Does the Face API Work?

Face API at a high level helps in detecting, identifying, verifying, and recognizing faces. It also can be used to get more insights about a face. Face detection and identification is not a new concept. It's been used across academia, government institutions, and industries for decades in one form or another. The Face API extends it by bringing years of Microsoft research into face detection and recognition in a simple-to-use API.

How Does Asclepius Achieve Strong Surveillance?

Asclepius has created various security groups to cater their security. Each hospital employee and person are added to one of those known groups (Visitors, Regular, Patients, Doctors, Vendors, Admin). By default, any unknown people are tagged as part of the Visitors group. All patients are tagged under the Patients group. All the doctors belong to the Doctors group and some of the doctors and hospital employees belong to the Admin group, which has access to all the bays. With the help of smart CCTV cameras, images are captured live via frames. Only authorized people from certain people groups will get access to certain rooms, as shown in Figure 6-14. The same process is followed to identify employees from people entering the office.

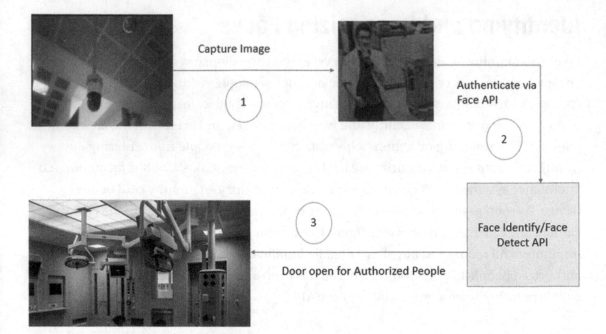

Figure 6-14. *How Asclepius consortium is using face recognition to recognize people and open the door for them*

Getting Keys for the Face API

As with all cognitive services, you must first get a subscription key for the Face API via the Azure Portal.

1. Go to the Azure Portal ➤ AI + Cognitive service blade.

2. Select the API type as Face API.

3. Fill out the location, pricing tier, and resource group, and then click Create to create a subscription.

Make sure the subscription key for the Face API is handy. You'll need it soon.

Creating a Person and Person Group

Follow these steps to attain face identification and verification:

1. Create a Person group.

2. Create a person.

3. Add faces to the person.

4. Train the Person group.

Once these tasks are achieved, the Person group can be used to authenticate and authorize people. While doing any face identification, you need to set the scope. The Person group determines the overall scope of the face identification. Each Person group contains one or more people. For example, only the Admin Person group has authority to access all security inventory. The Person group contains many people and each person internally contains multiple face images to get it trained, as shown in Figure 6-15.

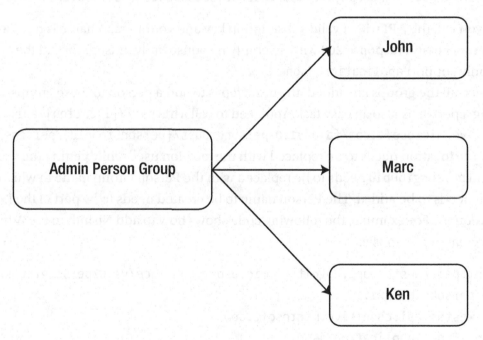

Figure 6-15. *The correlation between the Person group and a person*

As shown in Figure 6-15, John, Marc, and Ken are part of the Admin Person group. Likewise, Asclepius has other person groups that handle authentication and authorization for other tasks. For example, the Regular Person group is for all the regular employees in the hospital. The Regular Person group is used to handle the automated attendance process by monitoring and validating all people entering the hospital using a secured bay.

Creating a Person group profile is a straightforward and easy process. You need to provide an HTTP PUT API, which is available at `https://[location].api.cognitive.microsoft.com/face/v1.0/persongroups/`, by passing the Person group name and the subscription key of the Face API that you created earlier.

```
PUT https://westcentralus.api.cognitive.microsoft.com/face/v1.0/
persongroups/Admin HTTP/1.1
Host: westcentralus.api.cognitive.microsoft.com
Content-Type: application/json
Ocp-Apim-Subscription-Key: 00000000000000000000000000000000000000000000000
```

If you call the API with a valid subscription key and your person name is unique, you will get successful response 200 with an empty response body. Ensure that all the Face APIs only support `application/json`.

Once all the groups are added, the next step is to add a person to these groups. Adding a person is also an easy task. You need to call a `https://[location].api.cognitive.microsoft.com/face/v1.0/persongroups/{personGroupId}/persons` where the location needs to be replaced with the location used while getting the Face API and `persongroupid` needs to be replaced with the Person Group name in which this person needs to be added. The Person name to be created needs to be part of the JSON body request. For example, the following code shows how to add Nishith to the Admin group created previously:

```
POST https://westus.api.cognitive.microsoft.com/face/v1.0/persongroups/
admin/persons HTTP/1.1
Host: westus.api.cognitive.microsoft.com
Content-Type: application/json
Ocp-Apim-Subscription-Key: 00000000000000000000000000000000
```

```
{
    "name":"Nishith",
    "userData":"User-provided data attached to the person"
}
```

Successful calls create a unique person ID with JSON response shown here:

```
Pragma: no-cache
apim-request-id: 845a9a5f-9c4f-4f96-a126-04f2916a602d
Strict-Transport-Security: max-age=31536000; includeSubDomains; preload
x-content-type-options: nosniff
Cache-Control: no-cache
Date: Sun, 31 Dec 2017 11:26:35 GMT
X-AspNet-Version: 4.0.30319
X-Powered-By: ASP.NET
Content-Length: 51
Content-Type: application/json; charset=utf-8
Expires: -1

{
    "personId": "91ec6844-2be9-46d9-bc7f-c4d2deab166e"
}
```

Each person is identified by his or her unique person ID. So now for future reference, Nishith would be referred as person ID 91ec6844-2be9-46d9-bc7f-c4d2deab166e. In order to call a successful person creation, you need to ensure that you are within the limit of creating a person and the person group for that subscription. The following table shows the limitation of each subscription.

Tier	Person per Person Group	Persons per Subscription
Free Tier	1K	1K
S0	10K	1M

If you exceed the limit, you will get the QuotaExceeded error. While creating a person, you didn't provide any faces.

Add Faces

In order to add faces, call `https://[location].api.cognitive.microsoft.com/face/v1.0/persongroups/{personGroupId}/persons/{personId}` via an HTTP Post. Be sure to replace the location, persongroupid, and person ID with the appropriate values. Pass the image as an URL in the application body. For example, use the following code to add Nishith's image to the Nishith Person in the Admin group:

```
POST https://westus.api.cognitive.microsoft.com/face/v1.0/persongroups/
admin/persons/91ec6844-2be9-46d9-bc7f-c4d2deab166e/persistedFaces HTTP/1.1
Host: westus.api.cognitive.microsoft.com
Content-Type: application/json
Ocp-Apim-Subscription-Key: 00000000000000000000000000000000

{
    "url":" https://pbs.twimg.com/media/DReABwzW4AAv7hL.jpg"

}
```

A successful call with this URL will result in returning a persisted face ID:

```
Pragma: no-cache
apim-request-id: 7e5f7e9d-4ad1-4cd4-a1df-ec81f4f37d33
Strict-Transport-Security: max-age=31536000; includeSubDomains; preload
x-content-type-options: nosniff
Cache-Control: no-cache
Date: Mon, 01 Jan 2018 09:55:08 GMT
X-AspNet-Version: 4.0.30319
X-Powered-By: ASP.NET
Content-Length: 58
Content-Type: application/json; charset=utf-8
Expires: -1

{
  "persistedFaceId": "185e9d95-d52b-4bd9-b6a9-f512c4dbd5a2"
}
```

Make sure the image is an URL and is specified in the request body; your application should be Internet accessible. Only files having extensions of JPEG, PNG, GIF, and BMP are supported and each image should not be more than 4MB. Each person can have multiple faces so efficient training can be done. You can tag up to 248 faces per person.

Training Is the Key

More training results in better accuracy. We must now train the Person group. Any changes to the faces would require training the Person group again before using it to identify faces. In order to train the Person group, give an HTTP POST call to `https://[location].api.cognitive.microsoft.com/face/v1.0/persongroups/ [persongroupname]/train` and pass the subscription key. Replace the `persongroupname` and location appropriately. For example, to train the Admin Person group, the HTTP request would be:

```
POST https://westus.api.cognitive.microsoft.com/face/v1.0/persongroups/
admin/train HTTP/1.1
Host: westus.api.cognitive.microsoft.com
Ocp-Apim-Subscription-Key: 00000000000000000000000000000000
```

A successful call to the API would result in Empty JSON.

Using the Face API for Authentication

Once a person and the Person group are trained, the Face API can then be used to authenticate or identify a face from an unknown Person group. As mentioned, all the bays and rooms of Asclepius have digital entrance mechanisms that are supported by Smart CCTV cameras. The digital locks are tied to one or more Person groups. Door locks are only open when the system authenticates and authorizes a person as being part of the Person group.

As and when a new person tries to enter a room, the CCTV camera first calls the Face Detect API by passing the captured image from CCTV to detect human faces in the image, which also returns face IDs for those faces. Those face IDs are then been passed to the Face Identify API to test it against person groups. When the Face Identify API returns a confidence score of more than .9, the door opens. The system also tracks the time spent in that room as well.

To call the Face Detect API for the image being captured, use the URL `https://westus.api.cognitive.microsoft.com/face/v1.0/detect?returnFaceId=true&returnFaceLandmarks=false`. Then pass the subscription key as the header and the image being captured from the CCTV camera as part of the JSON request body. For example:

```
POST https://westus.api.cognitive.microsoft.com/face/v1.0/detect?returnFace
Id=true&returnFaceLandmarks=false HTTP/1.1
Host: westus.api.cognitive.microsoft.com
Content-Type: application/json
Ocp-Apim-Subscription-Key: 00000000000000000000000000000000

{
    "url":"https://asclepius.com/media/DReABwzW4AAv7hL.jpg"
}
```

The response will return an array of face entries in JSON, along with face ID, as shown in this code.

```
Pragma: no-cache
apim-request-id: b6a209c3-fd26-422c-8baa-99b54e827d86
Strict-Transport-Security: max-age=31536000; includeSubDomains; preload
x-content-type-options: nosniff
Cache-Control: no-cache
Date: Mon, 01 Jan 2018 10:35:37 GMT
X-AspNet-Version: 4.0.30319
X-Powered-By: ASP.NET
Content-Length: 113
Content-Type: application/json; charset=utf-8
Expires: -1
[{
  "faceId": "1e685d67-43b9-470f-8c06-e9b0cd5d6584",
  "faceRectangle": {
    "top": 134,
    "left": 525,
    "width": 74,
    "height": 74
  }
}]
```

In this code, a face is returned along with the face ID. Use the face ID and pass it to the Face Identify API, as shown in the following code, to validate whether the face ID captured is part of the Person group that's authorized to enter the bay:

```
POST https://westus.api.cognitive.microsoft.com/face/v1.0/identify HTTP/1.1
Host: westus.api.cognitive.microsoft.com
Content-Type: application/json
Ocp-Apim-Subscription-Key: 00000000000000000000000000000000

{
    "personGroupId":"admin",
    "faceIds":[
        "1e685d67-43b9-470f-8c06-e9b0cd5d6584"
    ],
    "maxNumOfCandidatesReturned":4,
    "confidenceThreshold": 0.9
}
```

In this code, the confidenceThreshold parameter is set to .9, which acts as a confidence score for determining the identity of a person. ConfidenceThreshold is an optional parameter and should have a value between O and 1. With proper subscription, it returns the result as a JSON API:

```
Pragma: no-cache
apim-request-id: de275faf-1cdf-4476-b19f-6466ebdbcbea
Strict-Transport-Security: max-age=31536000; includeSubDomains; preload
x-content-type-options: nosniff
Cache-Control: no-cache
Date: Mon, 01 Jan 2018 10:45:48 GMT
X-AspNet-Version: 4.0.30319
X-Powered-By: ASP.NET
Content-Length: 135
Content-Type: application/json; charset=utf-8
Expires:  1
[{
```

```
  "faceId": "1e685d67-43b9-470f-8c06-e9b0cd5d6584",
  "candidates": [{
    "personId": "91ec6844-2be9-46d9-bc7f-c4d2deab166e",
    "confidence": 1.0
  }]
}]
```

In this code, the face is being detected with 100% accuracy, so the digital door opens.

Your Assignment

As part of their digital strategy to make video processing more powerful, Asclepius is planning to use surveillance to get more useful insights. It plans to achieve this by getting powerful insights through the video streaming, all of which is possible through the use of Video AI. Video content has been developing at such a rapid pace that manual processing or creating manual video surveillance system doesn't work. The need of the hour is to get a surveillance system that monitors the video, takes immediate actions, and generates insights to help serve the need. Asclepius Consortium plans to handle queries like the following:

- How many patients and people came into the hospital yesterday?

- Were the patients happy after consulting with the doctor?

- Who entered or attempted to enter the secured inventory warehouse?

- What are all the products and tools taken out of inventory?

- How do we respond to critical and severe patients 24X7?

- Can we monitor people activity and ensure that people get proper support whenever and wherever required?

- When did Dr. John (for example) enter the hospital and where is he currently? Or when was the patient named Mike last attended to?

- How can we identify instruments, doctors, and other inventory objects?

Hint   We discussed Video AI briefly in Chapter 4, but essentially Video AI helps in processing videos, generating insights such as the face recognition and tracking, detecting voice activity, performing sentiment analysis, detecting scenes, and much more. You need a couple of APIs of Video AI to do this. You need an Index API to index, a Search API to do a search, a Visual Insights API to get insights, and then the Streaming API to do the actual streaming. This is achieved by discovering content in the video and generating insights. To learn more about it, visit `https://Vi.microsoft.com`. At the time this book was written, Video Indexer is in preview mode.

Recap

In this chapter, you learned about some of the powerful ways to use Microsoft Cognitive Services and apply them to the Asclepius hospital example. You got an in-depth understanding about LUIS and learned how to create, train, test, and publish a LUIS application. You also learned how to convert text to speech and speech to text by calling the Speech API. Later in the chapter, you learned how to use the Face API to identify and recognize faces and to create a strong surveillance system.

CHAPTER 7

Understanding Blockchain

In last decade, we have seen the emergence of various computer technologies, each of which was disrupting and revolutionary. Some of these technologies paved the way for a newer generation of technologies to make our lives easier. Some of these technologies are in the category of invention, as they change and disrupt the entire ecosystem. There was a big wave that produced a lot of new billionaires and millionaires. What was available for just 2 cents in 2009 is now available for more than $15,000 US. Yes, we are talking about Bitcoin and Blockchain. Blockchain is the technology behind Bitcoin. Cryptocurrency and especially Bitcoin have certainly divided the world into two zones—one that supports cryptocurrency and the other that opposes it. The use of cryptocurrency has been such a craze that there are around 1400+ cryptocurrencies like Bitcoin in the market, having more than 17+ million accounts. People have raised doubts about the future of Bitcoin. A few countries don't allow cryptocurrencies in their economies, but almost all of them have provided tremendous support for Blockchain. Bitcoin is just one of the finest implementations of Blockchain, but Blockchain is certainly going to stay and is currently transforming the way we trust across work and business.

Until this point, we have assumed the role of intermediaries to be important. They are part of our core ecosystem of daily life. Everything that we do, such as buying vegetables or buying a house, getting an insurance claim, signing a contract, or even booking a hotel destination for our upcoming vacation, includes intermediaries. Apart from bringing a few advantages, it also brings several disadvantages, like cost, lack of transparency, and brokerage percentages. Wouldn't it be great if we had a technology that reduced all intermediaries? Wouldn't it benefit the producer and the consumer? Yes, this technology has arrived and it's called Blockchain. Bitcoin and the rise of cryptocurrency is possible with the technology behind it, which we call Blockchain.

© Nishith Pathak and Anurag Bhandari 2018
N. Pathak and A. Bhandari, *IoT, AI, and Blockchain for .NET*, https://doi.org/10.1007/978-1-4842-3709-0_7

Blockchain and Bitcoin are so interrelated that a lot of times people use these terms interchangeably. Well before we go further and drill down more in detail, let's understand how Blockchain is not Bitcoin.

In this chapter, you learn about:

- History of the exchange medium

- Need and emergence of Bitcoin

- What Blockchain is

- How Blockchain is different from Bitcoin

- Features of Blockchain

- Various types of Blockchain

Blockchain will change the way we trust. It is important for you to understand the core reason for creating a technology like Blockchain. Hence, it is important to understand the history behind cryptocurrency, as it will help you understand the underpinnings for creating a technology like Blockchain.

The History of Cryptocurrency

Since the evolution of mankind, there has been various types of exchanges, each of which has pros and cons. Back in 6,000 BC, it all started with the barter system. The barter system is about trading services and goods. It was definitely a good system—a person was required to produce or offer services that he is specialists in and then exchange those for the goods that he/she requires. The barter system continued successfully for centuries but had a few fundamental flaws including the absence of a common unit of value for exchange. This results in creating a different valuation for the different exchange of good. For example, buying a few apples in exchange of a liter of milk might be good, but the same liter of milk might not be traded for rice. It requires a new valuation, which may or may not be accepted by all parties involved. Apart from this, few of the goods were perishable in nature and few goods were large and heavy, making them transport-unfriendly. Another flaw with the barter system was proof of ownership. There was no way to tie goods to a person. These flaws led to the emergence of the gold coins era.

Era of Gold Coins

The era of gold coins started around 650 BC. The use of coins resolved some of the basic and fundamental problems with the barter system. For example, gold coins serve as a common unit of value. Now a certain number of goods could be exchanged with a gold coin. Gold is also non-perishable in nature and can be easily transportable. Gold coins also have a couple of flaws, primarily that they are expensive and insecure. Anyone can easily steal gold coins. Moreover, it was not easy to mine gold. All of these issues led to paper-based currency, aka FIAT currency.

FIAT Currency

The paper currency era started around 960 AD. During the initial days of paper currency, people deposited gold coins to third-party financial corporations. Some of these financial parties are now called banks. In lieu of gold coins, these third party gave IOU notes, which were treated as standard currency notes. These IOU notes were also termed the first form of FIAT currency.

Tip   FIAT currency is the standard currency being supported by government regulations and institution. Currencies like the Dollar, Yen, Rupee, Euro, Pound, etc., are current FIAT currencies. We use FIAT currency terminology later in the due course of the chapter.

People who have these IOU notes can exchange them for goods. There are many advantages to using paper currency. It is lighter than gold and easy to mine. It was initially backed by a tangible commodity like gold, and later by an intangible commodity like banks and governments that issue these notes. All the government institutions that back various currencies have a standard acceptance of exchange rates. FIAT currency has been used across the world in one form or another, as shown in Figure 7-1.

Figure 7-1. *Some of the currently used FIAT currencies*

In spite of paper currency being successful and used currently as well, it has its flaws. FAIT currency is unsecured, inflationary, and untraceable. There is no way you can tie paper currency to a person. Anyone can steal your currency and use it again. Government institutions backing currency have no way of knowing who owns the currency. Once the currency is in the market, there is absolutely no way to trace it. This can create a lot of inflation in the market, leading to economic issues like black money hoarding and parallel economies. Some of the countries also use demonetization drives to replace the running currency with new currency notes to stop creating parallel economy.

Using Checks

With the rise of all these issues, government institutions brought another exchange medium in the market, i.e. checks. The first checks were created in 1717 AD. Checks resolve some of the issues with currency and have quite a lot of similarity with existing cryptocurrency. First and foremost, they resolved the security issue. Checks contain the sender's and receiver's identities. Checks also used a very elementary form of cryptography (i.e., the signature) to validate the actual sender, as shown in Figure 7-2. Each check can have a different value than any others, which means two checks can have different amounts. Checks were successful in resolving some of the vital issues with previous medium exchanges.

Figure 7-2. *A sample check from a checkbook, where the user is filling in the receiver's info*

However, checks also have a few issues, especially transaction verification time. Consider a normal case, when a buyer needs a good and he issues a check in lieu of getting those goods. The buyer gets the good but the seller now has to verify the authenticity of the check only when the seller's bank talks with the buyer bank and gets the clearance of debt. Currently, check clearance takes from 1-4 working days. There are chances that the check is fraudulent and in practical scenarios, the seller now needs to chase the buyer. Checks also have a very basic version of cryptography, via the signature, but that can easily be forged.

Promises of E-Wallet

With so many flaws with FIAT currencies and checks, there was a need to create a new medium of exchange, based on which e-wallet was introduced. E-wallet is almost a perfect medium of exchange. There is no need for paper currencies and you don't need to carry a wallet with you. It is fast, convenient, and efficient, with transaction verification happening in a couple of seconds. This solves the biggest issues with checks. It can easily be installed and accessed from any device, including mobile devices. By using various mobile biometric and IRIS security measures, the validating transaction can reach the highest level of security compared to using signatures on checks. As there is no paper currency involved, it's easy for a regulatory authority to track the transaction and track the money usage and its supply. It thereby reduces illegal money uses and black money hoarding.

The Financial Crisis Broke the Trust

At a high level, e-wallet looks to be very promising, without any flaws, and addresses all the concerns with the medium exchange. The biggest problem with e-wallet is that it is still tied up with an existing financial structure. Now if you remember the financial crisis back in 2008, you will know that financial systems can have a good degree of corruption. The financial crisis of 2008 was considered the largest recession since 1929. The subprime mortgage crisis spurred financial markets to crash.

The worldwide financial crisis in 2008 had a lot of consequences. Financial companies collapsed and some governments verged on bankruptcy. Large investment banks were bankrupt and the government started bailing out banks that they deemed too big to fail. Banks, of course, were most largely impacted, because ultimately that is where the crisis originated. These financial crises caused people to lose faith in existing financial systems. People used to feel that the bank was the safest option to keep their hard earn money, safe and secure.

People started making mass withdrawals from banks. They had two options at that time. Either to keep all their money at home, which is not a great idea, or keep it in a bank, which they no longer trusted. There was a need for an alternate financial system. In addition, if you look over the current financial transaction, some of these take a couple of days to get transferred over the wire if two parties are in different countries. Another problem is the unfavorable exchange rates that lack transparency and thereby trust.

Blessings in Disguise: Bitcoin

While all these issues were happening, a group of people (or a single individual) under the name of Satoshi Nakamoto published a paper titled "Bitcoin: A Peer-to-Peer Electronic Cash System," shown in Figure 7-3. It challenged the very concept of money and having intermediaries to deal with it. In this paper, Nakamoto proposed a system that is comprised of a chain of blocks, which is later called *Blockchain*. In this paper, Nakamoto coined the term *Bitcoin* as a peer-to-peer electronic cash system supported by a distributed decentralized network.

192

Bitcoin: A Peer-to-Peer Electronic Cash System

Satoshi Nakamoto
satoshin@gmx.com
www.bitcoin.org

Abstract. A purely peer-to-peer version of electronic cash would allow online payments to be sent directly from one party to another without going through a financial institution. Digital signatures provide part of the solution, but the main benefits are lost if a trusted third party is still required to prevent double-spending. We propose a solution to the double-spending problem using a peer-to-peer network. The network timestamps transactions by hashing them into an ongoing chain of hash-based proof-of-work, forming a record that cannot be changed without redoing the proof-of-work. The longest chain not only serves as proof of the sequence of events witnessed, but proof that it came from the largest pool of CPU power. As long as a majority of CPU power is controlled by nodes that are not cooperating to attack the network, they'll generate the longest chain and outpace attackers. The

Figure 7-3. A snapshot of the Satoshi Nakamoto paper, through which Bitcoin and Blockchain emerged

The idea of Bitcoin is peer-to-peer, without requiring a third-party trust-based intermediary. The Bitcoin system comprises the following:

- Resolving the double spending issue through the use of a peer-to-peer network.

- Ensuring participants identity can be hidden and they can be anonymous.

- No requirement of trusted parties. In fact, you don't need to trust any one but the system.

- New coins of cryptocurrency can be generated through hash cryptography proof of work.

Tip   Although we have tried to give you a good overview of the paper, we still suggest you take some time and go through the actual paper written by Nakamoto. This paper is around nine pages long and is available at `https://bitcoin.org/bitcoin.pdf`.

The progress of cryptography and the emergence of some clever solutions like proof of work, mentioned in Nakamoto's paper, opened the door to create a new kind of digital currency. The release of this paper issued in the era of cryptocurrency. Bitcoin, as shown in Figure 7-4, is the most popular and the oldest of the cryptocurrencies.

Figure 7-4. *The actual Bitcoin currency, which is another form of Bitcoin*

Thank you, Satoshi Nakamoto! Bitcoin, among others, is now a real alternative to banking dominance. While writing this book, there were around 1400+ cryptocurrencies in the market, with Bitcoin being the oldest one.

What Is Bitcoin?

Bitcoin is defined in one sentence as follows:

Bitcoin is a **digital**, **disintermediated**, **decentralized trust based** cryptocurrency

Each of the words marked in bold in this definition is very important. We are going to discuss in more detail each one, but for now just understand that Bitcoin is a digital currency so it doesn't have a physical form. Unlike other digital cash, it has its own value and has corresponding denomination value for other currencies.

There is a lot of discussion about Bitcoin being trustless and anonymous. This is not correct. In fact, trust is the main issue that led to the emergence of cryptocurrencies like Bitcoin. What Bitcoin and other cryptocurrencies have done is ensure that trust is moved from centralized to decentralized systems. Even Bitcoin is a FIAT currency in nature, which means it is not backed by tangible value, but rather intangible value, i.e., trust. It has value just because a member of the group believes it has value and Bitcoin should be used to exchange in lieu of a good just like any currency. The only difference is a normal currency's trust comes from government backing. Out here, it is from the people.

Bitcoin, being decentralized, is very secure in nature. The Bitcoin system can't be faked. The system can be trusted with full transparency. In fact, identities in Bitcoin are hidden and each identity is referenced through alphanumeric codes done using hash cryptography rather than names.

The Blockchain is the underlying technology behind Bitcoin. Bitcoin is just an application created using Blockchain. Before delving more into Blockchain, it is important to understand the difference between centralized, decentralized, and distributed systems.

Centralized Systems

Centralized systems, as shown in Figure 7-5, are the systems that have single point of authority (POA). All the control is concentrated in this authority, which ensures all processes and decisions are carried out at this location. Centralized systems have a couple of advantages. As there is just one point of authority, the decision can be faster and easier to implement. Each point in the authority is responsible for one task. This prevents any single task from being done by multiple points, ensuring no duplicity and faster change management. Some of the examples of the centralized system include banks, Department of Motor Vehicles, credit agencies, title companies, and server CPUs, to name a few.

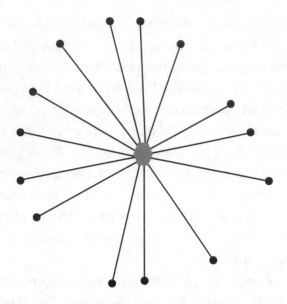

Figure 7-5. *A pictorial representation of a centralized system, where one node governs the other nodes*

The centralized system introduces a lot of advantages and hence it's been popular even now. However, centralized systems also have a lot of flaws. A single POA brings the notion of having a single point of failure. This means if this point goes down for any reason, the entire system will collapse. We witnessed such failure during the financial crisis of 2008. Another flaw with these systems is that centralized system lacks transparency and is prone to fraud and distrust. Centralized systems works like a black box and people using centralized systems might get influenced with fraud and loss of trust. A centralized system has a lot advantages and are more suited for systems that can accept a single point of trust, require fast growth, and of course, don't require growing systems at scale.

Decentralized Systems

Decentralized systems have multiple points of authority, as shown in Figure 7-6, which ensured that there is no single point of failure and that authority tasks are more diversified. Unlike centralized systems, decentralized systems also ensure a flat hierarchy. You can think of decentralized systems as containing lots of nodes, with few nodes having additional tasks to authority and instead broadcasting that authority to several other nodes.

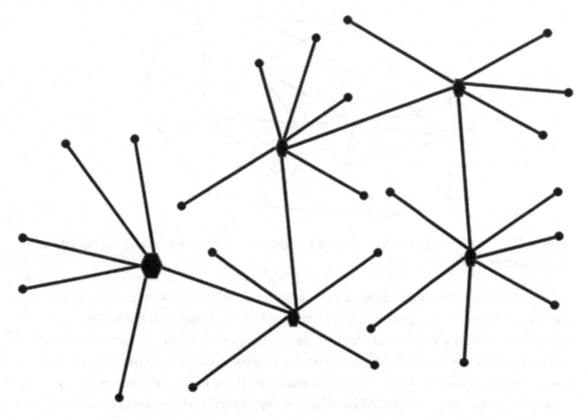

Figure 7-6. *A pictorial representation of classic decentralized systems*

Decentralized systems are advantageous when you want to make a decision closer to the consumer rather than doing this at one central location. Some of the classic examples of decentralized systems include a Cloud database and state authorities, to name a few. One of the disadvantages of the decentralized system is that, since there is multiple points of authority, chances of a duplicate task is higher, which can affect economies of scale. A decentralized system is more secure than a centralized one, but is still not 100% secure.

Distributed Systems

Distributed systems are the third type of system in which everyone is an authority. Each node has equal power. This is the most secure among the three systems. This doesn't mean the system can't be hacked or faked, but to do it, you must have more than 50 percent control over the points of authority. The time needed to fake and hack would nullify any benefits and hence distributed systems are considered most secure systems. See Figure 7-7.

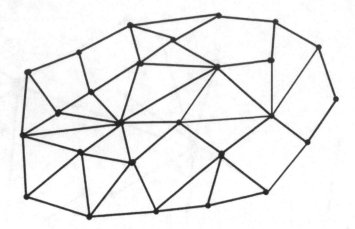

Figure 7-7. *A pictorial representation of distributed systems, where all nodes have equal power*

The distributed system ensures a flat hierarchy, which ensures everyone is equal. There are a lot of advantages to having distributed systems. Since all the nodes are equal, it removes the need for an intermediary. Changes are replicated across all nodes and verified by at least 50 percent of the nodes, making it very transparent. Distributed systems make perfect options for a system requiring third-party trust, intermediary, or even trusting another node. While using the distributed system, you don't need to trust anyone but the system itself. Some of the examples of distributed systems include cryptocurrency and of course, Blockchain.

With decentralization and disintermediation at the core of the Bitcoin system and Blockchain, there is no requirement for people to trust each other, just the system. Distributed systems, however, take some time to set up and require a good initial amount of investment. Among all the three systems, distributed systems are the most stable. Another benefit of using distributed systems is that they are infinitely scalable and hence any process involving scalability issues at large scale can safely vouch for using distributed systems.

What Is Blockchain?

All we have learned about Bitcoin is possible due to the Blockchain implementation behind it. We also learned that Blockchain is the underlying technology behind Bitcoin. In fact, Blockchain has a broader scope than just being a technology beneath Bitcoin, as shown in Figure 7-8. In fact, Blockchain is a mother of lot of future technologies and systems. We have just seen one implementation of Blockchain, i.e. Bitcoin, but more systems implementing Blockchain across various verticals are soon going to disrupt the entire ecosystem.

Figure 7-8. *Blockchain is far bigger than Bitcoin and Bitcoin is just one implementation of Blockchain*

To understand the power of Blockchain, let's look at it from another angle. Trust is inevitable and part of our daily life. Everything that we do involves some sense of trust associated with it. Whether you are buying a car or house, doing any financial transactions, viewing a website, buying products online or from the market, or even getting a degree from a university, the ledger in one form or another is the fundamental source of trust. Take the case of financial transactions. Hundreds of trillions of transactions happen every year across the globe. Historically, we maintain ledgers, shown in Figure 7-9, to handle and store information about the transaction.

Figure 7-9. *A classic ledger*

These ledgers have been either kept in lockers for safety or have been given to the third parties such as banks, universities, or another third-party trusted source. In the last few decades, we saw some of these ledgers moved to the centralized database. One of the benefits of using these ledgers is that they are easily accessible whenever required. For example, if you want to get a copy of a transaction statement that's 10 years old, it's just a matter of clicking your banking site. Similarly, you can always get a copy of your degree from a university in case you lost it, because universities safely store your records. This benefit of making it available also makes it vulnerable to errors, making it fake, or even modifying it with ease. We have already discussed issues related to centralized systems.

- Think about your transaction records kept in the bank. If someone has access to the central database, a person can modify and hack the records. Such hacking has happened to many banks and customers have suffered.

- Take another case of you going to buy a property. How are you going to do a valuation of the property and ensure that it belongs to the person from whom you are buying it? Property information can easily be tampered with, making you pay more than it's worth.

- Take another use case of identifying organic vegetables from non-organic one. It would be hard to just trust those labels, which can easily be stamped on.

- Take another case of leasing a car for a couple of years. How do you ensure that car is insured and within regulations for that country for driving?

- Take another case of buying products from sites like Amazon and relying on them that they would deliver the authentic item you choose from the site.

- You are also showing trust on email exchange providers while exchanging emails, on social networking site while doing social tasks, and so on.

These examples are cases where people have a greater level of trust. Moreover, due to digital technologies, we create copies of that data while sharing it. When one of your colleagues asks you to send an important spreadsheet via email, for example, you are sending a copy of the spreadsheet to him over email. This results in creating multiple copies of the important sheet. We keep on creating multiple copies of the same data, creating different owners. Trusting one of those copies as an original is a great challenge, as anyone who has ownership has the opportunity to modify any of the cells and then claim that it's the original.

The rationale of trust is more important in the IoT era. As we have seen in previous chapters, more and more devices are getting connected and emitting data. It is important to ensure that data coming from these devices can be trusted. For all these use cases and many more, you can identify that the current system is either caged with a lot of paperwork, creating multiple copies, stored in the central custody of some third-party trusted source, either in the hard or soft copy. These ledgers can easily be modified and even faked.

The Blockchain is a revolutionary disruptive technology, as shown in Figure 7-10, that is going to change the way we trust across work and business. The Blockchain is transforming the way we maintain ledgers.

Figure 7-10. *Blockchain evolving to change the way we trust and getting it applied to various verticals*

There are a lot of unique features that Blockchain brings as a ledger, which resolve all the previous issues with its predecessors. Consider these features:

- Blockchain is distributed and decentralized in nature. Every computer that joins the Blockchain network, as shown in Figure 7-11, gets a copy of Blockchain immediately. These computer nodes are then used to validate and relay transactions.

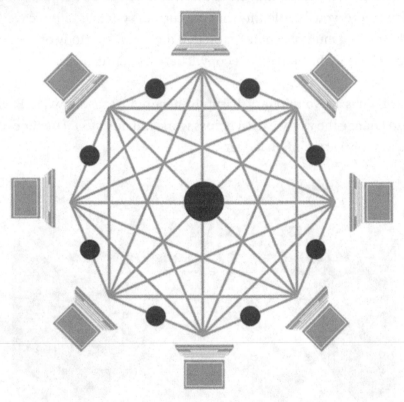

Figure 7-11. *All computer nodes joining the Blockchain network have equal writes and get a copy of Blockchain software immediately as they join network*

- The Blockchain, as shown in Figure 7-12, is immutable in nature. This means the Blockchain transaction cannot be edited or deleted. If you want to modify or undo a transaction, you must propose new transactions, which go through the same process of approval. Only when the majority of nodes approve it will it be accepted.

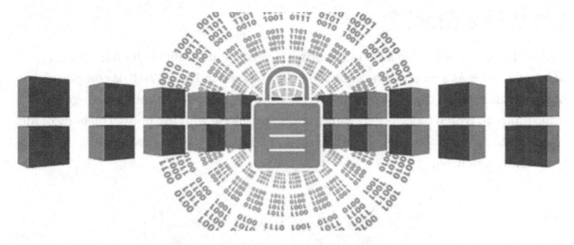

Figure 7-12. *The Blockchain network is very secure and immutable*

- Blockchain is fully secure in nature as it uses hash cryptography for handling identities.

- Every record added to the Blockchain ledger has a unique key associated with it.

- Every record added is trusted and stamped by the party that added that record.

- When the next record is written, everything from the first record including the key and the content of the second record is put in the formula, generating the key for the second record.

In a one-liner, *Blockchain is an immutable distributed ledger that can be used to record everything of value.* This statement provides the true testimony to the usage of the Blockchain. Most of the use of Blockchain until now has been associated with financial transactions, but eventually, Blockchain can be used to record and manage anything that has value.

Blockchain technology delivers unbelievable traceability that is autonomous and trusted by creating permanent records of data and transactions. It thereby brings the single source of truth and no single point of failure to all stakeholders, as everything related to data and transactions are always visible on the network.

What Is a Block?

A *block* is a unit containing a set of confirmed transactions. If Blockchain is a ledger, think of a block as a page or book. Each block, as shown in Figure 7-13, is composed of the header, which contains information like the previous block hash reference, the timestamp on which block is generated, and so on, along with the body. The body of the block contains a list of the accepted transaction. The header is hashed cryptographically to generate a new block.

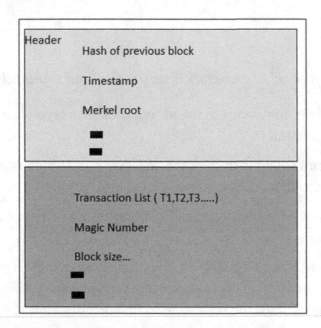

Figure 7-13.   *The items available in a block of a Blockchain*

Every transaction is encrypted (hashed) with a public-private key and every header is hashed to generate a new block. Due to this implementation, every transaction has a record associated with the new block. The header also contains the address of the previous block, thus the chain becomes incorruptible. As more and more transactions happen, the Blockchain transaction appends only and creates a chronologically growing timestamp database of transactional data, as shown in Figure 7-14. It thereby creates a chain block, hence the name Blockchain.

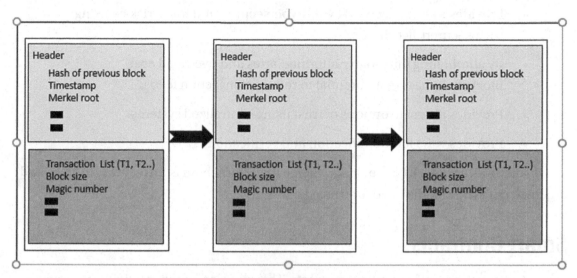

Blockchain

Figure 7-14. *The classic representation of Blockchain*

Benefits of Blockchain

Blockchain brings numerous benefits by storing and organizing the data in a novice
way. Various industry verticals have been researching and exploring unique ways to
use Blockchain in an effective manner. As mentioned earlier in the chapter, Blockchain
can organize data for anything that has value. You can also use Blockchain in all the
scenarios where it requires you to trust someone. Here are some of the benefits of using
Blockchain:

- Improves the efficiency of the system.

- All the changes on the public Blockchain can be viewed publicly by
  all parties, thereby creating transparent systems.

- Ensures transactions are immutable in nature, which means
  transactions cannot be altered or deleted. In order to modify existing
  transactions, the new transaction needs to be proposed.

- Blockchain transaction is processed 24/7 and can also help reduce
  transaction time to minutes.

- Provides a secured way to avoid cybersecurity and fraud risk by using trust secured algorithms.

- By eliminating third-party intermediaries and overhead cost, Blockchain has great potential to reduce transaction feeds.

- Provides alternate options of trust using centralized systems.

- Provides ways for identification and verification.

If you think about it a bit, you might agree that Blockchain is a great way to store and organize data without the need for trusted authority.

Smart Contracts

Smart Contracts are self-executing contracts. They are also known as digital contracts. Smart Contracts are not a new concept. In fact, two decades back, Nick Szabo, a computer scientist, proposed and emphasized the need for the Smart Contract while designing and implementing the decentralized based system.

The Smart Contract can be treated as a computer program that helps in executing contracts digitally. Unlike any other contract, Smart Contracts don't just define instructions and consequences around an agreement, but also enforce them. With the use of Smart Contracts, computers can take an action if some requirements get fulfilled. In raw terms, Smart Contracts are a suite of various if-else statements. Take a betting scenario case. If Real Madrid wins the La Liga, Nishith gets the money; otherwise, he pays.

In most cases, you might not trust the other party during the betting. In these scenarios, self-executing contracts bring a lot of trust on the table. Smart Contracts also bring options to revise, execute, or even propose contracts, thereby ensuring the highest level of traceability and trust. Take a use case of insurance claims. Currently, all insurance companies use the manual process of paperwork, complex execution, administration costs, etc. It would indeed be beneficial to execute these claims using Smart Contracts to ensure a hassle-free claiming process, less administration cost, and the highest level of transparency. Take another case of payment where you pay to the contractors only when they fulfills your requirement. Smart Contracts and Blockchain can be used to remove a lot of inefficiencies that exist in the contracts management process.

Ethereum

In 2013, various bloggers and Blockchain enthusiasts explored the use cases through Bitcoin. One of the bloggers named Vitalik Buterin found few limitations of Bitcoin. Bitcoin doesn't allow you to create your own smart contract or even your own currency. Earlier in this chapter, we discussed how important and impactful the smart contract can be. Vitalik reached out to the Bitcoin team with a few recommendations, such as the ability of Bitcoin to build its own currency or smart contract without requiring the need to build the entire Blockchain. Moreover, Vitalik insisted on the need for a scripting language on top of the Bitcoin system so it can be used for application development and more broader uses. Since Bitcoin implementation of Blockchain is more public and based on the shared distributed ledger, it was not possible for the Bitcoin team to implement this suggestion and they refused. Vitalik wrote a whitepaper explaining Ethereum and got a lot of funding, through which he built Ethereum, as shown in Figure 7-15.

Figure 7-15. *The Ethereum coin*

Ethereum is a shared computing platform that enables people to build smart contracts and cryptocurrencies without having people to build their own Blockchain. On top of that, it has its own Turing complete programming language that allows developers to create custom applications. Ethereum is a game changer in Blockchain implementation, as it allows everyone to adopt the Blockchain technology.

Types of Blockchain

The original concept for using Blockchain was primarily as a public, transparent, disintermediate way to store cryptocurrency. The initial success of cryptocurrency and its usage pushed across industry verticals to ensure and utilize Blockchain in an effective manner. This has led to different flavors of the original Blockchain implementation. At a high level, various implementations of Blockchain across industries can be placed into three different models, having differences in access control and network type. This means each model is different in terms of who can be part of the Blockchain network (public, on demand, etc..), who can execute a consensus protocol, and who can access Blockchain records:

- **Public Blockchain**: The original form of how Blockchain was coined. Anyone from the public can join the network, write the data under the consensus protocol, and read it. The advantage of this Blockchain type lies in being fully decentralized, transparent, and anonymous. These types of public Blockchains are applicable across various cryptocurrencies, including Bitcoin, Ethereum, litecoin, etc.

- **Private Blockchain**: Also known as internal Blockchain, this type of Blockchain implementation is designed for private networks and governed by one organization. This organization is responsible for setting up the rules to join the network and read data. Some of the trusted nodes get the higher privilege of providing acceptance of the transaction. Such types of Blockchain implementation are less expensive, faster, confidential, and only allow authenticated parties to participate in the network. Some of the examples are the Kadena chain, Iroha, and Blockchain implemented by organization internally for their processes.

- **Hybrid Blockchain**: Hybrid Blockchain is a combination of public and private Blockchain so it is a partly private, permissioned Blockchain. These types of Blockchain implementations are owned by a group of companies, forming a consortium. Such a Blockchain is efficiently used for working in a shared platform. These Blockchains only allow specific parties or nodes to be part of the Blockchain, participating in the transaction. Some of the examples include R3 Corda, Multichain, etc.

Recap

In this chapter, you learned about the history of various exchange mediums and the need of cryptocurrency. You also got a good understanding of how Bitcoin is different from Blockchain. Later in the chapter, you learned about the various types of systems (centralized, decentralized, and distributed) and learned why distributed systems are the most secure ones. The latter part of the chapter introduced you to the need for smart contracts and Ethereum. At the end of the chapter, you learned about various types of Blockchain implementation currently available. In the next chapter, we start working on the development of Blockchain and applying it to the hospital use case.

CHAPTER 8

Implementing Blockchain as a Service

In the last chapter, you learned about the emergence of Blockchain and the very core reason for building Blockchain was cryptocurrency, especially Bitcoin. Over the years, various industry verticals started using Blockchain technology for non-payment systems. As we mentioned in the previous chapter, Blockchain changes the way we trust. While writing this book, various industries across verticals are transforming their individual business cases with the power of Blockchain. Every day new use cases are getting evolved on how Blockchain technology can transform a specific vertical. There is absolutely no denial of the fact that Blockchain is going to disrupt every vertical in the very massive way that one can imagine and would be the source of the next industrial revolution.

One of the core roadblocks of utilizing technologies like Blockchain is to have the necessary infrastructure to support it. Setting up the initial Blockchain requires a huge investment in terms of infrastructure. Apart from setting your own closed virtual private network, it also involves some of the servers reserved for doing the transaction and others reserved for doing mining, making them available always and if required, adding more transaction and mining nodes. Setting this environment is not just time-consuming, complex, and costly. Most of the non-technology and mid-size technology companies might find it difficult to create their own infrastructure.

This problem of infrastructure is quite similar to infrastructure problems that led to the emergence of the Cloud infrastructure. This resulted in the eruption of new technology infrastructure commonly known as Infrastructure as a Service (IaaS). Various Blockchain pioneer companies also felt the need to provide Blockchain infrastructure in the Cloud so they could just focus on development rather than worrying about infrastructure. The setup done by these companies was called Blockchain as a Service (BaaS). Companies providing BaaS are called BaaS providers and companies and people

© Nishith Pathak and Anurag Bhandari 2018
N. Pathak and A. Bhandari, *IoT, AI, and Blockchain for .NET*, https://doi.org/10.1007/978-1-4842-3709-0_8

consuming them are called BaaS consumers. As a BaaS consumer, you pay for the BaaS infrastructure most preferably on a pay-as-you-use basis. BaaS emergence has paved the way for rapid adoption of Blockchain technologies.

Tip   While writing this book, each industry leader created their own BaaS offering. This creates a thought of relying on just one centralized third party. In the future, we expect companies to collaborate on BaaS and to have a more decentralized BaaS offering

---

Microsoft provides a suite of BaaS offerings, ranging from R3 corda, hyperledger fabric, Ethereum, and so on, all of which sit on Microsoft Azure. Depending on your business use case, you can pick one of the Azure Blockchain predefined templates to get started. Like all other Microsoft Azure offerings and services, BaaS offerings for each of the Blockchain implementations come with free and paid tiers. At the end of this chapter, you'll understand

- The Enterprise Ethereum Alliance

- The Ethereum jargon

- Understand how to set up a Blockchain leader Consortium in Azure

- How to transfer Ether within Blockchain

- How to build, test, and deploy smart contracts

Enterprise Ethereum Alliance

Started in 2015, Ethereum has slowly been adopted across the globe. In 2017, industry leaders and academia titans understood the need for collaboration to support Ethereum and so formed the Enterprise Ethereum Alliance (EEA). EEA is a non-profit cooperation supporting fortune 500 companies and academia across the globe, as shown in Figure 8-1.

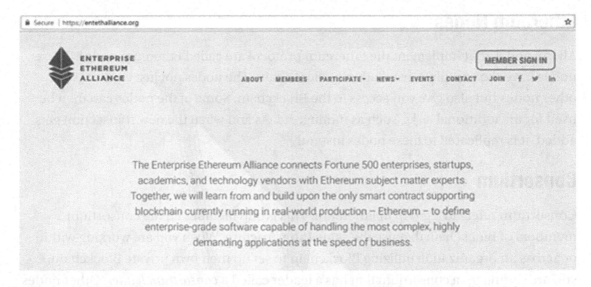

Figure 8-1. *The home page of Enterprise Ethereum Alliance. If you haven't visited EEA, we suggest you visit the page and view the list of member companies supporting the Ethereum.*

Understanding Ethereum Jargon

Before we look at the Ethereum terms, it is important to know why Ethereum has been so popular and has created deep roots at the enterprise level. There are multiple reasons for it, but primarily it's because Ethereum is open source and is more suited for creating a private Blockchain. Compared to Bitcoin, Ethereum can execute transactions faster. While writing this book, Ethereum community support has rapidly increased so developers get a lot of community support and help, which contributes to faster development. Let's quickly look at the Ethereum terms that are widely used in the Ethereum community.

Ethereum Virtual Machine (EVM)

The Ethereum network is made up of various computers or large decentralized computers that are together called the Ethereum Virtual Machine (EVM).

Ethereum Nodes

All the nodes that implement the Ethereum protocol are called Ethereum nodes. These nodes have the complete installation of Blockchain. The nodes not just connect with other nodes but also give you access to the Blockchain. Some of the nodes can then be used for an additional tasks, such as mining, etc. As and when the new transaction gets added, it is replicated to these nodes instantly.

Consortium

Consortium refers to a group in Ethereum. This group includes all the consortium members of Blockchain that use the same infrastructure. When you are working within or across an organization utilizing Blockchain to set up their own private Blockchain, you are setting up a consortium that has a leader called a *consortium leader*. Other nodes being part of the consortium are called *consortium nodes*.

Consortium Leader

Like any group leader, the first and foremost thing to do when setting up an Ethereum consortium is to identify the consortium leader, as shown in Figure 8-2. The consortium leader is responsible for the following:

- Setting up and configuring a private Blockchain
- Deciding on the criteria for joining the privately owned network
- Setting up criteria for allocation of Ether, etc.

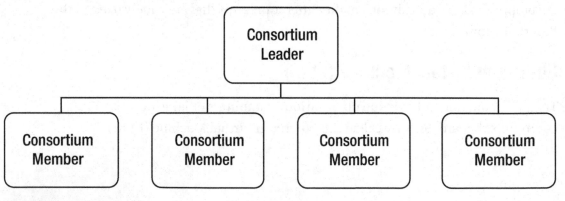

Figure 8-2. *The hierarchical structure of the consortium leader with the members in Ethereum*

The consortium leader heads the privately owned Blockchain and all other consortium members follow the rules and criteria set by the consortium leader. Once the consortium leader is set up, other members can join with their own infrastructure or use the existing one. Asclepius (our fictitious hospital) is using Blockchain to track a distributed ledger for a lot of work. It also collaborates with other hospitals and branches. The main branch of Asclepius is working as the consortium leader.

Ether

Ether is the currency used for transactions in Ethereum. There are many other cryptocurrencies along with Ether that can be used in Ethereum, as shown in Figure 8-3.

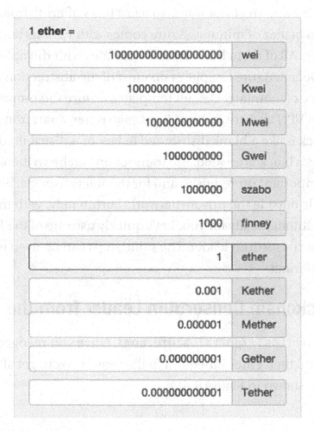

Figure 8-3.   The Ether conversion to other Ethereum used cryptocurrencies. Image source https://forum.ethereum.org/discussion/1518/ether-unit-converter-wei-finney-szabo-btc

Ether can be used as a payment mechanism or even to authenticate the user.

Gas

Every EVM node requires a good amount of processing power to execute code. While working on Blockchain, it is important to understand the computational effort required to execute specific code, which is denoted as Gas in the Blockchain world. Once an EVM node has enough gas to run the code, it is later awarded goodies like additional Ether for the proof of work. Let's now look at how to set up Ethereum using Azure.

Setting Up Ethereum

There are many ways to set up the Ethereum network. One way is to set up the entire infrastructure of your own. An easier way is to use a BaaS offering from Azure to quickly set up Ethereum in a matter of minutes. Azure comes with various templates for creating a Blockchain offering. All of them have default templates with the option to customize each one of them. Default Azure templates do most of the abstraction and should be your preferred choice of template. Default templates ensure the transaction and mining nodes are part of the VPN and are isolated from each other, apart from creating a genesis block. A genesis block is like a blank distributed ledger or a distributed ledger with no data. Once the genesis block is created, the transaction can be written on top of the block. It is also an important prerequisite and for the safety aspects, that mining node should not accessible outside the private network. Fortunately, with the default Azure template, it is done automatically for you. Let's quickly use one of the Blockchain Azure templates to create a consortium leader. The same steps can be used to create other Blockchain Azure offerings.

Creating a Blockchain Consortium Leader from the Azure Portal

Open and navigate to `https://portal.azure.com/`. Once you're logged in, click on Create a Resource and then enter Ethereum in the search box to get all the Ethereum related templates, as shown in Figure 8-4.

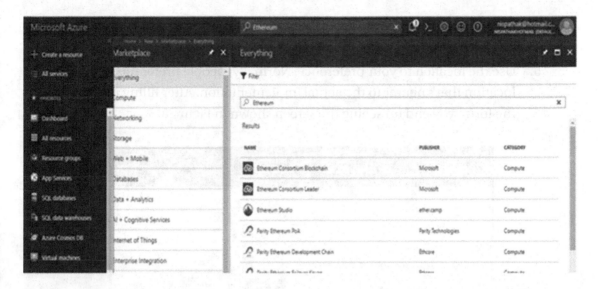

Figure 8-4. *The Ethereum related templates in Azure Portal. Microsoft is developing new templates. As you read the book, there will much more Ethereum related templates than shown here.*

Select Ethereum Consortium Leader. Use the same deployment model and Click on Create to start the Ethereum Consortium leader wizard interface, as shown in Figure 8-5.

1. Specify the resource prefix to differentiate it from another template. For our convenience, we will use eth. You can use a prefix of your own choice.

2. In order to log in to the various nodes, a username is required. For convenience, we stick with the default username, gethadmin. For the password, you have an option to either use a SSH public key or a password. For the demo, we are using a password for now but you can opt for the SSH public key. The password should have at least one uppercase, one lowercase, one number, and one special character.

3. Choose the subscription as assigned. If you haven't purchased a paid subscription, you get the Free Trial option. If you are going to use it in production, it's better to use a paid subscription instead of a free trial.

4. Create a new resource group to have future permissions and
    policy consistent.

5. Use the location to your preference. Normally, people prefer the
    location that's nearer to the actual implementation. After filling in
    the form, you end up seeing the screen shown in Figure 8-5.

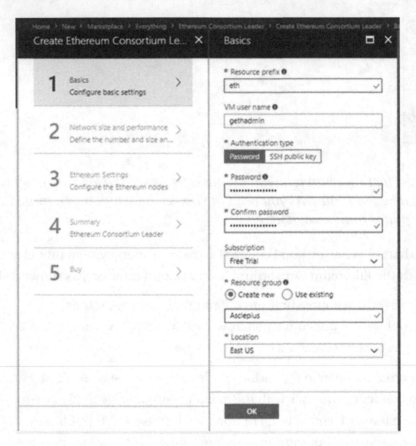

Figure 8-5. *The first screen of the Ethereum consortium leader wizard interface*

Click OK to navigate and specify the network size and performance for the transaction and mining nodes, as shown in Figure 8-6.

1. Each consortium member is identified with a separate ID. As we are creating the consortium leader, let's keep it set to 0 for now. Additional nodes can be added later as well.

2. Specify the mining nodes per member. This value should be set depending on your availability requirements. A maximum of 15 can be set. For now, we are using the default value of 2. It can be changed later.

3. Choose the mining node storage from standard or premium. Azure provides various node storage options to create mining node storage. Standard uses a normal magnetic drive while Premium uses solid state drives. If you require higher IO, use Premium. By default, a virtual machine size of 2x Standard D1 v2 is set. If you need it higher, you can change it by clicking the > sign next to the mining virtual machine size.

4. While setting the storage node, you can set the redundancy locally or globally.

5. Apply the default settings for the transaction node.

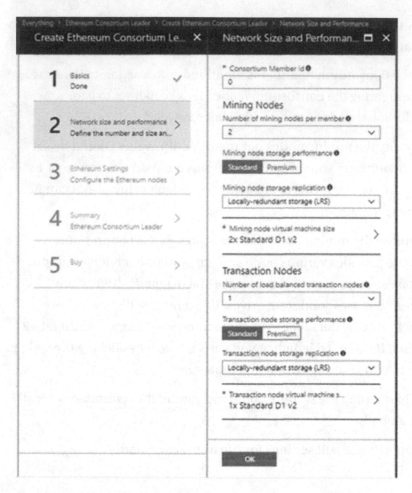

Figure 8-6. *The network size and performance setting in the Ethereum consortium leader wizard*

Click OK and navigate to the Ethereum account setting, as shown in Figure 8-7.

1. The Network ID is the unique ID through which the Ethereum account is identified. This ID eventually is used for pairing nodes. All nodes having the same ID can be paired with each other. You can go with the default Ethereum network ID or specify a custom one.

2. Specify whether you want the portal to automatically create a new genesis block or whether you want to customize it. For now, let Azure create a genesis block for you.

3. Specify the password for the default account created.

4. Specify the passphrase, as shown in Figure 8-7.

Figure 8-7. *Configuring the Ethereum related settings*

Click OK and review the summary to double validate your options. If everything looks good, click OK, as shown in Figure 8-8.

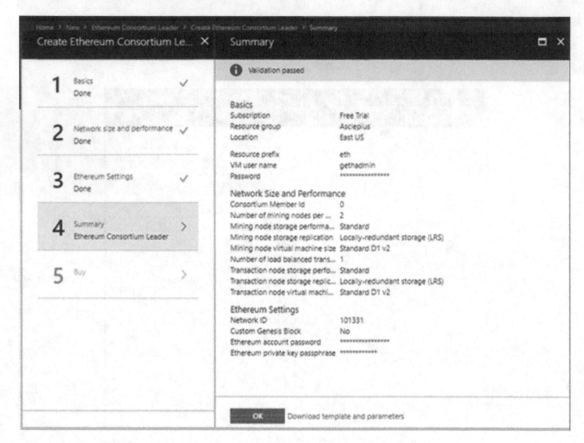

Figure 8-8. *The summary of all the settings you have done to configure the Ethereum consortium network*

Read the permissions, check the terms of use, and click Create, as shown in Figure 8-9.

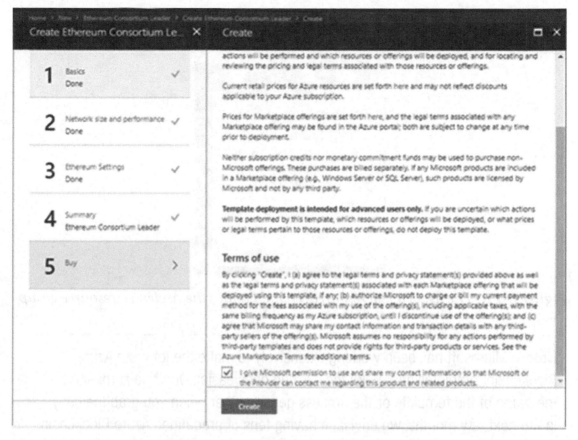

Figure 8-9. *The terms of use for the Ethereum Blockchain consortium leader*

It will take some time to create the Azure Blockchain. Notification in Azure, as shown in Figure 8-10, will keep informing you about the progress.

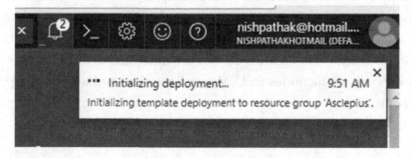

Figure 8-10. *The notification for initializing the deployment of the Asclepius group*

After initializing, procuring, and deploying the Ethereum Blockchain account, you will see it as shown in Figure 8-11.

Figure 8-11. *The list of a few resources created under the Asclepius resource group*

Note   Microsoft has been working extensively to make the lot more Azure Blockchain templates and make the existing ones easier. Don't be surprised if the name of the template or the process get smoother when you grab the copy. In the next few months, we envisage having tens of predefined Azure Blockchain templates for your business case to promote Blockchain as a Service extensively.

Exploring the Newly Created Ethereum Account

Open your Azure Portal and then the resource group, as mentioned in the left rail. Select the Asclepius resource group link previously created while setting up the Ethereum account. Click on the Asclepius link. Your resource name might be different based on how you set it up, as shown in Figure 8-12. You are navigated to the Asclepius resource group that shows you all the nodes and VMs previously created while setting up the Asclepius account.

Figure 8-12. *The list of all the resources created*

As shown in Figure 8-12, behind the scenes, a lot of activities were happening that included the creation of a load balancer, VMs, and security groups, to name a few. Imagine how much time it would take to create these at your infrastructure. This is a classic example of the power of using a Cloud infrastructure like Azure. Thanks to the Azure Ethereum Leader template, abstracting it and developing the necessary infrastructure takes just a few clicks. Click on Deployments on the left rail to see all the deployments, as shown in Figure 8-13.

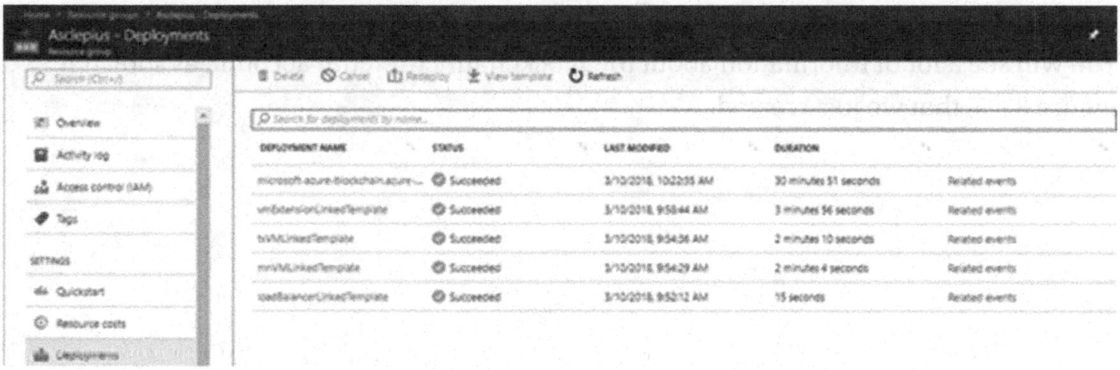

Figure 8-13. *The Deployments list. The first one starting with Microsoft Azure is the deployment of the private Ethereum network.*

Click on the first link, Microsoft-azure-Blockchain, to get overview details and then click on the output link to view all the information, as shown in Figure 8-14. It contains all information and endpoints details, such as the URL of the Admin site, the Ethereum RPC endpoint to connect, and the Gateway ID, to name a few.

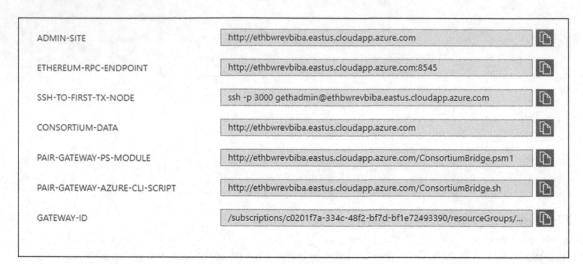

Figure 8-14. *All the Ethereum related links. The first two links—the Admin site and Ethereum-RPC-Endpoint—will be used extensively.*

It's time to quickly open the Ethereum Admin site.

Ethereum Default Admin Site

Open the Admin site by copying the address of Admin site previously created in Figure 8-14. You will see a lot of information about the Blockchain Ethereum account, as shown in Figure 8-15, that we just created.

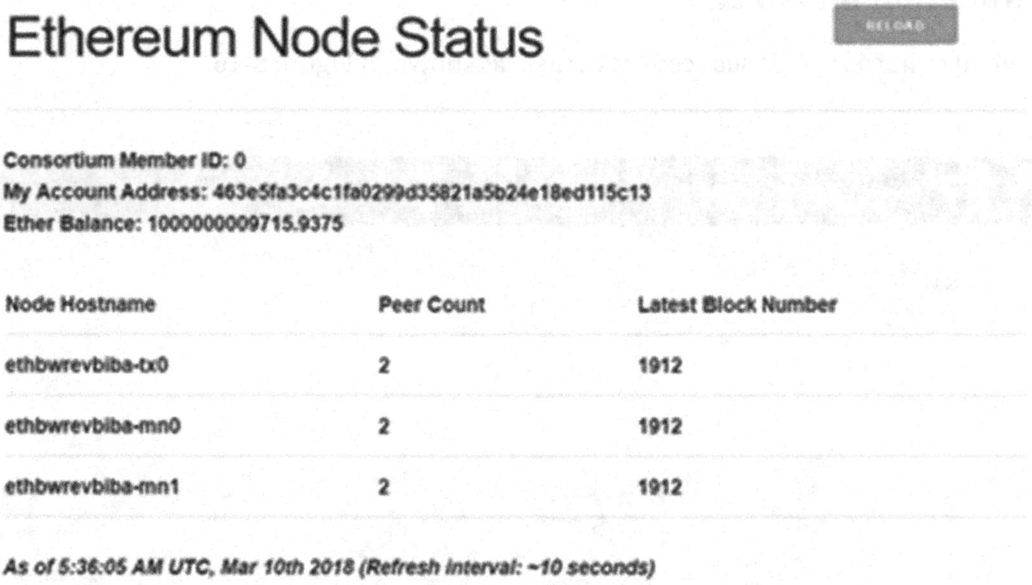

Ethereum Node Status

RELOAD

Consortium Member ID: 0
My Account Address: 463e5fa3c4c1fa0299d35821a5b24e18ed115c13
Ether Balance: 1000000009715.9375

Node Hostname	Peer Count	Latest Block Number
ethbwrevbiba-tx0	2	1912
ethbwrevbiba-mn0	2	1912
ethbwrevbiba-mn1	2	1912

As of 5:36:05 AM UTC, Mar 10th 2018 (Refresh interval: ~10 seconds)

Figure 8-15. *The home page of the default Ethereum Admin site*

You will see the address of the default genesis account that Azure created. You will also see a good amount of private Ether being allocated to this account for testing purposes.

Tip   It is important to understand that these private Ethers can't be transacted, transferred, or even used in public or any other Blockchain account.

We now see how to transfer this Ether to other accounts. This requires having two nodes sharing the same network ID. This is one of the ways to test whether your Ethereum consortium leader network is working properly. The best and fastest way is to test via a browser plugin called MetaMask.

Installation MetaMask

Navigate to `https://github.com/metamask`, as shown in Figure 8-16.

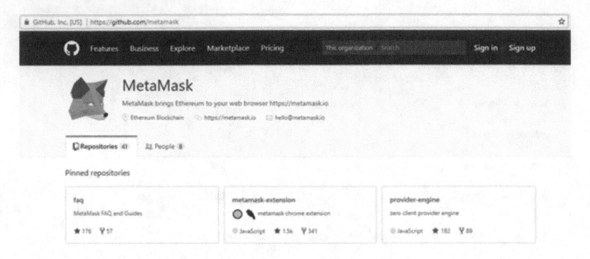

Figure 8-16. *The MetaMask home page in GitHub*

Click on metamask-extension and then on Releases. Download the chrome extension version. Extract the ZIP file to some folder. Open Chrome, navigate to Extensions, and click on Developer Mode, as shown in Figure 8-17.

Figure 8-17. *The Chrome extension page for enabling developer mode*

Click on Load Unpacked extension after checking Developer mode. Navigate to the folder where the `metamask.zip` file was extracted. Click OK. Once you're done, you will see the fox icon on your chrome extension, as shown in Figure 8-18.

Figure 8-18. *The MetaMask extension installed a Chrome extension*

Disabled the developer mode. Click on the fox icon again and accept the terms. Create a new password that you can remember. It will then give the user a set of 12 words that can be used to restore all your accounts. You will now be logged in to Ropsten Test. net and have less Ether, as shown in Figure 8-19.

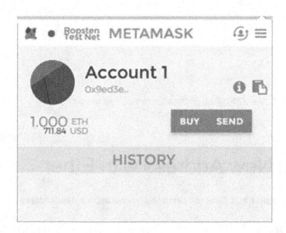

Figure 8-19. *The default home page of MetaMask plugin when opened for the first time*

In order to transfer the Ether from the newly created Blockchain, copy the Ethereum RPC endpoint link that was previously created (see Figure 8-14). Click Settings on the top right of MetaMask plugin. Paste the Ethereum endpoint link that you copied and click on Save. Once you're done, your UI of MetaMask will show that you are now connected to a private network (instead of Ropsten Test Net), as shown in Figure 8-20.

Figure 8-20. *The MetaMask plugin connected with private Blockchain network rather than the default network*

Copy the address of newly created account and navigate back to the Admin Ethereum site. Scroll down and paste the address as shown here. Then specify the number of Ethers to transfer and click on Submit, as shown in Figure 8-21.

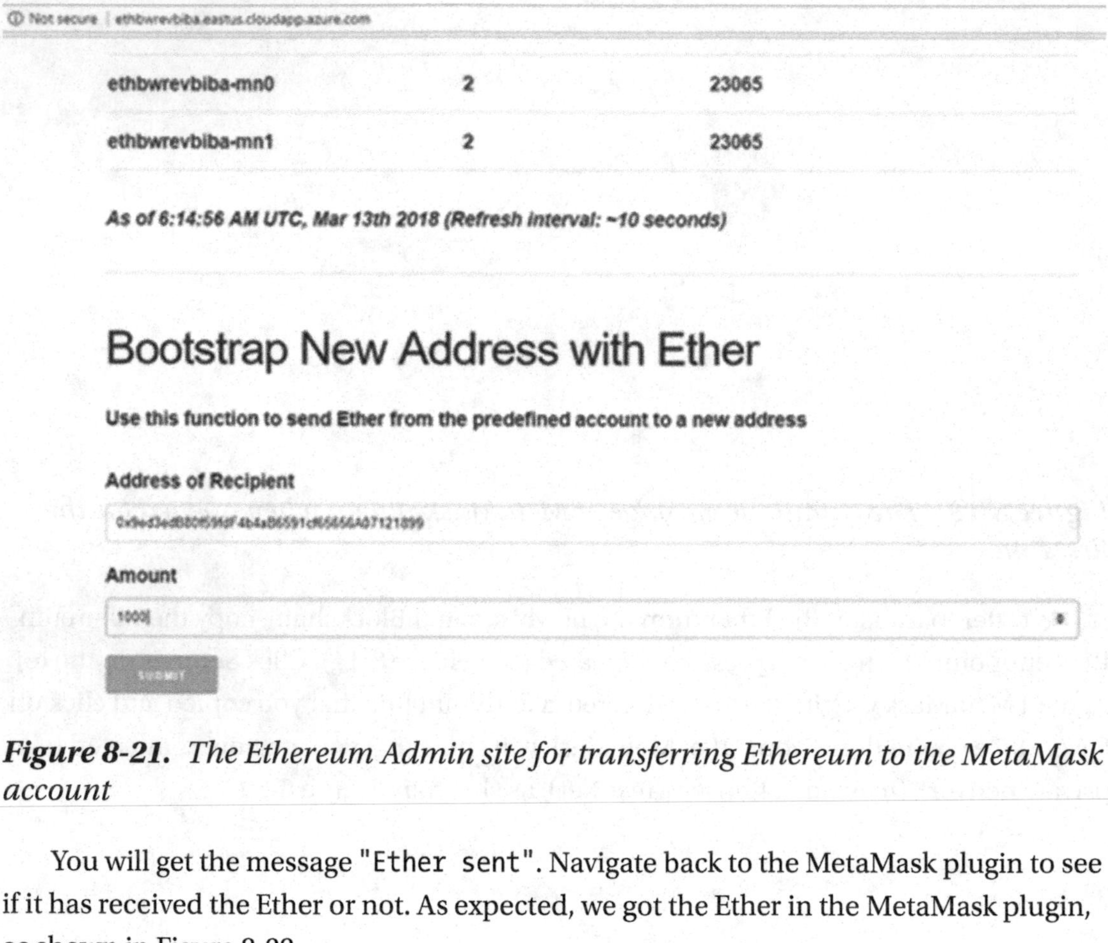

Figure 8-21. *The Ethereum Admin site for transferring Ethereum to the MetaMask account*

You will get the message "Ether sent". Navigate back to the MetaMask plugin to see if it has received the Ether or not. As expected, we got the Ether in the MetaMask plugin, as shown in Figure 8-22.

Figure 8-22.   *The Ether received in the MetaMask plugin from the Ethereum Admin site*

Congratulations! Your Blockchain network is working and you are good to add more consortium members, transfer Ethers, and use it for further development. Normally, Ethers are only rewarded to consortium members when they execute a specific computational task. Most of these tasks go hand in hand with the execution of smart contracts. Let's now look at how to create Smart Contracts.

Smart Contracts in Asclepius

In the previous chapter, we discussed the importance of Smart Contracts. In Asclepius, the Smart Contract is widely used in various scenarios to avoid paperwork for tasks such as maintaining health records, prescriptions, insurance claims, etc. Two of the other uses of the Smart Contract are briefly discussed:

- The Smart Contract is used in Asclepius during the claims adjustment process. Previously, when the Smart Contracts were not introduced, patients had a lot of paperwork, including negotiation with health payers or insurance providers, and most of the time, patients ended up in paying claims. This process has been greatly reduced through the introduction of Smart Contracts and using the power of Blockchain.

- Patient information and medical records, including medical prescriptions and doctor details, are stored in Blockchain and only authorized users as per patient and healthcare provider Smart Contracts are eligible to access this data. This helps not only to

231

maintain immutable medical historic records of the patients, but ensures data integrity. Every treatment of the patients is added to this smart contract. This also enables instant verification of medical records without the need of a third party.

These are just two of the many use cases in which Asclepius uses Smart Contracts. With Blockchain and Smart Contracts, Asclepius can become a trusted partner, by ensuring that they are storing all patients' records digitally and securely, and making relevant data easily accessible with proper authorization.

Developing Smart Contracts

You can write Smart Contracts easily using Notepad and a Smart Contracts compiler. It would be very tedious to build, test, and deploy Smart Contracts on your own. In order to develop Smart Contracts, the following software is required for ensuring a proper development environment.

Package Managers

Install the Node Packet Manager (NPM). Navigate to https://nodejs.org/en/ and download the latest version available.

Truffle

Truffle provides a built-in compiler for Smart Contracts that help in compiling and deploying the solution. Once the solution is built, Truffle also provides development, testing, and deployment of Smart Contracts very easily. In order to install the Truffle toolset, open PowerShell in administrative mode and run the command shown here:

```
C:\> npm install -g truffle
C:\Users\nishith\AppData\Roaming\npm\truffle -> C:\Users\nishith\AppData\
Roaming\npm\node_modules\truffle\build\cli.bundled.js
+ truffle@4.1.3
updated 1 package in 13.964s
```

Note   Truffle is a great tool for compiling, deploying, and testing smart contract solutions. However, there are quite a number of other tools available in the market, like Remix (`http://remix.ethereum.org`), Mist browser, and others that provide GUI based interface. One real advantage of using tools like Remix is that you don't need to install anything on your machine. However, we personally prefer Truffle, as while developing enterprise application, you do need to worry about enterprise policies that don't support using web-based solutions to compile and deploy.

Once Truffle is installed, you can initialize it to get the basic project structure and get started quickly, as shown here:

```
C:\samplecontract> truffle init
Downloading...
Unpacking...
Settingup...
Unbox successfully. Sweet !

Commands :
Compile:        truffle compile
Migrate:        truffle migrate
Test contracts:        truffle tests
```

It ends up creating a couple of folders, as shown in Figure 8-23.

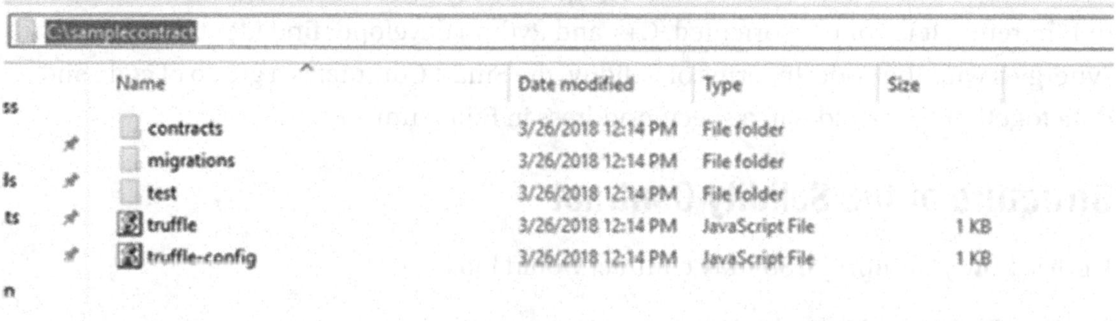

Figure 8-23. Folders created after initializing the Truffle template on a folder

Each of the folders contains specific files.

- The Contracts folder contains all Solidity contracts. Place all your newly created contracts in the Contracts folder.

- The Migrations folder contains scripts for deploying contracts. Once new contracts are created, the migration scripts need to be updated to include new contracts.

- The Test folder contains files for testing applications and contracts.

In order to work properly with Truffle, ensure you create the right files in their appropriate folders.

Code Editor

The Truffle toolset provides the great tool for development. However, you still need a code editor for writing Smart Contracts. You are free to use any code editor, including Notepad. If you are from a .NET background, we suggest you use Visual Studio. While writing this book, Solidity (the language used to create a Smart Contracts for Ethereum) has extension support only up to Visual Studio 2015 (and not Visual Studio 2017). However, Solidity extensions are supported in Visual Studio code for 2017. You can opt to install any version of Visual Studio 2015 or you can use Visual Studio code. Our personal preference has been the latter, as it provides faster development. Install the latest version of your preferred editor.

Solidity

There are a couple of languages that create Smart Contracts. Of those, the most popular and widely used is Solidity. It's the most popular language for creating Smart Contracts in Ethereum. It is contract oriented. C++ and Python developer find identical syntax and synergies with the code. In terms of Solidity, the Smart Contract is a group of code and data together that resides in a specific address in Ethereum.

Structure of the Solidity Contract

Here is how your normal Solidity contract would look:

```
Pragma Solidity ^<versionname>;
Contract <<contractname>>
{
```

```
Contract fields
Contract events
Contract functions
}
```

The first line of any Solidity contract is always `pragma solidity ^<versionname>`, where the version name is replaced by an actual version of Solidity. This line is an instruction to the Solidity compiler. What it means is the Solidity source code is written to the version name. The application will only compile in the same major version. Any change to a major version would not compile the program. This line ensures that the code written in earlier versions doesn't suddenly break. Any contract has the contract name followed by all the fields, events, and function declarations, and definitions with those two braces { and }. Here is the solidity contract for storing patient details:

```
pragma solidity ^0.4.2;

contract PatientDetail {
    enum Gender { Male, Female }
    struct PatientName {
        String PatientId;
        String name;
        String Description;
        uint age;
        Gender gender;
        uint admissionDate;
        uint releaseDate;
    }

     PatientDetail patient;
    function getPatientDetail(string id) public view returns (struct
    patient) {
        //code for returning patient detail
    }

}
```

This code as the `pragma` instruction for the compiler, followed by a contract containing a structure to store patient details. It has the function of fetching patient details. Let's look at a Smart Contract used by Asclepius for storing the `medicalasset`. Open the Smartcontract folder previously created in the Visual Studio code. Navigate to the Contracts folder. Right-click to choose a new file, create a new file called `medicalcontracts.sol.`, and copy the contract to it. Click Save.

```solidity
pragma solidity ^0.4.2;

contract MedicalAssestStorage {
struct AssetDetail {
    string assetName; //store the asset name
    string desc; //store the description of the asset
    string prodOrigin; //store the actual origin of the asset
    bool isAvailable; // determine where this asset is available or not
}

mapping(string  => AssetDetail)  assetinfo;
string[] public assetList;
mapping(address => mapping(string => bool))  myWallet;

event evtCreateAsset(address account, string assetId, string prodOrigin);
event evtRejectAsset(address account, string assetId, string message);
event evtTransferAsset(address from, address to, string assetId);
event evtTransferReject(address from, address to, string assetId, string message);

function createAsset(string assetName, string assetId, string description, string prodOrigin) public {

    if(assetinfo[assetId].isAvailable) {
        evtRejectAsset(msg.sender, assetId, "This Asset ID already exists.");
        return;
    }

    assetinfo[assetId].assetName = assetName;
    assetinfo[assetId].desc = description;
    assetinfo[assetId].prodOrigin = prodOrigin;
    assetinfo[assetId].isAvailable = true;
```

```
        myWallet[msg.sender][assetId] = true;
        evtCreateAsset(msg.sender, assetId, prodOrigin);
}

function transferAsset(address to, string assetId) public {

    if(!assetinfo[assetId].isAvailable) {
        evtTransferReject(msg.sender, to, assetId, "No asset with this
        Asset Id exists");
        return;
    }

    if(!myWallet[msg.sender][assetId]) {
        evtTransferReject(msg.sender, to, assetId, "Sender does not own
        this Asset.");
        return;
    }

    myWallet[msg.sender][assetId]= false;
    myWallet[to][assetId] = true;
    evtTransferAsset(msg.sender, to, assetId);
}

function getAsset(string assetId) public view returns (string, string,
string) {

    return (assetinfo[assetId].assetName, assetinfo[assetId].desc,
    assetinfo[assetId].prodOrigin);

}

function isOwnerOf(address owner, string assetId) public view returns (bool) {

    if(myWallet[owner][assetId]) {
        return true;
    }

}
}
```

Understanding the Code

First and foremost, the contract with the name MedicalAssestStorage is created. To store the necessary asset, the structure name AssetDetail is being created.

```
struct AssetDetail {
    string assetName;
    string desc;
    string prodOrigin;
    bool isAvailable;
}
```

AssetDetail as a structure is used to store and track the assets. These assets can be used to track instruments and hospital equipment while getting transferred across assets. Asclepius is a chain of hospitals, so it wants to ensure transparency in maintaining laboratory inventory and ensuring that if required, assets can be transferred from one hospital to another. For tracking, the asset is first mapped to a string.

```
mapping(string  => AssetDetail)  assetinfo;
```

Various events are created to track whenever an asset is created, transferred, or rejected.

```
event evtCreateAsset(address account, string assetId, string prodOrigin);
event evtRejectAsset(address account, string assetId, string message);
event evtTransferAsset(address from, address to, string assetId);
event evtTransferReject(address from, address to, string assetId, string message);
```

Later, functions like createAsset and transferAsset are created to add a new asset to Asclepius or to transfer it to any other Asclepius chain.

```
function createAsset(string assetName, string assetId, string description, string prodOrigin) public {

    if(assetinfo[assetId].isAvailable) {
        evtRejectAsset(msg.sender, assetId, "This Asset ID already
        exists.");
        return;
    }
```

```
        assetinfo[assetId].assetName = assetName;
        assetinfo[assetId].desc = description;
        assetinfo[assetId].prodOrigin = prodOrigin;
        assetinfo[assetId].isAvailable = true;
        myWallet[msg.sender][assetId] = true;
        evtCreateAsset(msg.sender, assetId, prodOrigin);
}

function transferAsset(address to, string assetId) public {

    if(!assetinfo[assetId].isAvailable) {
        evtTransferReject(msg.sender, to, assetId, "No asset with this
        Asset Id exists");
        return;
    }

    if(!myWallet[msg.sender][assetId]) {
        evtTransferReject(msg.sender, to, assetId, "Sender does not own
        this Asset.");
        return;
    }

    myWallet[msg.sender][assetId]= false;
    myWallet[to][assetId] = true;
    evtTransferAsset(msg.sender, to, assetId);
}
```

Lastly, to track who owns the asset and where the actual asset lies, the getAsset and isOwnerof functions are created.

```
function getAsset(string assetId) public view returns (string, string,
string) {

    return (assetinfo[assetId].assetName, assetinfo[assetId].desc,
    assetInfo[assetId].prodOrigin);

}
```

```
function isOwnerOf(address owner, string assetId) public view returns (bool) {

    if(myWallet[owner][assetId]) {
        return true;
    }
}
```

Compiling a Contract

Once the contract is created, the next step is to make the Truffle built-in compiler aware of the new contracts created. Modify the JavaScript file under the Migration folder to include the newly created medicalcontracts.sol, as shown here:

```
var medicalcontract = artifacts.require("./medicalcontracts.sol");
module.exports = function(deployer) {
 deployer.deploy(medicalcontract);
  };
```

In this code, we first created the variable that points to the newly created medicalcontracts. We then add the variable to the deployer. Modify the truffle.js file to point to the endpoint previously created in the Azure Portal. The new file should be something like what's shown here:

```
module.exports = {
  // See <http://truffleframework.com/docs/advanced/configuration>
  // to customize your Truffle configuration!
  networks: {
    development: {
      host: "ethbwrevbiba.eastus.cloudapp.azure.com",
      port: 8545,
      network_id: "*" // Match any network id
    }
  }
};
```

Note   In this example, we are deploying directly to Ethereum private Blockchain endpoint. It is always advisable to test the contracts before deploying to the private Blockchain. The best way to test your contract locally is to install `testrpc` from Ethereum.js using the command `npm install -g ethereumjs-testrpc` and then run the `testrpc`. Once you install `testrpc`, it runs under the localhost with port 8545 by default.

Once the contracts are created, navigate to:

```
C:\samplecontract> truffle compile
Compiling .\contracts\medicalcontracts.sol...
Writing artifacts to .\build\contracts
```

Once this is compiled, you are ready to deploy your contract to the Blockchain. Use the `truffle deploy` command to deploy the contract on Blockchain. Congratulations! Your contract is now being deployed on the Blockchain. Once your transaction is deployed, you can see transaction being sent in detail, as shown in Figure 8-24.

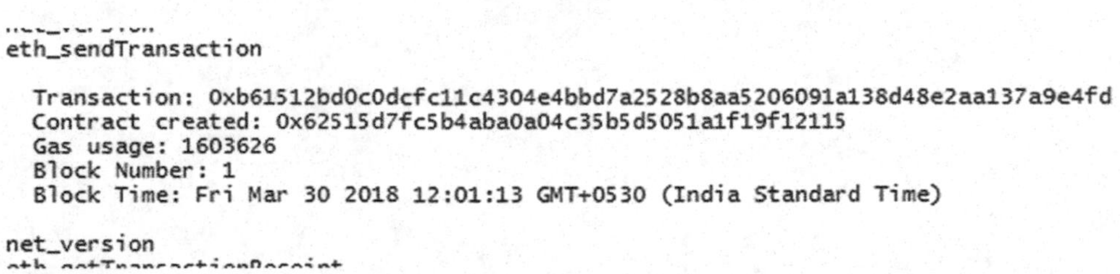

```
eth_sendTransaction

  Transaction: 0xb61512bd0c0dcfc11c4304e4bbd7a2528b8aa5206091a138d48e2aa137a9e4fd
  Contract created: 0x62515d7fc5b4aba0a04c35b5d5051a1f19f12115
  Gas usage: 1603626
  Block Number: 1
  Block Time: Fri Mar 30 2018 12:01:13 GMT+0530 (India Standard Time)

net_version
```

Figure 8-24. *The execution of a transaction in the console*

Recap

In this chapter, you learned about Ethereum and learned how to set up Ethereum quickly using built-in Azure templates. Microsoft has invested in promoting Blockchain using built-in Azure templates. Solidity is a language for building Smart Contracts and is developing as we speak. Every week new changes are being proposed, accepted, and taken forward. As mentioned earlier, while you read these chapters, some of the options change with new options coming that make it easier to use the Blockchain infrastructure. Concepts for using Blockchain and using Solidity to create Smart Contracts remain the same. There is no doubt that we have an exciting time ahead in the Blockchain arena. All of the technology for AI 2.0, like Blockchain, IoT Hub, and consuming Cognitive Services have one thing in common—they generate a humungous amount of data. Data is of no use unless you can analyze it and get insights to make decisions quickly. In the next chapter, you learn how to use this data to capture, analyze, and visual real-time data quickly.

CHAPTER 9

Capturing, Analyzing, and Visualizing Real-Time Data

Having come this far, you are now equipped with the knowledge of how to create next generation AI 2.0 applications. In your arsenal, you have weapons, such as Cognitive Services, IoT Hub, and Blockchain, to help you create truly cutting-edge intelligent solutions for clients, customers, or your own organization. From a developer's perspective, you are fully equipped. However, developing solutions is only part of a bigger picture, no matter how big it is.

While solutions solve problems, they usually generate a ton of data along the way, some of which is consumed by the application itself to make instantaneous decisions. It is no longer uncommon for an application to generate massive mountains of data (think several gigabytes per hour), something that is not always possible to consume and analyze simultaneously by the application itself. This is especially true in scenarios involving IoT. Such data is then stored (in cloud) for later analysis using Big Data techniques. "Later" could be minutes, hours, or days.

However, real-time analysis of such massive amounts of data is sometimes desirable. Healthcare is one domain where real-time analysis and notifications could save lives. For example, monitoring the pulse rate of all patients in a hospital, to keep tabs on their heart conditions, and raising alarms when abnormal rates are detected. Timely attention can make all the difference in saving a patient's life.

You saw a preliminary form of real-time analysis in Chapter 3, where our solution backend was continuously reading all data written to our IoT Hub to detect high temperature conditions. To keep things simple, our solution catered to only one patient (we had exactly one simulated device to fake sending a virtual patient's vitals to the hub).

© Nishith Pathak and Anurag Bhandari 2018
N. Pathak and A. Bhandari, *IoT, AI, and Blockchain for .NET*, https://doi.org/10.1007/978-1-4842-3709-0_9

In the real world, a sufficiently large hospital may have hundreds or thousands of patients at any given point in time. Although the solution in Chapter 3 is designed to be scale up to millions of devices—thanks to Azure's IoT Hub service—our primitive solution backend application will crash when trying to analyze such volumes of data in real time.

Azure Stream Analytics (ASA) provides a way to perform complex analyses on large amounts of data in real time. Power BI complements ASA by providing beautiful visual charts and statistics—based on results produced by ASA—that even completely non-tech-savvy staff can use to take decisions.

By the end of this chapter, you will learn to:

- Create, configure, start, and stop an Azure Stream Analytics job

- Use a storage backend (Azure Blob Storage) to store ASA analysis results

- Create graphical dashboards in Power BI to show ASA analysis results in real time

Azure Stream Analytics

Data that systems deal with is in one of two forms—static or stream. Static data is unchanging or slow changing data usually stored in files and databases. For example, historic archives, old log files, inventory data, etc. For a thorough analysis of such data, no matter how large, one can use data analytics applications, libraries, and services. Azure HDInsight, Hadoop, R, and Python are commonly used tools for this purpose. You may use Stream Analytics for analysis of static data, but that is not what it is made for.

Streaming data, on the other hand, is a continuous, real-time chain of data records that a system receives at a rate of hundreds or thousands of records per second. You may have heard the terms "stream" and "streaming" in the context of online videos, especially when they are being made available live (directly from recording camera to viewers, in real time). Apart from being consumed by end users, video streams can also be analyzed to produce key statistics, such as occurrences of a person or object through the video, dominant colors, faces, and emotions, etc. We saw hints about video analytics using AI (cognitive services) in Chapters 4 and 5. But analyzing video streams is not as common as analyzing other data streams.

Some examples of data streams that are frequently analyzed are shown in Table 9-1.

Table 9-1. *Examples of Streaming Data and Analysis That Can Be Performed on Them*

Data Stream	Example Analysis Use Case
Pages visited and elements clicked (buttons, textboxes, links, etc.) on a website by all its visitors. Plus, data about visitors themselves— IP address (location), browser, OS, etc. Collectively known as clickstream.	Finding out most visited pages, most read sections, most popular visitor locations, etc.
Social media posts for a trending topic.	Finding out the overall and location-based sentiments about the topic.
Stock market prices.	Calculating value-at-risk, automatic rebalancing of portfolios, suggesting stocks to invest in based on overall intra-hour performance.
Frequent updates (telemetry data) from a large number of IoT devices.	Depends on the type of data collected by the devices.

Azure Stream Analytics is specially designed to deal with streaming data. As a result, it excels in situations requiring real-time analysis. Like other Azure services, ASA is highly scalable and capable of handling up to 1GB data per second.

It provides an easy-to-use SQL-like declarative language, called Stream Analytics query language, to perform simple to complex analysis on streaming data. You write queries exactly the way you write in SQL—SELECT, GROUP, JOIN—everything works the same way. The only major difference here is that since you are dealing with never-ending streaming data, you need to define time-specific boundaries to pick the exact data set to analyze. In other words, since static data changes very slowly or docsn't change at all, analysis is performed on the whole data. Streaming data is continuous with no predefined end. In most situations, the system performing analysis cannot predict when the data will end. So, it must pick small, time-bound pieces of data stream to analyze. The shorter the time window, the closer the analysis is to real time.

Note   It is important to note that performing extremely complex analyses of the scale of Big Data takes significant time. For this reason, Stream Analytics solutions (ASA, Apache Storm, etc.) are not recommended for very complex analyses. For situations where running an analysis may take minutes to hours, streaming data should first be stored in a temporary or permanent storage and then processed like static data.

A typical workflow in ASA starts with defining one or more input sources of data. ASA can out-of-the-box work with IoT Hubs, event hubs, and blob storages. ASA can use streaming data from a hub together with reference static data to perform analysis. Additionally, functions defined in Azure machine learning may also be used in an ASA job to perform real-time predictions on the data being analyzed. You will learn more about machine learning in Chapter 10. The output of an ASA job may be stored in a permanent storage (blob, SQL database, data lake, etc.) or sent directly to Power BI to generate dashboards, or both. An IoT Hub solution backend may also subscribe to an ASA job's output to send commands to devices based on the output received. Figure 9-1 summarizes this workflow.

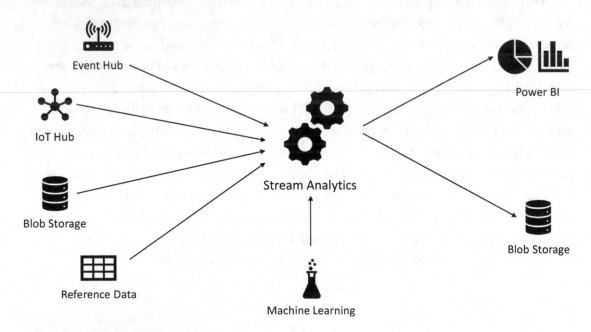

Figure 9-1. *Azure Stream Analytics workflow*

Performing IoT Stream Data Analysis

Let's start with something basic. In Chapter 3, we created an IoT Hub in Azure and a simulated device in C# that could send to the hub a patient's vitals every three seconds. We'll reuse these to perform real-time analysis for just one patient. Later, we'll create more simulated devices to generate fake data for more patients and use that data for perform more complex real-time analytics.

Creating an Azure Stream Analytics Job

Visit Azure Portal (`https://portal.azure.com`) and click on the Create a Resource button at the top of the left side menu. Go to Data + Analytics ➤ Stream Analytics job. Or, search for "stream analytics" if you are unable to find this option otherwise. Fill in the form, as shown in Figure 9-2. As this job is going to be our way to test ASA, you will not need more than one streaming unit. Ideally, you should start small and scale up when your hub starts receiving large volumes of data.

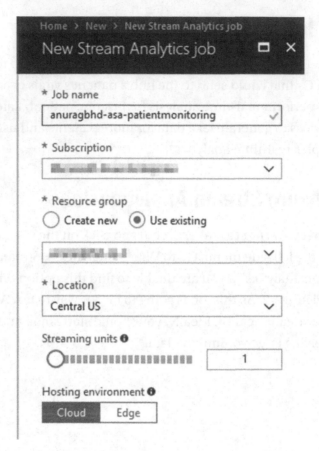

Figure 9-2. *Creating a new ASA job*

Click on the Create button and wait a few seconds for the deployment to complete.

Adding an Input to an ASA Job

By default, an ASA job is created in stopped mode. We'll first configure it by specifying input and output before starting the job. Once the job starts, you cannot edit input and output settings.

From the newly created ASA job's overview page in Azure Portal, go to Job Topology ➤ Inputs. You will see two options to add an input—Add Stream Input and Add Reference Input. The latter option lets you add reference data, which is static data that we can use to complement our streaming data. In a lot of situations, it may be metadata that can be joined with streaming data to aid in analysis. For example, a reference input may be a list of all patients along with their names, ages, and other attributes. These are things that are not present in streaming data records to reduce redundancy and save network bandwidth. While running a real-time Stream Analytics query, we may need a patient's age to more accurately determine diseases.

Choose Add Stream Input ➤ IoT Hub. Fill in the resulting form, as shown in Figure 9-3. The easiest way to select an existing IoT Hub is to choose one from the same Azure subscription. If your hub is in a different subscription than your ASA job, you will have an option to specify the hub's connection string. The Input alias can be anything that describes your input uniquely in the context of the job.

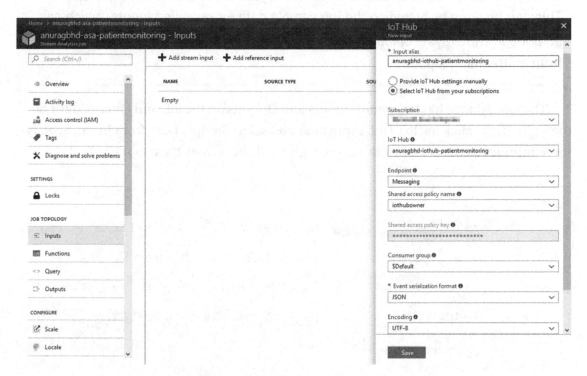

Figure 9-3. *Adding an existing IoT Hub as a stream input to an ASA job*

Clicking Save will add the input to your job and immediately perform a test to check the connection to the specified hub. You should receive a `"Successful Connection Test"` notification post.

Testing Your Input

Before moving to the next step—specifying an output in our ASA job—it's a good idea to run a sample SA query on the input data stream just to ensure that the job is configured correctly. We'll run the query directly on real-time data received by our IoT Hub. For this, we'll have to fire up the simulated device that we created in Chapter 3 to start sending data to our hub.

Open the IoTCentralizedPatientMonitoring solution in Visual Studio. With only the SimulatedDevice project set as the startup project, run the solution. When our simulated device is up and sending messages to the hub, return to Azure Portal. From the ASA job's side menu, go to Job Topology ➤ Query.

Note   You do not need to start a Stream Analytics job in order to run test queries. This can be done by providing the job sample data for specified inputs, which can be done in two ways—uploading the data file (.json, .csv, etc.) or sampling data from a streaming input.

The Query page has two panes: Inputs and Outputs on the left and Query Editor on the right. Right-click the IoT Hub input alias and select Sample Data from Input. Specify three minutes as the sampling duration. Figure 9-4 shows how these options look.

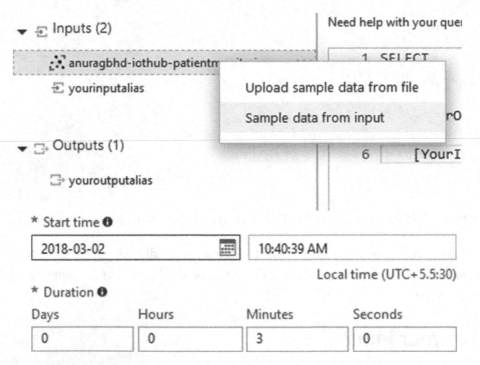

Figure 9-4. *Sampling data from a streaming input, such as IoT Hub*

Azure will start collecting data (for the next three minutes) being received by the hub in a temporary storage. After it is finished sampling, Azure will notify you about it. If, at this point, you close your browser's tab or navigate to another page, the sampled data will be lost.

Testing with a Pass-Through Query

Once the data is sampled and ready to be queried, you may stop the simulated device to prevent your IoT Hub from being metered further. Now, modify the query in the editor to update YourInputAlias to the name of your hub input. You may leave YourOutputAlias as is.

```
SELECT
    *
INTO
    [YourOutputAlias]
FROM
    [your-iothub-input-alias]
```

As you may recall from your SQL knowledge, SELECT * FROM <table> picks up and displays all rows and columns from the specified table. In the context of Stream Analytics, this is what is called a "pass-through" query. It selects all data from the given input and sends it to the given output. Ideally, you'd specify constraints and filters (e.g., the WHERE clause) to perform analysis and send only those records to an output that match your criteria.

Click the Test button. In the absence of a permanent storage output, the pass-through query generates results in a browser, as shown in Figure 9-5. ASA is smart enough to automatically generate column names from attributes of data records.

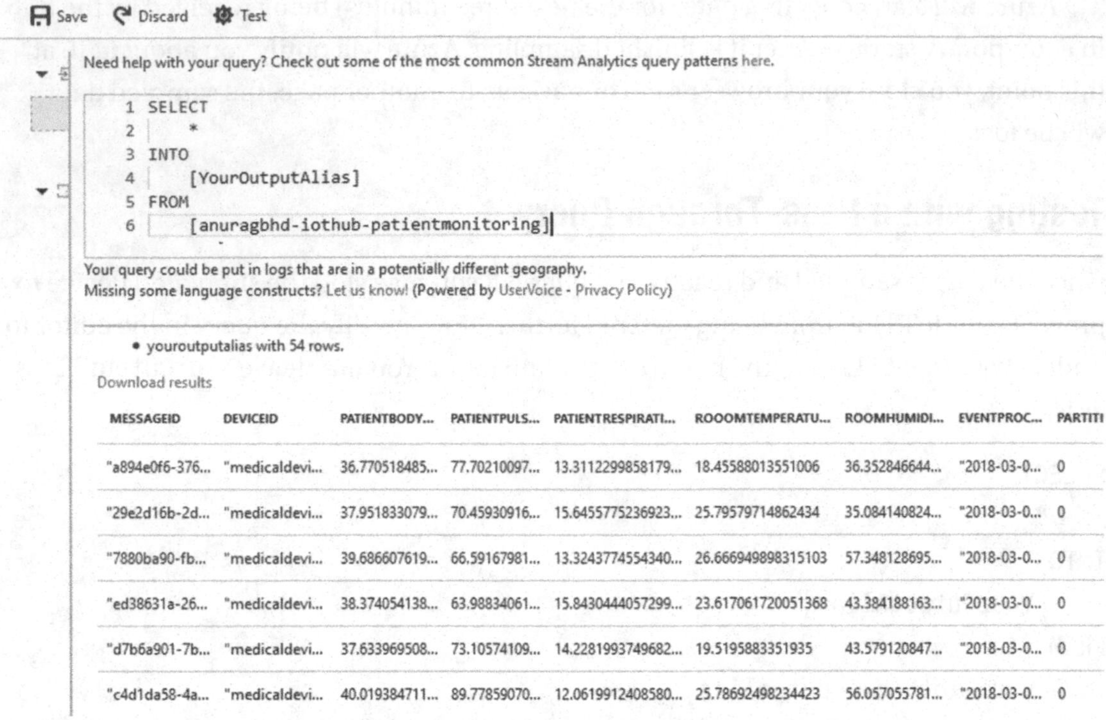

Figure 9-5. *Results from the pass-through query*

To recall, a message from a device looks like this:

{"messageId":"1e7c7cf7-5d6b-4938-aac0-688cb870b70e","deviceId":"medicaldevice-patient1","patientBodyTemperature":40.471381505937956,"patientPulseRate": 76.017155878253817,"patientRespirationRate":15.639444097708651,"rooomTemperature":29.475085872912352,"roomHumidity":54.724774525838335}

You can match column names in the SA query result with the attribute names in the sample message. Apart from these, we see IoT Hub specific columns such as EventProcessedUtcTime, PartitionId, etc.

Testing with a Real-World Query

Let's try a more complex query to cater to a real-world scenario. In Chapter 3, we wrote our solution backend to detect high body temperature conditions. Along similar lines, we'll write a query to detect high pulse rate conditions. Our solution backend was very basic and naïve in checking for high temperatures in each message received from a medical device. We will not do the same to detect high pulse rates. Instead, we will check for high values among pulse rates averaged from within time intervals of 30 seconds each. In other words, we want to tag pulse rates as high if they are consistently above a certain threshold (say, 90) during a period of 30 seconds.

The query for this sort of condition will look like this:

```
SELECT
    System.Timestamp AS Time,
    Avg(PatientPulseRate) AS AvgPulseRate
INTO
    [YourOutputAlias]
FROM
    [your-iothub-input-alias]
    TIMESTAMP BY EventEnqueuedUtcTime
    GROUP BY TumblingWindow(second, 30), DeviceId
    HAVING Avg(PatientPulseRate) > 90
```

If you run this query, you may get none to three results, depending on the sample data. In this case, we received a single result, as shown in Figure 9-6.

TIME	AVGPULSERATE
"2018-03-02T11:34:10.0000000Z"	93.70949969023599

Figure 9-6. *Result from running a constraint-bound SA query*

In the real-world, an ASA job will deal with data from hundreds or thousands of devices, lending this query its real worth. Let's break the query down for better understanding.

The most unusual thing in the entire query is the keyword `TumblingWindow`. Stream Analytics deals with streaming data. Unlike static data, streaming data has no start or end; it's just a continuous stream of incoming data records that may or may not end in the near future. A question then arises: starting when and how long should streaming data be analyzed in one go? A bit earlier in the chapter, we talked about analyzing time-bound windows of streaming data. `TumblingWindow` provides us with those time-bound windows while performing aggregate operations using `GROUP BY`. An equivalent keyword we use with a `JOIN` is `DATEDIFF`.

TumblingWindow takes in two parameters—unit of time and its measure—in order to group data during that time interval. In our query, we group incoming data records every 30 seconds and check for the average pulse rate of the patient during that time interval.

Tip   If you are still confused, do not forget that we ran this query on sampled data, which was already a snapshot—a three-minute window—of an ongoing stream. So, ASA created six 30-second groups and displayed the final result after analyzing them. When we start our ASA job, it will start working with an actual stream. Analysis will be performed and a result spat out (to specified outputs) every 30 seconds.

TIMESTAMP BY provides a way to specify which time to consider while creating time-bound windows. By default, Stream Analytics will consider the time of arrival of a data record for the purpose. This may be fine in some scenarios, but it's not what we want. In healthcare applications, time when data was recorded by the IoT device is more important than the time when that data was received by Azure (IoT Hub or Stream Analytics), since there may be a delay of a few milliseconds to a couple of seconds between the two events. That's why, in our query, we chose to timestamp by EventEnqueuedUtcTime, which is closer to when the data was recorded.

Selecting System.Timestamp provides us with the end time for each window.

Adding an Output to an ASA Job

While running test queries on sampled input, ASA generated its output directly in the browser. However, this is not how it works in a real-world scenario. ASA requires you to specify at least one output sink (container) where the results will be stored or displayed on a more permanent basis. Stored results may be analyzed further to arrive at decisions.

Although ASA supports a long list of output options, we'll go with a popular choice called *blob storage*. Azure's blob service provides a highly-scalable storage for unstructured data. It also provides a RESTful API to access data stored in it. In most cases, you'd want to stored ASA results as JSON in a blob and retrieve it later in a web or mobile app via its REST API.

Before we can specify a blob storage as an output in our ASA job, we need to create it in Azure. The process is the same as for other Azure services. In the portal, visit Create a Resource ➤ Storage ➤ Storage Account – Blob, File, Table, Queue. Create a new blob, as shown in Figure 9-7.

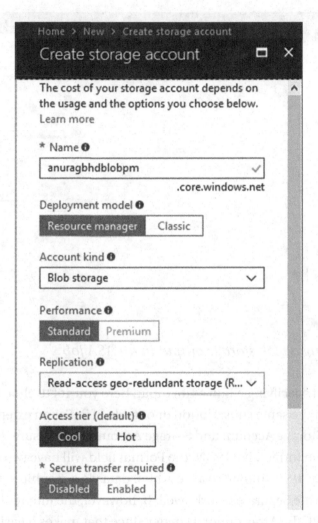

Figure 9-7.   *Creating a new blog storage to store ASA job output*

The name cannot contain special characters (even hyphens and underscores). That is why we have deviated here from our usual naming scheme. The access tier you choose will impact your pricing. Blob storage does not have a free tier, but the cost of storing data is negligible (almost zero) for small amounts of data. You choose Hot if the blob data is going to be accessed frequently; choose Cool if data is going to be stored more frequently than accessed. We will use the latter in this case.

When Azure has finished creating our new storage, we should return to our ASA job and go to Job Topology ➤ Outputs ➤ Add ➤ Blob storage. Fill in the form, as shown in Figure 9-8.

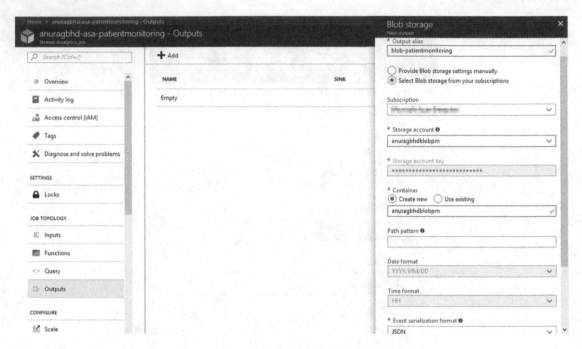

Figure 9-8. *Adding a blob storage output in an ASA job*

As in the case of specifying a hub as an input, here you get to choose an Azure Blob storage from within the same subscription or outside of it. For an external blob, you need to manually enter Storage Account and Storage Account Key. Ensure that you have JSON select as serialization format. For JSON, the Format field will have two options—Line Separated and Array. If you intend to access blob data via a graphical tool (e.g., Azure Storage Explorer), Line Separated works well. If, however, the intention is to access blob data via its REST API, the Array option is better since that makes it easier to access JSON objects in JavaScript. Leave the rest of the fields as is and click on Create. Azure will perform a connection test immediately after the new output is added.

Testing Your Output

Return to your ASA job's query editor and paste the same query that we used earlier, except this time specify your blob's output alias after INTO.

```
SELECT
    System.Timestamp AS Time,
    Avg(PatientPulseRate) AS AvgPulseRate
INTO
    [blob-patientmonitoring]
FROM
    [anuragbhd-iothub-patientmonitoring]
    TIMESTAMP BY EventEnqueuedUtcTime
    GROUP BY TumblingWindow(second, 30), DeviceId
    HAVING Avg(PatientPulseRate) > 90
```

Click Save to save the query. Go to the Overview page and start the job. It may take a couple of minutes for the job to start. You'll be notified when it's started. When a job is running, you may not edit query or add/edit inputs and outputs.

From Visual Studio, start the simulated device again if you'd earlier stopped it. You may want to increase its update frequency to 10 or 20 seconds to reflect a more realistic value.

```
// Wait for 10 seconds before repeating
await Task.Delay(10000);
```

Let it run for a few minutes to allow for our specified high pulse rate condition to be met. In the meantime, download and install Azure Storage Explorer from http://storageexplorer.com. This is a nifty little desktop application for accessing Azure storage accounts, such as blob, data lake, Cosmos DB, etc.

When you open Azure Storage Explorer for the first time, you will be greeted with the Connect to Azure Storage wizard. If you are not, manually open the wizard by right-clicking on Storage Accounts in the Explorer pane on the left and selecting Connect to Azure Storage. In the wizard, select the Use a Connection String or a Shared Access Signature URI option and click Next. Copy your Blob's connection string from Azure Portal ➤ <your-blob> ➤ Settings ➤ Access Keys ➤ key1 ➤ Connection String and paste it into the wizard's Connection String textbox, as shown in Figure 9-9.

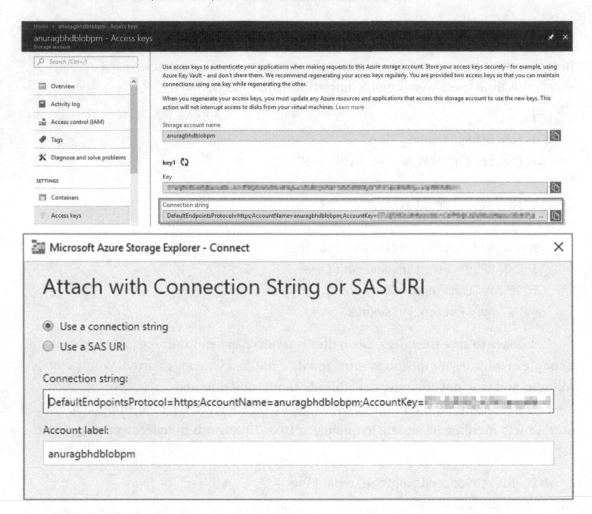

Figure 9-9. *Copying the blob storage's connection string from Azure Portal to Azure Storage Explorer*

Once the application has successfully connected to your blob storage, you will see its name under Storage Accounts in the Explorer pane. Expand it and go to Blob Containers ➤ <your blob container name>. In the Details pane on the right, you should see a listing corresponding to a `.json` file. If you do not see anything there, the high pulse rate condition has never been met. You could wait for a few minutes more or relax the condition a bit by setting `Avg(PatientPulseRate) > 80` (you will need to stop your ASA job, edit the query, and start the job again). Double-click the `.json` file to open it locally in your default text editor. You should see something similar to the following.

{"time":"2018-03-03T05:55:30.0000000Z","avgpulscratc":91.907351640320385}
{"time":"2018-03-03T05:56:00.0000000Z","avgpulserate":94.212707023856254}
{"time":"2018-03-03T06:05:00.0000000Z","avgpulserate":94.652964749677551}
{"time":"2018-03-03T06:06:00.0000000Z","avgpulserate":93.091244986168064}
{"time":"2018-03-03T06:14:00.0000000Z","avgpulserate":91.6573497614159}
{"time":"2018-03-03T06:14:30.0000000Z","avgpulserate":90.980160983425321}
{"time":"2018-03-03T06:15:00.0000000Z","avgpulserate":92.107636040126735}

Note   Each time an ASA job is stopped and started again, the subsequent outputs from the job are written to a new `.json` file (blob) in the same blob container. You will see as many blobs in Azure Storage Explorer as the times the ASA job was started.

You can access these results programmatically in the web and mobile apps using blob storage's comprehensive REST APIs. Check `https://docs.microsoft.com/en-us/rest/api/storageservices/list-blobs` and `https://docs.microsoft.com/en-us/rest/api/storageservices/get-blob` for more details.

Let your simulated device run for a while longer and keep refreshing the Details pane in Azure Storage Explorer to see how Stream Analytics processes streaming input and generates output in real time.

Visualizing ASA Results Using Power BI

While blob storage provides an easy, scalable method to store Stream Analytics results, it is difficult to visualize the stored results using either Azure Storage Explorer or REST API. Power BI is a collection of business intelligence and analytics tools that work with dozens of types of data sources to deliver interactive, visual insights via a GUI interface. Some data sources it supports include SQL databases (SQL Server, Oracle, and PostgreSQL), blob storage, MS Access, Excel, HDFS (Hadoop), Teradata, and XML.

Power BI is offered as a web, desktop, and mobile app to quickly create dashboards and visualizations filled with charts (line, bar, pie, time-series, radar, etc.), maps, cartograms, histograms, grids, clouds, and more. Dashboards can be generated and viewed within Power BI or published to your own website or blog.

> **Important** In order to sign up for or use Power BI, you need a work email address that is integrated with Microsoft Office 365. You cannot use personal email IDs (Gmail, Yahoo Mail, or even Hotmail) to sign up for Power BI.

Adding Power BI as an Output in an ASA Job

Stop your ASA job in Azure Portal, if it's running. Then go to Job Topology ➤ Outputs ➤ Add ➤ Power BI. Fill in the details, as shown in Figure 9-10.

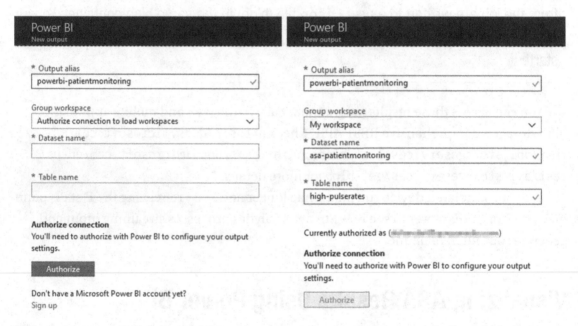

Figure 9-10. *Adding Power BI as an output in the Stream Analytics job: before and after authorizing a connection to Power BI*

Make note of the values you fill in for Dataset Name and Table Name. We kept these as `asa-patientmonitoring` and `high-pulserates`, respectively, which are consistent with the naming scheme we follow. Azure will automatically create the specified dataset and table in Power BI, if it's not already present. The existing dataset with the same name will be overwritten.

Updating the SA Query

With the output created, let's head back to query editor. We'll need to update our query to redirect results to our Power BI output. There are two ways to do it—replace the current output alias (blob) with the new (Power BI) or add a second SELECT INTO statement for the new output. Both approaches are shown next.

Replacing the existing output:

```
SELECT
    System.Timestamp AS Time,
    Avg(PatientPulseRate) AS AvgPulseRate,
    COUNT(*) AS HighPRInstances
INTO
    [powerbi-patientmonitoring]
FROM
    [anuragbhd-iothub-patientmonitoring]
    TIMESTAMP BY EventEnqueuedUtcTime
    GROUP BY TumblingWindow(second, 30), DeviceId
    HAVING Avg(PatientPulseRate) > 90
```

Adding additional output:

```
WITH HighPulseRates AS (
    SELECT
        System.Timestamp AS Time,
        Avg(PatientPulseRate) AS AvgPulseRate,
        COUNT(*) AS HighPRInstances
    FROM
        [anuragbhd-iothub-patientmonitoring]
        TIMESTAMP BY EventEnqueuedUtcTime
        GROUP BY TumblingWindow(second, 30), DeviceId
        HAVING Avg(PatientPulseRate) > 90
)
SELECT * INTO [blob-patientmonitoring] FROM HighPulseRates
SELECT * INTO [powerbi-patientmonitoring] FROM HighPulseRates
```

Notice carefully that we have selected another value—the count of each recorded high pulse rate instance. Although this value will be 1 for each instance, we'll need it for plotting our line chart a little later.

It is also possible to send different results to different outputs. You do that by writing a separate SELECT ... INTO ... FROM statement, one after the other, for each output. Update your query, click Save, and start the job again. This is also a good time to fire up that simulated device once again. Go to Visual Studio and start the project.

Creating Dashboards in Power BI

Go to https://powerbi.com and log in with your work account. If you expand the My Workspace section in the left sidebar and look at DATASETS, you should see the name of the dataset you specified earlier if the ASA job produced at least one result.

Navigate to Workspaces ➤ My Workspace from the sidebar menu. We'll start by creating a dashboard that displays a count of all high pulse rate instances for our patient. Choose Create ➤ Dashboard. Give your dashboard a name and click Create. In your newly created dashboard, click Add Tile and choose Custom Streaming Data, as shown in Figure 9-11. Click Next.

Figure 9-11. *Adding a new tile in a dashboard in Power BI*

On the Choose a Streaming Dataset screen, select the name of your dataset and click Next. On the Visualization Design screen, select Card as the visualization type, and then add highprinstances in the Fields section. On the next screen called Tile Details, fill in a title and a subtitle and click Apply. Your new tile will be live immediately.

Similarly, let's add a new tile for tracking high pulse rates over 10-minute periods. Add Tile ➤ Custom Streaming Data ➤ <your dataset>. On the Visualization Design screen, choose Line Chart as the type, Time as the axis, avgpulserate as the value, and Last 10 Minutes as the time window to display. Once this tile is live, you should see a line chart for your selected data. At this point, your dashboard should look like Figure 9-12.

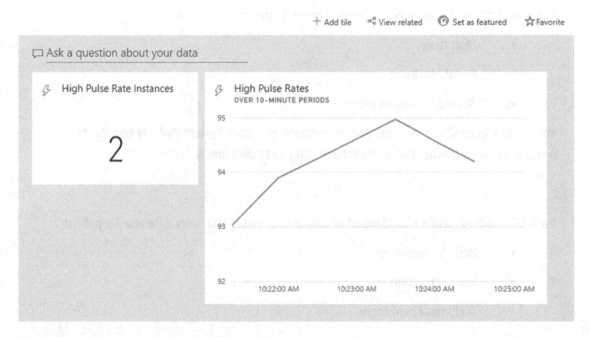

Figure 9-12. *A Power BI dashboard with two tiles*

Feel free to create more titles using the data at hand and then watch them update in real time.

Next Steps

With the power of Stream Analytics and Power BI in your hands, we encourage you to try slightly more complex scenarios. Try solving the problem mentioned in the following exercise, or take hints from it to solve a different problem.

REAL-TIME DENGUE OUTBREAK DETECTION

Dengue fever is a mosquito-borne viral disease, common in certain South and Southeast Asian regions, such as India and Singapore. If not detected and treated early, dengue can be fatal. As per online statistics, hundreds of millions of people are affected by the disease each year and about 20,000 die because of it. The disease starts as a regular virus and gradually becomes severe in some cases (within 7-10 days). Dengue outbreaks recur every year in certain areas, and timely detection of such outbreaks may help in timely and effective public health interventions.

Symptoms of the diseases include, among several others:

- High fever

- Rapid breathing

- Severe abdominal pain

Your task is to design a real-time dengue outbreak detection system that one hospital or several hospitals (perhaps on a Blockchain) can use to take timely action.

System Design

Each IoT medical device should report at least the following telemetry data about a patient:

- Body temperature

- Respiration rate

- Abdominal pain score

- Location

The location of a person can be easily tracked via GPS. As for determining a pain score, there are devices in the market that do this. Check this: http://gomerblog.com/2014/06/pain-detector. Alternatively, a proper measurement of functional magnetic resonance imaging (fMRI) brain scans can also give indications of pain levels, as reported here https://www.medicalnewstoday.com/articles/234450.php.

Your job initially is not to use such sophisticated medical devices for taking measurements, but to create about a dozen simulated devices for the job that report telemetry data for each patient.

You can then write an SA query to perform aggregate operations on incoming data stream and count the number of cases where telemetry values are above certain thresholds at the same location. If you get multiple locations reporting a bunch of dengue cases around the same time, you have the outbreak pattern.

Recap

In this chapter, you learned how to perform complex real-time analyses on streaming data, such as that received by an IoT Hub from hundreds or thousands of connected devices. You learned how to:

- Create a new Stream Analytics job in the Azure Portal

- Add (and test) an input (hub) to an ASA job

- Write queries that work on time-bound windows of streaming data

- Add (and test) a blob storage output to an ASA job

- Access Stream Analytics results stored in a blob using Azure Storage Explorer

- Add Power BI as an output to an ASA job

- Create a dashboard with multiple tiles in Power BI to visualize ASA results

In the next chapter, you will take data analytics to the next level by using Azure machine learning.

Making Predictions with Machine Learning

Our adventures in AI 2.0 are nearing their conclusion. If you have gone through all of the previous nine chapters, you have almost all the skills needed to build the next generation of smart applications. You are almost AI 2.0 ready. Almost.

Reflecting on your journey so far, you now have a clear big-picture understanding of how AI, IoT, and Blockchain together form the AI 2.0 architecture (Chapter 1), know how to design and build highly scalable IoT solutions using Azure IoT Suite (Chapters 2 and 3), are capable of adding intelligence to your applications and IoT solutions by AI-enabling them using Cognitive Services (Chapters 4, 5 and 6), know how to integrate your applications with decentralized, transparent and infinitely scalable smart networks using Azure Blockchain as a Service (Chapters 7 and 8), and can analyze and visualize real-time data using Azure Stream Analytics and Power BI (Chapter 9).

In the space of a few chapters, you learned so many "new" technologies. But this knowledge is incomplete without the technology that is a major enabler for AI and a key accompaniment in real-time data analytics. As you saw in Chapters 1 and 9, that technology is *machine learning*.

Recapping from Chapter 1, machine learning is the ability of a computer to learn without being explicitly programmed. This tremendous ability is what makes a computer think like a human. ML makes computers learn to identify and distinguish real-world objects through examples rather than instructions. It also gives them the ability to learn from their own mistakes through trial and error. And ML lends computers the power to make their own decisions once they have sufficiently learned about a topic.

Perhaps the most useful aspect of ML—that makes it slightly better than human intelligence—is its ability to make predictions. Of course, not the kind we humans make by looking into crystal balls, rather informed, logical ones that can be made by looking at data patterns. There are machine learning algorithms that, if supplied with sufficient

© Nishith Pathak and Anurag Bhandari 2018
N. Pathak and A. Bhandari, *IoT, AI, and Blockchain for .NET*, https://doi.org/10.1007/978-1-4842-3709-0_10

historic data, can predict how various data parameters will be at a point in the future. Weather, earthquake, and cyclone predictions are made through this technique, and so are predictions about finding water on a remote celestial body such as the Moon or Mars.

How does machine learning do all this, you'll learn shortly. By the end of this chapter, you will have learned about:

- Machine learning (ML)

- Problems ML solves

- Types of machine learning

- Azure Machine Learning Studio—what and how

- Picking the right algorithm to solve a problem

- Solving a real-world problem using ML

What Is Machine Learning?

Now that we have a fair high-level functional idea about machine learning, let's look at its more technical definition. ML is a field of computer science—evolved from the study of pattern recognition—that enables machines to learn from data to make predictions and progressively improve over time.

It is commonly used in scenarios where designing software applications using explicit programming is not possible. These are scenarios where a computer may have to deal with completely new and previously unseen data to make predictions based on that data, making it practically impossible to write an exhaustive set of if-conditions to cover all possibilities. Some examples of such scenarios include:

- **Natural language understanding**: There can be hundreds of ways to say the same sentence in just one language, owing to different dialects, slangs, grammatical flow, etc.

- **Email spam filtering**: Spammers are consistently producing new kinds of spam and phishing emails every day.

- **In-game AI**: When playing a computer game against non-human enemies (bots), the behavior and actions of bots must adapt according to your unique style.

- **Face recognition**: One just cannot explicitly train a computer to recognize all the faces in the world.

In the video series Data Science for Beginners, Brandon Rohrer, Senior Data Scientist at Microsoft, explains that machine learning can really answer only these five questions:

- Is this A or B? (classification)

- Is this weird? (anomaly detection)

- How much or how many? (regression)

- How is this organized? (clustering)

- What should I do now? (reinforcement learning)

These are the problems that ML can solve. We'll look at some of them in detail very soon.

There are a bunch of algorithms associated with machine learning. Some of these are linear regression, neural network regression, two-class SVM, multiclass decision forest, K-means clustering, and PCA-based anomaly detection. Depending on the problem being solved, one algorithm may work better than all others. Writing ML algorithms is not a trivial task. Although it's possible to write your own implementation of a well-established algorithm, doing so is not only time consuming but most of the times inefficient.

When performing machine learning tasks, it's best to use existing known and well-written implementations of these algorithms. There are free and open source machine learning frameworks—such as Torch, Tensorflow, and Theano—that effectively let you build machine learning models, albeit with the assumption that you know the internals of machine learning and statistics at least at a basic level. Alternatively, you can use Azure machine learning to build robust ML models through an interactive drag-and-drop interface, which does not require data science skills. You'll see Azure ML in a bit.

Using an existing ML framework not only greatly decreases the time to build the actual software application, it also ensures that you are using ML the way it's meant to be. No matter what ML algorithm or framework you use, its high-level functioning never changes. Figure 10-1, repeated from Chapter 1, shows how ML works at a high level.

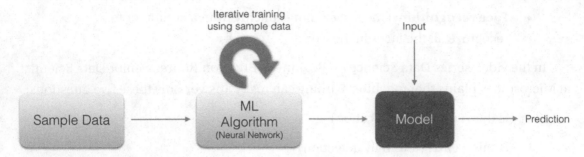

Figure 10-1. *High-level picture of how machine learning works*

All ML algorithms rely heavily on data to create a model that will generate predictions. The more sample data you have, the more accurate the model. In the case of machine translation (automated machine-based language translation), sample data is a large collection (corpus) of sentences written in the source language and their translations written in a target language. A suitable ML algorithm (typically an artificial neural network) trains the system on the sample data—meaning that it goes through the data identifying patterns, without explicitly being told about language grammar and semantics. It then spits out a model that can automatically translate sentences from source to target language, even for ones it was never trained on. The trained model can then be incorporated inside a software application to make machine translation a feature of that application.

It is important to note that training is an iterative and very resource- and time-consuming process. On regular computers, this may take months to complete when running 24x7. ML algorithms typically demand high-end computers, with specialized graphical processing units (GPUs), to finish training in reasonable amounts of time.

ML and Data Science

Machine learning is a confluence of computer science and statistics. Figure 10-2 illustrates this point. To perform their tasks, ML algorithms borrow heavily from well-established statistical techniques. Its data-driven approach and use of statistics sometimes makes it look synonymous with *data science*. Although both fields are technically similar, they differ heavily in terms of applications and use. In other words, machine learning *is not the same as* data science.

Figure 10-2. *Machine learning is the progeny of computer science and statistics fields, both in turn descended from mathematics*

While both the fields deal with massive amounts of data to produce models, their focus areas are different. On one hand where data science focuses on data analytics to arrive at actionable insights that can help the management at an organization take effective decisions, on the other hand machine learning focuses on creating predictive models that can be used by other software components (rather than human beings) to produce accurate, data-driven results. Table 10-1 lists the common differences between the two fields.

Table 10-1. *Major Differences Between Data Science and Machine Learning*

Data Science	Machine Learning
Focus on performing analysis on data to produce insights.	Focus on using data for self-learning and making predictions.
Output: Graphs, Excel sheets.	Output: Software, API.
Audience: Other humans.	Audience: Other software.
Considerable human intervention.	Zero human intervention.

A Quick Look at the Internals

With tools like Azure Machine Learning Studio, one is no longer required to know the internal workings of machine learning. Yet, brief knowledge about the internal technical details can help you optimize training, resulting in more accurate models.

Until now, we have repeatedly been using terms such as model and training without explaining what they actually are. Sure, you at least know that training is the process through which an ML algorithm uses sample data to make a computer learn about something. You also know that model is the output of training process. But how is training done and what does a model actually look like?

To answer these questions, consider the following example. The cars we drive vary in terms of engines, sizes, colors, features, etc. As a result, their mileage (miles per gallon/liter) varies a lot. If a car A gives x MPG, it's difficult to say how many MPGs would a totally different car B would give. B may or may not give the same mileage x, depending on several factors, horsepower being a major one. Usually, with higher horsepower you get a lower mileage and vice versa.

Note Of course, horsepower is *not* the only factor that affects a car's mileage. Other factors include number of cylinders, weight, acceleration, displacement, etc. We did not consider all these in our example for the sake of simplicity.

Suppose that we have horsepower and mileage data for a large number of car models. But this list is not exhaustive and does not cover all models (or horsepower values). So, we want to use existing data so that given a new, previously unseen horsepower value, our system can predict the corresponding mileage. Table 10-2 shows an incomplete snapshot of the data.

Table 10-2. *Horsepower vs MPG Courtesy Dua, D. and
Karra Taniskidou, E. (2017). UCI Machine Learning
Repository [*`http://archive.ics.uci.edu/ml`*]. Irvine,
CA: University of California, School of Information and
Computer Science.*

Car Name	Horsepower	Mileage (MPG)
Chevrolet Chevelle Malibu	130	18
Buick Skylark 320	165	15
Plymouth Satellite	150	18
AMC Rebel SST	150	16
Ford Torino	140	17

Features and Target

We want to use horsepower to predict mileage. In machine learning terminology,
horsepower is a *feature* that will be used to determine our *target* (mileage). In order to
design a model capable of accurately predicting MPG values, just five rows of data will
not do. We'll need a very large number of such rows with as distinct data as possible.
Fortunately, we have close to 400 rows of data.

   If we were to plot a graph using 25 feature versus target data values, it will look as
shown in Figure 10-3.

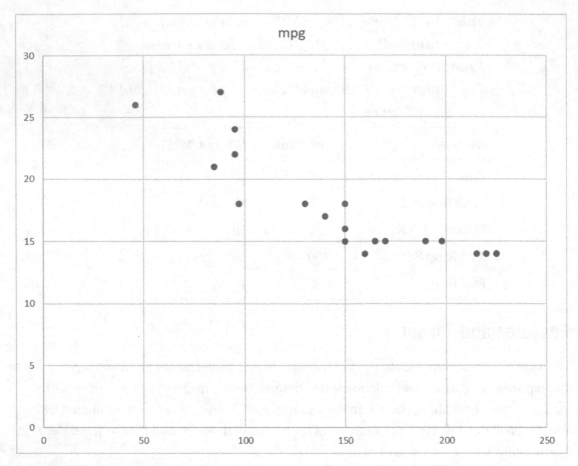

Figure 10-3. *A scatter plot with horsepower on the x-axis and MPG on the y-axis*

Model

Now if we carefully draw a line so that it passes through as many dots as possible, we'll arrive at what looks like Figure 10-4a. This line represents our model. Yes, in linear regression this simple line *is* the model; the chart represents *linear* regression since we have drawn a straight line.

Predicting MPG values for unknown horsepower is now easy. In Figure 10-4a, we can see that there does not seem to be a corresponding MPG for horsepower 120. If we draw a dotted line at 120—perpendicular to the x-axis—the point where it intersects our model is the predicted MPG. As seen in Figure 10-4b, the predicted value is roughly 19.5.

Programmatically, we can draw our model using the well-known mathematical equation $y = mx + b$ (do you remember this from your high school days?), where m is line's slope and b is its y-intercept. Since our y-axis represents target (MPG) and x-axis feature (horsepower), predicting MPG is as easy as plugging in the value of x to arrive at the value of y.

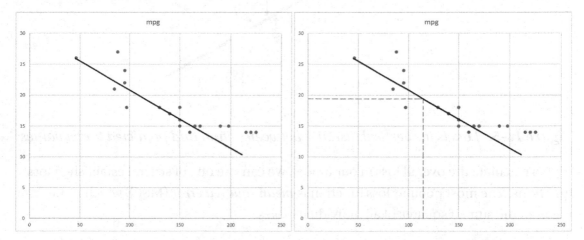

Figure 10-4. *(a) Creating our linear regression model by drawing a line (left). (b) Predicting a value using our model (right)*

Training and Loss

The line we drew was just an approximation. The goal while drawing the line—in order to create a model—is to ensure it is not far away from most of the dots. In more technical words, the goal of plotting a model is to minimize the loss. But what is *loss*?

The vertical distance between a dot and the line is called *loss*. That is, the absolute of difference between actual target value (dot on chart) and predicted target value (point on line) for the same feature value. Figure 10-5 shows individual loss values for the initial three dots.

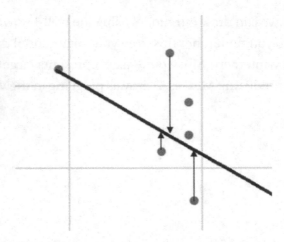

Figure 10-5. *Loss is the vertical distance between actual and predicted target values*

To calculate the overall loss in our model, we can use one of several established loss functions. The most popular loss function is *mean squared error* (MSE), which is the mean of the sum of squares of all individual losses.

$$MSE = \frac{1}{N} \sum_{(x,y) \in D} \left(y - prediction(x) \right)^2$$

Thus, we define training as the iterative process of minimizing loss. That is, plotting and replotting the model until we arrive at a reasonably low value of MSE (overall loss). As with plotting model and calculating loss, there are several well-established ways to minimize overall loss. Stochastic Gradient Descent (SGD) is a common mathematical technique to iteratively minimize loss and, thus, train a model.

Where Do We Go From Here?

That's it! This is all you needed to know about the internals of ML. Suddenly, the innocuous high-level terms you'd been hearing since Chapter 1 seem too mathematical. But if you have followed us up until now and understood most of ML internal concepts, congratulations! You have unlocked some confidence in getting started with an ML framework.

What open source ML frameworks, such as Tensorflow and scikit-learn, do is they provide you with ready-made methods to create a model, calculate loss, and train the model. However, you are required to have good working knowledge of cleansing data, picking features, and evaluating a trained model, among other things—all of which again require a decent hold on statistics and mathematics. An ML framework just makes dealing with multiple algorithms and multi-feature scenarios easier.

Azure Machine Learning Studio takes ease-of-use of ML a bit further by automating all of the above, while still giving expert ML engineers and data scientists control over the underlying processes.

Problems that ML Solves

Machine learning has literally unlocked an infinite amount of possibilities to get things done by machines that could not be done using traditional programming techniques. If we start listing down all the problems that ML can solve, we'll run out of paper very soon. Fortunately, all these problems can be categorized into a handful of problem types. Let's explore the most common types.

Classification

Identifying whether something is of type X or Y is a very common ML task. Humans gain the ability to discern various types of objects at a very early age. We can look at an animal with our eyes and instantly say, "it's a dog." So easy for a human, so humungous a task for a computer.

Thinking logically about how a computer may perform this task using explicit programming, it's not uncommon to propose a solution where the computer would use a camera to take a picture of the animal (simulating human eyes) and compare it with the set of dog images it has in its image bank. Odds would be heavily against the possibility of getting a match for a photo captured of that exact dog at that specific spot. How do we make computers "learn" to recognize dogs, no matter what their pose or location? That's a very good example of a classification problem. Figure 10-6 shows classification at work.

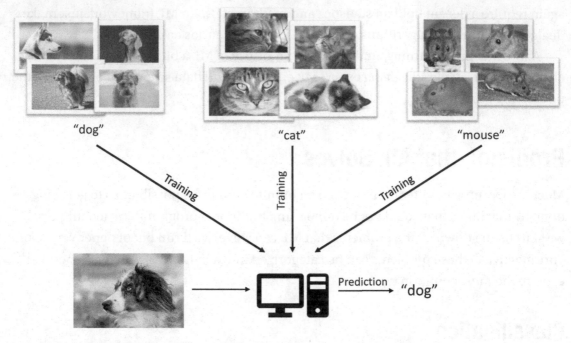

Figure 10-6.   Multi-class classification to identify the kind of animal. For each class, hundreds of images are used to train the computer

Classification problems appear in two varieties—*two-class (is it X or Y?)* and *multi-class (what kind is it?)*. Given an IoT device's age, average temperature, and wear and tear, will it fail in the next three days (yes or no)? Is this a two-legged animal or a four-legged animal? These are two examples of two-class classification problems. Examples of multi-class classification are detecting the type of animal and species of a dog. In both examples, our system would need to be trained with several different animal types and dog species respectively, each animal type or dog species representing one class.

Who tells a computer what picture is a dog or a cat in the first place? Short answer—humans. Each picture is manually tagged with the name of the class it represents and supplied to the computer. This process is called *labeling*, and the class name supplied with training data is called a *label*.

Regression

This type of supervised learning (more on this later) is used when the expected output is *continuous*. Let's see what we mean by output being continuous. We read about regression earlier in the section called "A Quick Look at the Internals". You now know that regression uses past data about something to make predictions about one of its parameters.

For example, using a car's horsepower-mileage data we could predict mileages (output) for unknown horsepower values. Since mileage is a variable, changing value— varies as per horsepower, age, cylinders, etc. even for the same car—it is said to be continuous. The opposite of continuous is *discrete*. Parameters such as car's color, model year, size, etc. are discrete features. A red-colored car will always be red, no matter what its age, horsepower or mileage.

Based on what you just learned about output types, can you guess the output type classification deals with? If you answered discrete, you were absolutely correct.

Regression problems are very common, and techniques to solve such problems are frequently used by scientific communities in researches, enterprises for making business projects, and even newspapers and magazines to make predictions about consumer and market trends.

Anomaly Detection

The ability to detect anomalies in data is a crucial aspect of proactively ensuring security and smooth operation (see Figure 10-7). Unlike classification, detecting anomalies is difficult for humans to perform manually, usually because of the amount of data one would have to deal with in order to correctly determine nominal trends.

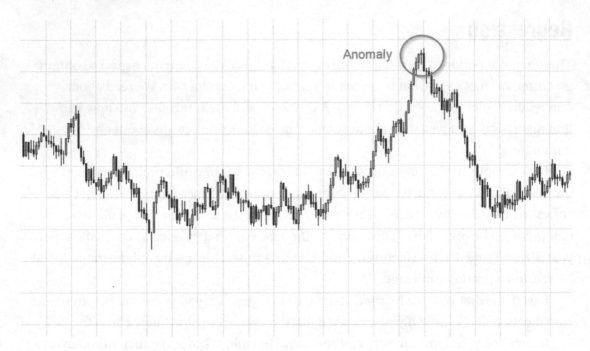

Figure 10-7. *Abnormal point in an otherwise consistent trend*

One of the most common anomaly detection use cases is detecting unauthorized transactions for a credit card. Consider this—millions of people use credit cards on a daily basis, some using them multiple times in a day. For a bank that has hundreds of thousands of credit card customers, the amount of daily data generated from card use is enormous. Searching through this enormous data, in real time, to look for suspicious patterns is not a trivial problem. ML-based anomaly detection algorithms help detect spurious transactions (on a stolen credit card) in real time based on customer's current location and past spending trends.

Other uses cases for anomaly detection include detecting network breaches on high-volume websites, making medical prognoses based on real-time assessment of a patient's various health parameters, finding out hard-to-find small or big financial frauds in banks, etc.

Clustering

Sometimes it is very useful to check certain patterns by organizing data first. For example, for a certain packaged snack company, it may be important to know which customers like the same flavor. They could use ML-based clustering to flavor-wise organize their users, as shown in Figure 10-8.

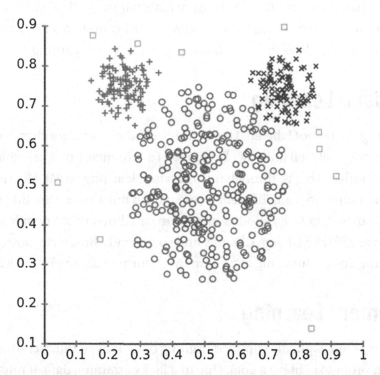

Figure 10-8. *Clustering allows you to organize data into criteria-based clusters for easy decision-making*

Types of Machine Learning

After having learned what machine learning is—including a quick dive into its internal details—and the problems ML can solve, let's take a quick look at the various types of ML. There really are only three types, based on how training is done.

Supervised Learning

Here, the training data is labeled. For a language detection algorithm, learning would be supervised if the sentences we supply to the algorithm are explicitly labeled with the language it's written in: sentences written in French and ones not in French, sentences written in Spanish and ones not in Spanish, and so on. As prior labeling is done by humans, it increases the work effort and cost of maintaining such algorithms. So far, this is the most common form of ML as with it we get more accurate results. Classification, regression, and anomaly detection are all forms of supervised learning.

Unsupervised Learning

Here, the training data is not labeled. Due to a lack of labels, an algorithm cannot, of course, learn to magically tell the exact language of a sentence, but it can differentiate one language from another. That is, through unsupervised learning an ML algorithm can learn to see that French sentences are different from Spanish ones, which are different from Hindi ones and so on. Similarly, another algorithm can differentiate people who like Tom Hanks from those who like George Clooney and so on, and, thus, form clusters of people who like the same actor. Clustering algorithms are a form of unsupervised learning.

Reinforcement Learning

Here, a machine is not explicitly supplied training data. It must interact with the environment in order to achieve a goal. Due to a lack of training data, it must learn by itself from the scratch and rely on a trial-and-error technique to take decisions and discover its own correct paths. For each action the machine takes, there's a consequence, and for each consequence it is given a numerical reward. So, if an action produces a desirable result, it receives "good" remarks. And if the result is disastrous, it receives "very, very bad" remarks. Like humans, the machine strives to maximize its total numerical reward—that is, get as many "good" and "very good" remarks as possible by not repeating its mistakes.

This technique of machine learning is especially useful when the machine has to deal with very dynamic environments, where creating and supplying training data is just not feasible. For example, driving a car, playing a video game, and so on. Reinforcement learning can also be applied to create AIs that can create drawings, images, music, and even songs on their own by learning from examples.

Azure Machine Learning Studio

There are multiple ways to create ML applications. We saw the mathematics behind linear regression in the section "A Quick Look at the Internals" earlier. One could write code implementation for linear regression by themselves. That would not only be time-consuming but also potentially inefficient and bug-ridden. ML frameworks, such as Tensorflow, make things simpler by offering high-level APIs to create custom ML models, while still assuming a good understanding of underlying concepts. Azure ML Studio offers a novel and easier approach to create end-to-end ML solutions without requiring one to know a lot of data science or ML details, or even coding skills.

ML Studio is a graphical, drag-and-drop interface to design and run ML workflows. It allows you to run simple to complex ML solutions right in the browser. Creating an ML workflow does not involve any coding, and it requires only putting different droppable components together. ML Studio comes with a huge list of tried and tested implementation of dozens of ML algorithms to target several different types of problems. Figure 10-9 gives a generalized overview of a typical ML workflow in ML Studio.

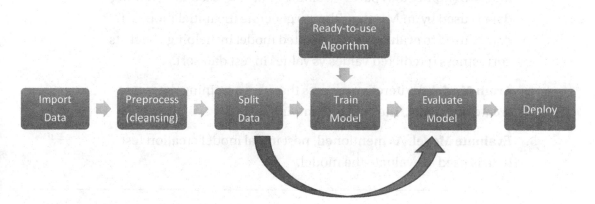

Figure 10-9.   Workflow of an ML solution in Azure ML Studio

Let's break down the workflow in steps:

1. **Import data**. The very first thing you do in ML Studio is import your data on which machine learning is to be performed. ML Studio supports a large variety of file formats, including Excel sheets, CSV, Hadoop Hive, Azure SQL DB, blob storage, etc.

2. **Preprocess**. Imported raw data may not be straight-away ready
   for ML analysis. For instance, in a tabular format data structure
   some rows may be missing values for one or more columns.
   Similarly, there may be some columns for which most rows do not
   have a value. It may be desirable to remove missing data to make
   the overall input more consistent and reliable. Microsoft defines
   three key criteria for data:

   a. Relevancy—All columns (features) are related to each other
      and to the target column.

   b. Connectedness—There is zero or minimal amount of missing
      data values.

   c. Accuracy—Most of the rows have accurate (and optionally
      precise) data values.

3. **Split data**. Machine learning (in general) requires data to be split
   into two (non-equal) parts—training data and test data. Training
   data is used by an ML algorithm to generate the initial model. Test
   data is used to evaluate the generated model by helping check its
   correctness (predicted values vs values in test dataset).

4. **Train Model**. An iterative process that uses a training dataset to
   create the model. The goal is to minimize loss.

5. **Evaluate Model**. As mentioned, post initial model creation test
   data is used to evaluate the model.

Tip   It is possible to visualize data at each step of the process. Azure ML Studio
provides several options for data visualization, including scatterplot, bar chart,
histogram, Jupyter Notebook, and more.

Picking an Algorithm

The most crucial step in an ML workflow is knowing which algorithm to apply after
importing data and preprocessing it. ML Studio comes with a host of built-in algorithm
implementations to pick from. Choosing the right algorithm depends on the type of

problem being solved as well as the kind of data it will have to deal with. For a data scientist, picking the most suitable one would be a reasonably easy task. They may be required to try a couple of different options, but at least they will know the right ones to try. For a beginner or a non-technical person, it may be a daunting task to pick an algorithm.

Microsoft have provided a quick reference diagram—that they call Machine Learning algorithm cheat sheet—to make picking an algorithm a hassle-free task. The cheat sheet is available at `https://bit.ly/2GywUlB`. Algorithms are grouped as per problem type, as shown in Table 10-3. Furthermore, hints are provided based on parameters such as accuracy and training time.

Table 10-3. *List of Algorithms Available in Azure ML Studio*

Problem	Algorithm(s)
Two-class classification	Averaged Perceptron, Bayes Point Machine, Boosted Decision Tree, Decision Forest, Decision Jungle, Logistic Regression, Neural Network, Support Vector Machine (SVM)
Multi-class classification	Decision Forest, Decision Jungle, Logistic Regression, Neural Network, One-vs-All
Regression	Bayesian Linear Regression, Boosted Decision Tree, Decision Forest, Fast Forest Quantile Regression, Linear Regression, Neural Network Regression, Ordinal Regression, Poisson Regression
Anomaly detection	One-class SVM, Principal Component Analysis-based (PCA) Anomaly Detection
Clustering	K-means Clustering

Using Azure ML Studio to Solve a Problem

Time to solve a real-world problem with machine learning!

Asclepius Consortium wants to use patient data collected from various IoT devices to reliably predict whether a patient will contract diabetes. Timely detection of diabetes can be effective in proactively controlling the disease.

This problem, which can also be stated as "will the patient contract diabetes?," is a two-class classification problem since the output can be either yes (1) or no (0). To be able to make any sort of predictions, we will, of course, need a lot of past data about real diabetes cases that can tell us which combination of various patient health parameters led to diabetes and which did not.

Let's start.

Note   This problem can also be solved using linear regression. But as the output will always be either 0 or 1, rather than a more continuous value such as the probability of contracting diabetes, it's best solved with a classification algorithm. During the course of your learning and experimenting with machine learning, you will come across a lot of problems that can be solved using more than one technique. Sometimes picking the right technique is a no-brainer, at other times that requires trying out different techniques and determining which one produces the best results.

Signing Up for Azure ML Studio

Using Azure ML Studio does not require a valid Azure subscription. If you have one, you can use it to unlock its full feature set. If you don't, you can use your personal Microsoft account (@hotmail.com, @outlook.com, etc.) to sign into ML Studio and use it with some restrictions. There's even a third option—an eight-hour no-restrictions trial that does not even require you to sign in.

Visit https://studio.azureml.net/, click the Sign Up Here link, and choose the appropriate access. We recommend going with Free Workspace access that gives you untimed feature-restricted access for free. This type of access is sufficient to allow you to design, evaluate, and deploy the ML solution that you'll design in the following sections. If you like ML Studio and want to try out restricted features and increase storage space, you can always upgrade later.

Choose the Free Workspace option and log into ML Studio. It may take a few minutes for Studio to be ready for first-time use.

Creating an Experiment

An ML solution in Studio is called an *experiment*. One can choose to create their own experiment from scratch or choose from dozens of existing samples. Apart from the samples that ML Studio provides, there is also Azure AI Gallery (https://gallery.azure.ai/) that has a list of community-contributed ML experiments that you can save for free in your own workspace and use them as starting point for your own experiments.

At this point, your workspace will be completely empty. The Experiments tab should look like in Figure 10-10.

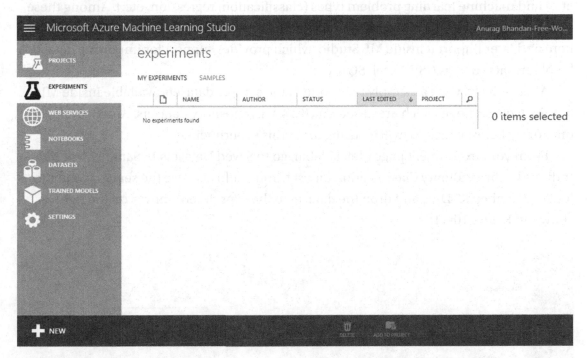

Figure 10-10. *Experiments tab in a new Azure ML Studio workspace*

Let's create a new experiment from scratch in order to better understand the various components in an ML workflow, and how to set them up correctly. Click the New button in bottom-left and choose Experiment ➤ Blank Experiment. After your new experiment is created and ready, give it an appropriate name, summary, and description. You can use the name—Diabetes Prognosis—that we used in our own experiment.

Importing Data

Data is the most important part of a machine learning solution. The very first thing to do is import data that will help us train our model. To be able to predict diabetes in a patient, we need data from past cases. Until we have a fully-functional, live IoT solution that captures from patients health parameters relevant to diabetes, we need to figure out another way to get data.

Fortunately, there are online repositories that provide access to quality datasets for free. One such popular option is University of California, Irvine (UCI) Machine Learning Repository (https://archive.ics.uci.edu/ml/). This repository is a curated list of donated datasets concerning several different areas (life sciences, engineering, business, etc.) and machine learning problem types (classification, regression, etc.). Among these datasets, you will find a couple of options for diabetes. You can download a dataset from here and later import it inside ML Studio, which provides support for importing data in a lot of formats such as CSV, Excel, SQL, etc.

Alternatively, you can simply reuse one of the sample datasets available inside ML Studio itself, some of which are based on UCI's ML repository datasets. Among them is one for diabetes, which we will be using for in this experiment.

From your experiment page's left sidebar, go to Saved Datasets ➤ Samples ➤ Pima Indians Diabetes Binary Classification dataset. You could also use the search feature to look for "diabetes." Drag and drop the dataset to the experiment canvas on the right, as shown in Figure 10-11.

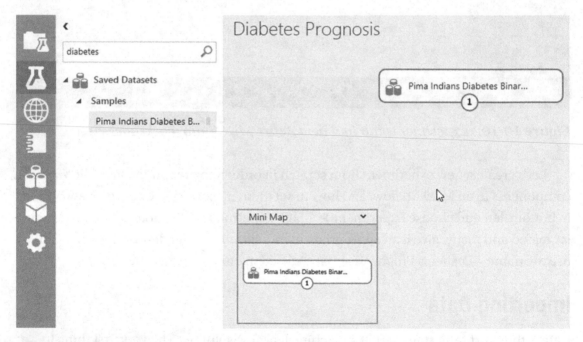

Figure 10-11. *Importing sample data in an ML Studio experiment*

It's a good idea to explore what's inside the dataset. That will not only give you a view of the data that Studio will be using for training, it will also help you in picking the right features for predictions. In experiment canvas, right-click the dataset and select dataset ➤ Visualize. You can also click the dataset's output port (the little circle at bottom-middle) and click Visualize.

Preprocessing Data

This diabetes dataset has 768 rows and 9 columns. Each row represents one patient's health parameters. The most relevant columns for our experiment include "Plasma glucose concentration after two hours in an oral glucose tolerance test" (represents sugar level), "Diastolic blood pressure," "Body mass index," and "age". The Class Variable column indicates whether the patient was diagnosed with diabetes (yes or no; 1 or 0). This column will be our target (output), with features coming from other columns.

Go through a few cases, analyze them, and see how various health parameters correlate to the diagnosis. If you look more carefully, you will see that some rows have a value of zero for columns where 0 just doesn't make sense (e.g., body mass index and 2-hour serum insulin). These are perhaps missing values that could not be obtained for those patients. To improve the quality of this dataset, we can either replace all missing values with intelligent estimates or remove them altogether. Doing the former would require advanced data science skills. For simplicity, let's just get rid of all rows that have missing values.

Notice that the 2-Hour Serum Insulin column appears to have a large number of missing values. We should remove the entire column to ensure we do not lose out on a lot of rows while cleaning our data. Our goal is to use as many records we possibly can for our trained model to be more accurate.

Removing Bad Columns

From the left sidebar, go to Data Transformation ➤ Manipulation and drag-and-drop Select Columns in Dataset onto the canvas, just below the dataset. Connect the dataset's output port with the newly added module's input port by dragging the former's output port toward the Select Columns module's input port. This will draw an arrow pointing from dataset to the module.

> **Note**   Modules in Azure ML Studio have ports that allow data to flow from one
> component to another. Some have input ports, some have output ports, and some
> have both. There are a few modules that even have multiple input or output ports,
> as you'll see shortly.

Clicking the Select Columns module once brings up its properties in the right
sidebar. From there, click the Launch Column Selector button and exclude the 2-Hour
Serum Insulin column, as shown in Figure 10-12.

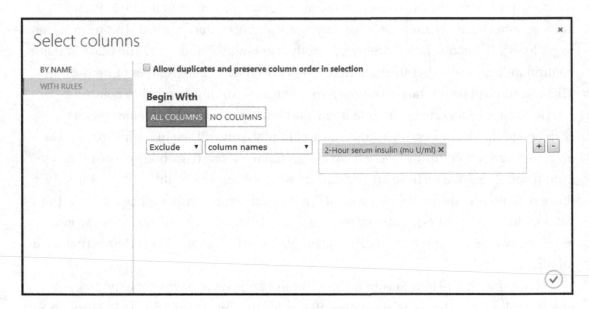

Figure 10-12. *Excluding a column in Azure ML Studio*

As a hint to yourself, you can add a comment to a module about what it does.
Double-click the Select Columns module and enter the comment `Exclude 2-Hour`
`Serum Insulin`.

Renaming Columns

The default names of columns in our dataset are too long and descriptive. Let's simplify the column names. Search for and add the Edit Metadata module in canvas, just below Select Columns. Connect it to the module above. In module's properties pane, click Launch Column Selector and select all columns except 2-Hour Serum Insulin. Coming back to the properties pane, add the following new names in the New Column Names field, leaving all other fields unchanged:

```
pregnancy_count,glucose_level,diastolic_blood_pressure,triceps_skin_fold_
thickness,bmi,diabetes_pedigree_function,age,diabetic
```

Click the Run button to run your experiment. After it's finished running, all modules that ran successfully will have a green check mark. At this point, right-click the Edit Metadata module and visualize the data. You should see the same dataset with renamed columns.

Removing rows with Missing Values

This is usually done using the Clean Missing Data module, which can remove rows where all or certain columns have no specified values. Since our data has no explicit missing values, this module will not work for us. We need something that can exclude rows where certain columns are set to 0 (e.g., glucose_level, bmi, etc.).

Search for and add the Apply SQL Transformation module in canvas, just below Edit Metadata. Connect its first input port to the module above. Enter the following query in the SQL Query Script field in the module's properties pane:

```
select * from t1 where glucose_level != 0 and diastolic_blood_pressure != 0
and triceps_skin_fold_thickness !=0 and bmi != 0;
```

Run your experiment. Once it's finished, visualize your data by right-clicking the Apply SQL Transformation module. You should now see only 532 rows out of the original 768 rows. Your experiment canvas should now look like Figure 10-13.

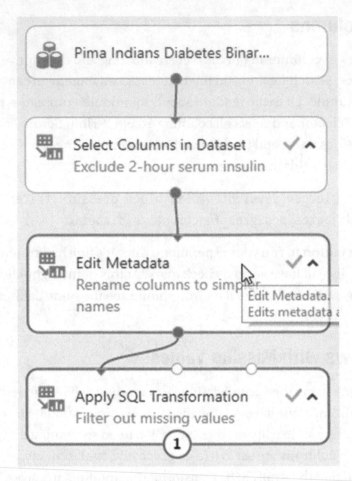

Figure 10-13. *Experiment canvas after performing data preprocessing*

Defining Features

Our data is now ready to be used for training. But before we perform training, we need to handpick relevant columns from our dataset that we can use as features.

Search for and add a second Select Columns in Dataset module in canvas, just below Apply SQL Transformation. Connect it to the module above. From column selector, choose glucose_level, diastolic_blood_pressure, triceps_skin_fold_thickness, diabetes_pedigree_function, bmi, and age.

Splitting Data

As discussed earlier in the chapter, a dataset should be divided into two parts—training data and scoring data. While training data is used to actually train the model, scoring data is reserved for later testing the trained model to calculate its loss.

Search for and add the Split Data module in canvas, just below the second Select Columns module. Connect it to the module above. In its properties page, set 0.75 as the value for Fraction of Rows in the First Output Dataset. Leave all other fields as such. Run the experiment to ensure there are no errors. Once it's completed, you can visualize the Split Data module's left output port to check training data and right output port to check scoring data. You should find both in the ratio 75-25 percent.

Applying an ML Algorithm

With data and features ready, let's pick an algorithm from one of the several built-in algorithms to train the model. Search for and add the module called Two-Class Decision Forest in canvas, just to the left of Split Data. This algorithm is known for its accuracy and fast training times.

Algorithm modules do not have an input port, so we will not connect it to any other module at the moment. Your experiment canvas should now look like Figure 10-14.

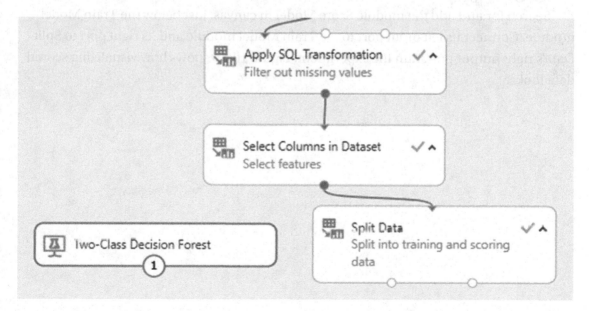

Figure 10-14. *With data and algorithm ready; we are all set to perform the training operation*

Training the Model

Search for and add the module called Train Model in canvas, just below the algorithm and Split Data modules. Connect its left input port to the algorithm module and its right port to Split Data's left output port.

From its properties pane, select the Diabetic column. Doing so will set it as our model's target value. Run the experiment. If all goes well, all modules will have a green checkmark. Like data, you can visualize a trained model as well, in which case you will see the various trees constructed as a result of the training process.

Scoring and Evaluating the Trained Model

Training using the selected algorithm takes only a few seconds to complete. Training times are directly proportional to the amount of data and selected algorithm. Despite Azure ML Studio's state-of-the-art implementations of ML algorithm, you should not be straight-away satisfied with the generated model. Just as with a food recipe one should taste a finished dish to determine if any modifications are necessary to make it more tasty, with a trained model one should score and evaluate it to see check certain parameters that can help ascertain if any modifications are necessary, for example changing the algorithm.

Search for and add the module Score Model in canvas, just below the Train Model module. Connect its left input port to the Train Model module and its right port to Split Data's right output port. Run the experiment. Figure 10-15 shows how visualizing scored data looks.

Diabetes Prognosis ❯ Score Model ❯ Scored dataset

rows   columns
133   9

ld_thickness	bmi	diabetes_pedigree_function	age	diabetic	Scored Labels	Scored Probabilities
	28.7	0.356	23	0	0	0
	45.6	1.136	38	1	1	0.625
	23.1	0.407	26	0	0	0
	33.8	0.088	31	0	0	0.25
	34.3	0.435	41	1	1	0.625
	34.3	0.196	22	1	0	0.125
	33.6	0.212	38	1	0	0.5
	35.7	0.258	22	1	1	0.875

Figure 10-15. *Visualizing scored data in Azure ML Studio*

As you can confirm from the figure, scoring is performed with the 25% output of Split Data module. Values in the Diabetic column represent the actual values in the dataset, and values in the Scored Labels column are predicted values. Also note a correlation between the Score Labels and Scored Predictions columns. Where probability is sufficiently high, the actual and predicted values are the same. If actual and predicted values match for most rows, you can say our trained model is accurate. If not, try tweaking the algorithm (or replacing it altogether) and running the experiment again.

Next, search for and add the Score Model module in canvas, just below the Score Model module. Connect its left input port with the above module. Run the experiment and visualize Evaluate Model's output. You will see metrics such as accuracy, precision, f-score, etc., that can be used to determine correctness of this model. For all aforementioned metrics, values closer to 1 indicate a good model. See Figure 10-16.

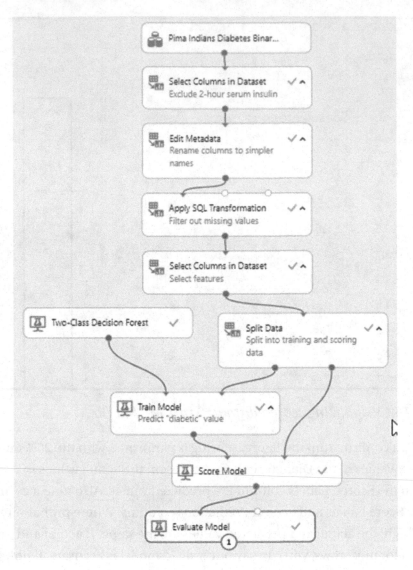

Figure 10-16. *Final preview of a two-class classification ML solution*

Deploying a Trained Model as a Web Service

Now that we have a trained and tested model, it's time to put it to real use. By deploying it as a web service, we'll give end-user software applications an option to programmatically predict values. For example, we use the diabetes prediction model's web service in our IoT solution backend or with Azure Stream Analytics to predict diabetes in real time.

Choose the Set Up Web Service ➤ Predictive Web Service option. This will convert our current experiment to what is called a Predictive Experiment. After the conversion is complete, your experiment will have two tabs—Training Experiment and Predictive Experiment—with the former containing the experiment that you set up in the previous sections and the latter containing its converted version that will be used with web service.

While in Predictive experiment tab, click the Run button. Once running completes successfully, click Deploy Web Service. You will be redirected to a new page, where you will find details about the deployed web service. It will also have an option to test the web service with specified values for features. Refer ML Studio's documentation at `https://bit.ly/2Eincl7` to learn more about publishing, tweaking, and consuming a predictive web service.

Recap

In this chapter, you learned about:

- Machine learning fundamentals—the what and why

- Differences between ML and data science

- Brief overview of ML internals—model and training

- The problems ML solves—classification, regression, etc.

- Types of ML—supervised, unsupervised, and reinforcement

- Azure Machine Learning Studio

- Creating and deploying your own ML solution

Congratulations! You are now officially AI 2.0-ready. In this book, you learned a host of new technologies that will separate you from your peers, and help you design the next generation of software applications. We encourage you to learn about each new technology in more detail and practice as much as possible to improve your hands-on skills.

Index

A

Printed in the United States
By Bookmasters